THE BEDFORD SERIES IN HISTORY AND CULTURE

The Japanese Discovery of America

A Brief History with Documents

Related Titles in
THE BEDFORD SERIES IN HISTORY AND CULTURE
Advisory Editors: Natalie Zemon Davis, Princeton University
Ernest R. May, Harvard University

The Origins of the Pacific War (forthcoming)
Edited with an Introduction by Akira Iriye, *Harvard University*

*Schools and Students in Industrial Society: Japan and the West
(1870–1940)* (forthcoming)
Edited with an Introduction by Peter N. Stearns, *Carnegie Mellon University*

THE BEDFORD SERIES IN HISTORY AND CULTURE

The Japanese Discovery of America

A Brief History with Documents

Edited with an Introduction by

Peter Duus

Stanford University

BEDFORD BOOKS   Boston ♊ New York

For Bedford Books
President and Publisher: Charles H. Christensen
General Manager and Associate Publisher: Joan E. Feinberg
History Editor: Katherine E. Kurzman
Developmental Editor: Beth Castrodale
Editorial Assistant: Joanne Diaz
Managing Editor: Elizabeth M. Schaaf
Production Editor: Stasia Zomkowski
Copyeditor: Cynthia Benn
Indexer: Steve Csipke
Text Design: Claire Seng-Niemoeller
Cover Design: Richard Emery Design, Inc.
Cover Art: Harper's Weekly. June 23, 1860. Collection of H. Kwan Lau, New York. (Photo: O. E. Nelson.) Courtesy of the Boston Public Library.

Library of Congress Catalog Card Number: 96–86768

Acknowledgments
 Aizawa Seishisai, excerpt from *Anti-Foreignism and Western Learning in Early Modern Japan: The New Theses of 1825* by Bob Tadashi Wakabayashi. Cambridge: Council on East Asian Studies, Harvard University, 1986.
 "A Bakufu Expulsion Edict," 1825 from *Anti-Foreignism and Western Learning in Early Modern Japan: The New Theses of 1825* by Bob Tadashi Wakabayashi. Cambridge: Council on East Asian Studies, Harvard University, 1986.
 Excerpt from *The Complete Journal of Townsend Harris.* Introduction and notes by Mario Emilio Cosenza. New York: Doubleday, Doran, & Co., 1930.
 "From St. Helena—Cruelty of the Japanese toward American Sailors." *New York Times,* June 15, 1852.

Foreword

The Bedford Series in History and Culture is designed so that readers can study the past as historians do.

The historian's first task is finding the evidence. Documents, letters, memoirs, interviews, pictures, movies, novels, or poems can provide facts and clues. Then the historian questions and compares the sources. There is more to do than in a courtroom, for hearsay evidence is welcome, and the historian is usually looking for answers beyond act and motive. Different views of an event may be as important as a single verdict. How a story is told may yield as much information as what it says.

Along the way the historian seeks help from other historians and perhaps from specialists in other disciplines. Finally, it is time to write, to decide on an interpretation and how to arrange the evidence for readers.

Each book in this series contains an important historical document or group of documents, each document a witness from the past and open to interpretation in different ways. The documents are combined with some element of historical narrative — an introduction or a biographical essay, for example — that provides students with an analysis of the primary source material and important background information about the world in which it was produced.

Each book in the series focuses on a specific topic within a specific historical period. Each provides a basis for lively thought and discussion about several aspects of the topic and the historian's role. Each is short enough (and inexpensive enough) to be a reasonable one-week assignment in a college course. Whether as classroom or personal reading, each book in the series provides firsthand experience of the challenge — and fun — of discovering, recreating, and interpreting the past.

Natalie Zemon Davis
Ernest R. May

Preface

A generation ago it was common for historians to speak of an "age of discovery" that began with the fifteenth-century European voyages of exploration. What they meant was that the Europeans discovered a world unknown to them, except through accounts like Marco Polo's that were thought too fantastic to be true. In recent years, critics have pointed out that the term "discovery" was a misnomer, demeaning to the peoples the Europeans "discovered," who already knew who they were and where they were. The point is well taken. But "discovery," I think, still remains a useful term if we remember that it describes a mutual process. As the Europeans were discovering the world beyond Gibraltar, the inhabitants of that world were discovering the Europeans too. We often forget that, just as the Spanish wrote histories of the conquest of Mexico, the Aztec people also produced their own narrative of Cortes and his intrusion into their lives, and that Chinese officials were no less eager to pick the brains of Jesuit missionaries than the missionaries were to send back glowing reports about the Middle Kingdom.

This book focuses on the Japanese encounter with the Americans in the mid-nineteenth century, an episode that took place rather late in the "age of discovery," as the last "unknown" lands of Africa and Asia were being probed by Western merchants, explorers, and travelers. Most of the documents assembled here—poems and political pamphlets, official memorials and private journals, newspaper reports and eyewitness accounts—were written (or drawn) by the Japanese, for whom the encounter raised the question of national survival. Their contents reveal the ignorance and curiosity, the anxiety and confusion, the admiration and disillusion that attended the meeting of these two rather different cultures. (I translated several of the Japanese documents especially for this book.) Documents from the American side are included too, but are fewer in number. Since the Americans were the intruders, their need to understand Japan was not nearly so urgent as the Japanese desire to grasp why the Americans had come and what they represented. Hence I have chosen to title the book *The Japanese Discovery of America.*

At the very least, these documents should remind readers of how difficult it is to comprehend a totally unfamiliar culture. But there are also more specific lessons useful for contemporary Americans: First, it should be clear that American society and institutions have never been as transparent or easily decipherable as Americans often assume them to be; second, even when outsiders take a close look at American society, not all of them like what they see, or conclude that it represents a better way of life. The missionary impulses of the nineteenth century, and even the buoyant American triumphalism of World War II, have now faded, but these lessons are still important. As the United States, the last of the superpowers, continues to engage itself intensely with the outside world, whether exporting action movies or dispatching peacekeeping missions, Americans must remain aware of how "foreign" or threatening their forays into the outside world often seem to others.

ACKNOWLEDGMENTS

In preparing this book I have enjoyed the help and encouragement of many. The staff at Bedford Books was central to its production: Niels Aaboe first suggested the project to me; Chuck Christensen seconded the proposal; and Beth Castrodale helped carry it to fruition. Stasia Zomkowski ably piloted the book through production, and managing editor Elizabeth Schaaf provided valuable support throughout the production process. Copyeditor Cynthia Benn helped bring clarity to the manuscript, and Joanne Diaz attended to many editorial details. I am also in the debt of several readers who kindly provided useful comments and suggestions on the first draft: Thomas W. Burkman, Warren I. Cohen, Suzanne Gay, Akira Iriye, Michael Lewis, and Fred G. Notehelfer. Needless to say, to all of the above I offer the usual absolution: All factual, orthographic, grammatical, or interpretive errors found in the volume are strictly of my own doing.

Peter Duus
Stanford, California

Contents

The Japanese Discovery of America

A Brief History with Documents

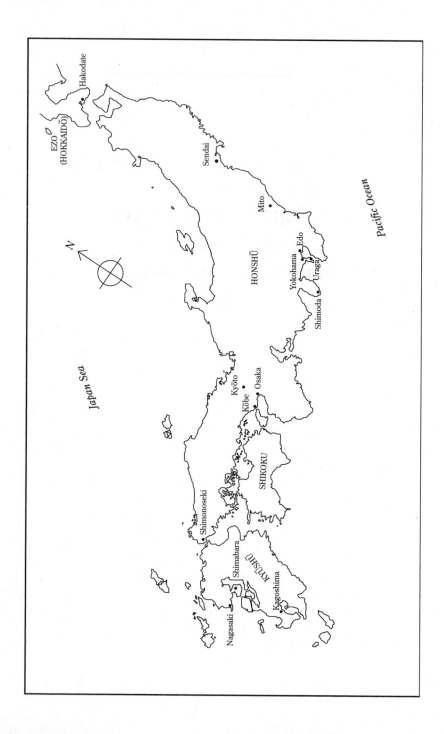

PART ONE

The Japanese Discovery
of America

It is difficult to imagine a cultural encounter more unsettling than Japan's mid-nineteenth-century confrontation with the United States. The two countries were separated not only by the Pacific Ocean but also by a cultural chasm that at times seemed nearly impossible to span. Japan was living in the shadow of a feudal past: Its society was divided by strict lines of hierarchy and status; its common people were peasants settled on the land for generations; and its ruling class, the samurai, looked to historical precedent and established custom for guidance on how to act. (Definitions for samurai and other terms used in this book can be found in the Glossary on page 205.) How different the Japanese were to find the United States, a country not yet a century old, whose laws and institutions proclaimed the equality of all, whose common people descended from immigrants seeking to escape the rigidities and conventions of "the Old World," and whose leaders prized liberty, worshiped progress, and looked endlessly to the future.

The Japanese, of course, would have preferred to avoid the encounter altogether, but they were overwhelmed by larger social and economic forces that were transforming the world into a single global market. As the king of Holland warned the Tokugawa shogun, the country's de facto ruler[1] in 1844: "The intercourse between the different nations of the earth is increasing with great rapidity. An irresistible power is drawing them together."[2] The irresistible force, of course, was the technological revolution that had harnessed steam power to the manufacture and movement

1

of goods across the globe. Armed with this new technology, the early industrializing nations, including the United States, burst into the world outside the West, seeking neither territory nor political domination but access to new markets. Historians have called this phase of Western expansion, which was justified by the doctrine that the wealth of nations would grow as artificial barriers to trade and intercourse were swept aside, the "imperialism of free trade."[3]

The outward thrust of the industrializing countries, however, involved more than the pursuit of trade. Convinced that they exemplified the future of humankind, the Westerners were determined to hurry the rest of the world in the same direction. Commodore Matthew C. Perry was sent to Japan as a first step toward "opening" the Japanese market, but Americans also hoped to induce the Japanese to adopt the customs, practices, and laws of the "civilized world." It was no accident that among the many gifts Perry brought to Japan were two potent symbols of Western technological superiority: a telegraph machine and a miniature railroad. As his official report gleefully noted, for the Japanese officials who eagerly sought to ride it, the railroad was a "triumphant revelation of the success of science and enterprise, to a partially enlightened people" (see Document 13). It was such cultural "revelations" that the Americans wished to export to Japan along with their goods.

In the long run the American cultural mission, dedicated to "uplifting" the "half-civilized" Japanese, was as significant as the diplomatic one. To be sure, the Japanese ruling elite—the bakufu (the shogun's government), the daimyo (regional territorial lords), and their samurai followers—initially responded to American ethnocentrism with an ethnocentrism of their own. While impressed by the technological accomplishments of the Americans and other "barbarians," they remained confident that their own culture was superior and that the new technology could be mastered with time and effort (see Documents 4 and 15). After all, even before Perry's arrival a few pioneering daimyo domains had already successfully experimented with Western-style iron smelting and gun making. But the American intrusion was profoundly disturbing nevertheless. Commodore Perry's fleet of "black ships" arrived at a historical moment when Japanese society seemed to be in a state of flux, its traditional institutions and class structure undermined by economic change. Members of the elite, gripped by a paranoid vision of the outside world, feared that the foreigners might win over the lower orders—the "ignorant people" *(gumin)*—perhaps setting in motion a complete disintegration of the whole society that would lead to barbarian rule (see Document 4).

The more the Japanese learned about the outside world, the more their fears abated. At the same time so did their cultural confidence. Stunned by the immense material gap between themselves and the Americans, they began to conclude that their country's problems lay not in popular gullibility or technical backwardness but in the failings of its culture, values, and institutions. Hesitantly, and often without deep understanding, a few Japanese began to ponder the advantages of adopting the peculiar laws, customs, and institutions they discovered in the outside world. Within fifteen years of Perry's arrival, an odd coalition of antiforeign, pro-Westernizing activists brought an end to the ancien régime. In 1868 a new regime, ostensibly led by the young Meiji emperor (1852–1912), launched the first modernizing nationalist revolution in the world outside the West. Its leaders, many of whom began their political lives as antibarbarian activists, committed themselves to "seeking knowledge throughout the world in order to strengthen the foundations of imperial rule."[4]

In this respect, the Japanese emerged from their encounter with the United States far less traumatically than many other societies whose leaders resisted the intrusions of the industrializing countries. The Japanese were eager to learn from the West but only on their own terms. For example, the United States at first seemed to offer a useful cultural model,[5] but as the Japanese leaders sorted out what best suited them from among the "advanced customs" of the world, they came to understand that American cultural standards were more useful to criticize the "evil customs of the past" than to serve as prototypes for new standards of their own. Not only did they discover more comfortable models in Europe, but they became acutely aware of how vastly different the brash, sprawling, diverse, and resource-rich United States was from their own tight little islands. In the end, the Japanese discovery of America proved more important in starting a process of cultural transformation than in shaping the direction it eventually took.

JAPAN'S ISOLATION POLICY

In the 1630s, as early English colonists were crossing the Atlantic to settle in the wilderness of North America, the rulers of Japan were relentlessly closing down their country's contacts with the outside world. Their policy of national isolation, also called a "seclusion" or "closed country" policy, grew out of their encounter with the Portuguese, the first Europeans to arrive in East Asia. A generation after Vasco da Gama had sailed around the horn of Africa, Portuguese trading ships put in regularly at ports in Kyūshū, bringing goods from the rest of Asia to exchange for

Japanese silver. The Japanese elite were deeply ambivalent toward the European newcomers: They welcomed the trade and were fascinated by the exotic ways of the "southern barbarians," who taught them how to make guns and smoke tobacco, but they grew increasingly wary of the foreigners' religion.

By the early seventeenth century, Jesuit missionaries who arrived with the Portuguese trading vessels had been so successful in making converts that there were reported to be 750,000 Christians in Japan, most of them concentrated in Kyūshū and around the imperial capital at Kyōto. The advisors of Tokugawa Ieyasu, the founder and first shogun of the Edo bakufu, were deeply hostile toward the foreign religion. Not only did they fear that missionary activity might pave the way to foreign invasion as it had in Mexico and the Philippines, they were also concerned that *Kirishitan* (i.e., Christian) believers were concentrated in regions where Edo's power was still weak. In 1612 the bakufu issued an edict prohibiting the practice of Christianity on its own territory, declaring it a "pernicious doctrine" that taught its believers to "contravene governmental regulations, traduce Shintō, calumniate the True Law [i.e., Buddhism], destroy righteousness, corrupt goodness."[6] Over the next several years, foreign missionaries were expelled, and native converts were forced to recant their faith or face execution (usually by crucifixion).

In the 1630s, to quarantine the country against further infection by the foreign religion, the bakufu authorities consolidated their anti-*Kirishitan* policy by severely restricting contacts with the outside world: The importation of Christian books was banned, travel and commercial voyages outside the country were prohibited, and the construction of oceangoing vessels was severely restricted. After a brutal and bloody crackdown against the Shimabara rebellion, an uprising of disgruntled peasants led by samurai Christian converts in 1637, confirmed its worst fears, the bakufu forbade further visits by Portuguese ships. All Japanese were ordered to demonstrate their religious orthodoxy by registering as parishioners at local Buddhist temples.[7] Within a few years the *Kirishitan* community had dwindled to a handful of believers, cut off from all missionary contact and driven to practicing their rites in secret.

In its determination to wipe out Christianity, the bakufu encouraged the publication of anti-Christian tracts. These works claimed to expose the irrationalities and contradictions in Christian mythology and doctrine, and they depicted the European missionaries as cunning and sinister creatures, more like demons or goblins than humans (see Document 1). But the conviction that the foreign religion was subversive of public morals and social stability remained at the heart of anti-Christian sentiment among the samurai elite. The doctrines of Christianity appeared to undercut the teaching of Confucianism, the source of the elite's moral code. Arai Hakuseki, a Confucian advisor to the sixth shogun, argued that the *Kirishitan* worshipers' devotion to God undermined both loyalty *(chū)* and filial piety *(kō)*, the two basic virtues on which the social order rested:

> If I have a Great Lord to serve beyond my lord and a Great Father to serve beyond my father, . . . then not only are there two sacred personages in the house and two lords in the land but the highest duty must be to be set at naught the lord and set at naught the father. Even if they do not go so far as teaching to set the father and the lord at naught, still the atrocious nature ingrained in their doctrine is of such enormity that even at the point of regicide or parricide they must not look back, and in the end think nothing of it.[8]

For the conventional Confucian, it was difficult to imagine a more horrendous set of beliefs.

The anti-Christian policies of the bakufu were not intended to cut Japan completely off from the rest of the world. The bakufu authorities encouraged trade with neighboring Asian countries—China, Korea, and the Ryūkyū Islands—and they continued profitable commercial dealings with the Dutch East India Company, run by canny Protestants who assured the Japanese that the company had no interest in propagating religion. To limit Dutch contacts with ordinary Japanese, the Japanese authorities confined them to Deshima, a small man-made island in the western port of Nagasaki. Since monopoly over trade with Japan made Deshima the Dutch East India Company's most profitable operation in Asia, the Dutch chief, or *kapitan,* at Deshima was willing to put up with the inconvenience. In any case, the restrictions on the Dutch were not so different from those placed on European merchants in India, China, and elsewhere in Asia.

After 1700 the Dutch trade at Nagasaki declined in importance for Japan. Technological innovation and economic growth made it possible to produce at home silk brocades and other goods the Dutch imported from other parts of Asia. Because the Japanese paid for Dutch imports in gold, silver, and copper, metals used in minting coinage, bakufu officials also began to fear that the country was exchanging the "bones and marrow" of its national wealth for superfluous luxury goods. In 1715 the bakufu placed limits on the number of Dutch vessels allowed to enter Nagasaki, and by the end of the eighteenth century their visits dwindled to one or two a year. Since the country suffered no ill effects from the new restrictions, the orthodox view was that Japan could survive easily with only limited links to the outside world. Even Engelbert Kaempfer, a Dutch physician stationed at Deshima in the late seventeenth century, argued that the Japanese could live "content and happy" within their own limits and without communication with foreign countries. "Ever since the Empire hath been shut up," he wrote, "nature, that kind mistress, taught them, and they themselves readily own it, that they can wholly subsist upon what it affords, and that they have no need of being supplied by foreigners with the necessaries of life."[9]

Despite the limits placed on trade, overseas travel, and immigration, cultural contacts with the West continued. The Japanese were aware that Dutch knowledge was superior to their own in the study of astronomy, calendar making, medicine and pharmacology, and other natural sciences. In 1720 the shogun Yoshimune loosened the ban on foreign books by permitting the import of Dutch scientific and technical works. A small but dedicated group of "Dutch Studies" [*rangaku*] scholars, working in Nagasaki and Edo, began to expand their understanding of contemporary European science and technology, laboriously reading and translating scientific and other works in the Dutch language. Although some of these scholars supported themselves by the practice of medicine, others enjoyed the patronage of the Tokugawa bakufu or the local daimyo regimes. By the end of the eighteenth century, Western scientific knowledge was familiar to many educated Japanese. The Copernican heliocentric view of the solar system was widely accepted, and local daimyo collected telescopes, clocks, and other Western devices as curiosities. Indeed, Dutch Studies had become something of a fad within the ruling class. Even Matsudaira Sadanobu, the shogun's chief minister, confessed to collecting Dutch books. "The barbarian nations are skilled in the sciences," he wrote in his autobiography, "and considerable profit may be derived from their works of astronomy and geography, as well as from their military weapons, and their methods of internal and external medicine."[10]

The Dutch were also a source of political intelligence about the outside world. Every year the Dutch kapitan at Deshima was required to submit a report on recent news from Europe and Asia. The kapitan often tailored the details to suit the interest of the Dutch East India Company, but these reports did nonetheless keep bakufu officials informed in a general way of what was going on in Europe. By the early nineteenth century, Dutch Studies scholars in the service of the bakufu amassed linguistic, geographical, and historical knowledge about foreign countries, compiling geographical tracts, encyclopedias, dictionaries, and maps (see

Document 10). Using Western surveying techniques, Inō Tadataka, a Dutch Studies scholar, drafted the first maps that gave the Japanese an accurate idea of the shape of their country. A few visionaries even argued that Dutch Studies was as important to the service of the country as the study of the Confucian classics and other traditional forms of learning.

Openness to Western learning, however, did not ease the isolation policy. On the contrary, it was Matsudaira Sadanobu, a collector of Dutch books, who reaffirmed it in the face of new foreign intrusions. During the eighteenth century the Russian empire, invigorated by the Westernizing reforms of Peter the Great, had extended its reach across Siberia to the Pacific Ocean. To supply their "breadless" colonies in Kamchatka and the Kurile Islands, the Russians thought of the Japanese as natural trading partners. Within Japan, however, where paranoia about the intentions of the Western "barbarians" ran strong, rumors spread that the Russians were preparing to attack Ezo, the sparsely populated island to the north of Honshū (now known as Hokkaidō) (see Document 2). When Adam Erkovich Laxman, an envoy dispatched by Catherine the Great, arrived there in 1792 to request trade relations, the bakufu turned him away. In a letter to the Russians Matsudaira declared that the Japanese had followed the "hallowed law of national isolation" since time immemorial.[11] Under his direction, orders were issued that no foreign ship, even those returning castaways, could call at any port but Nagasaki and that any ship from a country that had no formal relations with Japan would be seized or destroyed if it approached Japanese shores.

With the exception of the capture and confinement of a Russian naval officer, Vasilii Golovnin, on the island of Kunishiro, the order to expel foreign ships was rarely carried out. When foreign ships arrived in Japanese coastal waters by accident or design, local officials found it much simpler to send them on their way. Even in 1808 when the *Phaeton,* a British naval frigate, pursued Dutch ships into Nagasaki during the Napoleonic wars, the bakufu's representative refrained from using force. But as Western trade and whaling in the Pacific expanded in the 1810s and 1820s, American and English vessels put into shore with requests for water, firewood, or food with increasing frequency. Some officials feared these encounters signaled a new round of foreign aggression. The memory of earlier contacts with the Portuguese and their missionaries kept alive the fear that the "barbarians" would use their contacts with the common people to spread their religion and corrupt the public morals. In 1825, at the urging of Takahashi Kageyasu, a leading Dutch Studies scholar, the bakufu issued an edict enjoining local officials to repel by force any foreign ship that approached the coast and to incarcerate any foreigners who had the audacity to land (see Document 5). Interestingly enough, Taka-hashi pointed out that it was the custom among Western countries to drive off ships from countries with whom they had no diplomatic rela-tions. Knowledge about the West, it appeared, could be a useful tool in maintaining the policy of isolation.

AMERICA'S APPROACH TO JAPAN

Until the 1840s the anxieties of the Japanese leaders remained focused on the English and the Russians, whose probes had been the most fre-quent and visible. The Americans, who were often confused with the Eng-lish, hovered only dimly on the edge of Japanese consciousness. Nishikawa Joken (1648–1724), a merchant scholar in Nagasaki, had described the country of "Quivira" in North America as a wild and for-bidding place where lions, bears, and tigers roamed, pine nuts were as big as dates, and people dressed in bird feathers and tiger skins.[12] By the end of eighteenth century, it was known that the English had settled in North America, but not until more than thirty years after the Declaration of Independence did bakufu officials learn that the American colonists had revolted against England and established a new nation called the United States. Gradually, however, fuller accounts of America, such as Mitsukuri Shōgo's *World Atlas (Konyo zushiki),* were published (see Document 10), and by the eve of Perry's arrival the Dutch kapitan were prompt in providing news of recent developments in the United States. The Japanese knew, for example, that Americans had won a war with Mexico, that gold had been discovered in California, that Millard Fillmore had been elected president, and that an English company planned to build a canal across Panama.

By contrast, educated Americans knew very little about current devel-opments in Japan. School geography books rarely mentioned the coun-try, and when they did it was often to stress the despotism, idolatry, or topsy-turviness of the Japanese.[13] Hardly any Americans could speak or read Japanese, and the handful who did learned it without the help of text-books, dictionaries, or even a grammar book. Popular knowledge of Japan came mainly from accounts written by European observers like Engelbert Kaempfer, Karl Peter Thunberg, Isaac Titsingh, and Philip Franz von Siebold, who had served at the Dutch trading post at Deshima. Their accounts were encyclopedic, and readers could draw from them quite contradictory and confusing conclusions, finding what they wished. Where one reader might decide that the Japanese prized honor, name, and courtesy, another might conclude that they were cruel, treacherous, and deceitful. A popular synthesis of these accounts published by Harper and Brothers in 1841, *Manners and Customs of the Japanese,* admitted that Japan remained "as much a *terra incognita* now as it was a hundred years ago."[14]

Limited knowledge of Japan did not prevent American commentators from pronouncing judgment on Japan's attitudes toward the outside world. All agreed that whatever their virtues, the Japanese were steeped in unconscionable conservatism at a time when the world was being swept by the whirlwinds of progress and change. As one prominent American put it, Japan had "no right to withhold its quota to the general progress of mankind."[15] Such views were not unique to the United States. Since the eighteenth century, educated Westerners had come to identify mechanical technology and scientific thinking with cultural and moral superiority.[16] While the sixteenth-century Jesuit missionaries had viewed the Japanese as heathens, they had not found them wanting compared with the Europeans in other respects. The invention of the steam engine, the railroad locomotive, the telegraph, and the steamship changed all that. Like other Westerners, mid–nineteenth-century Americans were convinced that they had reached a new and higher plane than the rest of humankind. They quickly forgot how recently — only two or three generations before — their material and scientific condition had not been so very different from the most developed societies outside the West.

To this general Western sense of superiority, the Americans added their own brand of ethnocentricism. By the mid-nineteenth century most Americans, brashly confident that their country represented the future, saw themselves as inhabitants of a fresh new land, untainted by the corrupt and decadent institutions of Europe, from whose cultural orbit they had broken. Unencumbered by a feudal past, they believed their free institutions were vastly superior to those of the rest of the world and that their religion was a truer faith than the empty rituals of the Old World churches. For most Americans the United States was a shining "city upon a hill," a model for the rest of mankind to emulate. As John Bingham, appointed as minister to Japan in 1873, put it:

> Born and reared in this land, it is not for me to forget that the United States, though the youngest, is one of the foremost of the nations, in the vastness of her domain, in the extent and diversity of her resources and production; in the rapidity of her growth and development; in the achievements of her intellect; . . . in her complex, but united and compact fabric of justice, which is for the shelter and protection of all by the power of all, and those graces of life which adorn and ennoble individual and collective man, the citizen, and the State. Let America, by

her example, teach all nations that it is their interest, as it is their duty, to help one another cultivate the works of peace and the arts of peace, to diffuse knowledge, to establish justice, to vindicate every right and redress every wrong, to recognize and accept the fact that the human race, however divided into nationalities, is one great family of intellectual, moral, and responsible beings, capable of indefinite progress here, and encouraged to hope for and aspire to an immortal life hereafter.[17]

Like his contemporaries, Bingham thought that his country had a mission to spread the doctrines of liberty, progress, and Christianity to the outside world whenever it had a chance to do so. What he envisaged was not a conquest of other people's territory but of their minds and spirit.

The voyage of the *Morrison,* a private American probe into Japan mounted in the summer of 1837 by expatriate American traders and missionaries in China, was prompted by "civilizing" motives mingled with a desire to open up trade.[18] To Americans already in Asia the two seemed to go hand in hand. The ostensible purpose of the voyage was the humanitarian mission of repatriating several Japanese castaways rescued by foreign ships, but its real purpose was to persuade the Japanese to relax their "antisocial" policy toward the outside world. The ship's owners, Olyphant and Company, loaded a cargo of machine-made cotton and woolen cloth they hoped to sell if the Japanese could be persuaded to trade, and the passengers included three Protestant missionaries curious to find out more about this potential new mission field. Although the probe was repelled by local authorities, one of the missionaries, Samuel Wells Williams, remained optimistic that Japan's "entrance into the family of nations was not far distant" and that "commerce, knowledge, and Christianity, with their multiplied blessings" would have full rein (see Document 7).

A new vision of the United States as a future commercial and naval power in the Pacific was probably the most powerful force propelling the Americans toward the opening of Japan. When the Ch'ing government opened four new ports to Westerners in China after the Opium War of 1839 to 1842,[19] merchants in Boston and New York saw new opportunities for trade not only with China but with Japan as well. The Pacific coast of the United States suddenly became important to journalists, businessmen, and politicians on the Atlantic seaboard. As one business journal breathlessly noted in 1845, "There is but little doubt that the United States are destined to command all the trade in the Indian and China seas. . . . For the past three centuries, the civilized world has been rolling westward; and Americans of the present age will complete the circle, and open a western steam route with the east."[20] In the early 1840s, however, the critical link in this great circle—the ports on the California coast—was still under the control of Mexico. Animated by fear that the English might take these ports first, expansionist journalists and politicians launched a crusade to bring California into the Union.

The drive to annex the Pacific coast was cloaked by an appeal to national mission: the doctrine of "manifest destiny." Like most grand political slogans, manifest destiny was specific neither as to ends nor means, an ambiguity that probably enhanced its appeal. Its vagueness licensed an amplitude of possibilities. Manifest destiny might mean that the United States had a mission to spread liberty and its institutions across the continent, or that Americans had a right to annex new territory from their "backward" neighbor to the south, or that new economic opportunities awaited on the Western frontier. To President Polk, who dispatched the first official expedition to Japan, manifest destiny meant securing a window on the Pacific. As he told Congress, control of the West Coast would "enable the United States to command the already valuable and rapidly increasing commerce of the Pacific" and "thus obtain for our products new and increased markets, and greatly enlarge our coastal and foreign trade, as well as augment our tonnage and revenue."[21] With victory over Mexico in 1848, the country's westernmost border finally reached the shore of the Pacific.

Although the desire for trade played a major role in the dispatching of expeditions to Japan, the initiative to "open" Japan was ultimately seized by the American navy, itself in the process of yielding to the "irresistible force" of steam power by shifting from sailing vessels to coal-burning steamships. A steam navy, whose vessels required periodic refueling, needed coaling stations at convenient and hospitable ports around the world. Forward-looking naval officers, including Matthew C. Perry, commander of the Brooklyn Naval Yard, believed (accurately as it happens) that there were rich coal deposits in Japan and that the United States should obtain access to them if the American fleet were to maintain a presence in the Pacific. The Navy was also concerned about the fate of castaway American sailors and whalers, whom local Japanese authorities often incarcerated for long periods before repatriating them at Nagasaki. Reports of allegedly inhumane treatment toward these sailors eventually reached the American press, provoking public demands that something be done to protect American sailors (see Document 9). Indeed, Herman Melville went so far as to predict in *Moby Dick,* "If that double-bolted land, Japan, is ever to become hospitable, it is the whale-ship alone to whom the credit will be due, for she is already on the threshold."[22]

In the late spring of 1846 two ships under the command of Commodore James Biddle arrived at Uraga at the mouth of Edo Bay, carrying a letter from President Polk expressing interest in opening trade. After a week or so of futile negotiations, the Japanese towed the American vessels out to sea and sent them on their way. The rejection was doubly humiliating for the Americans since at one point in the negotiations Biddle lost face when he was shoved unceremoniously by a Japanese guard. A second unsuccessful mission led by Commander James Glynn arrived in Nagasaki in 1849 to secure release of seven American sailors, allegedly castaways but actually deserters, who had been held in captivity on the island of Ezo, and a third mission under Commodore James H. Aulicke in 1852 aborted when he was forced to return home to face charges of official misconduct.

By the time Commodore Perry made his first visit to Japan in the summer of 1853 it was clear what American public officials and private citizens wanted to achieve by the "opening" of Japan. First, at the most basic level, the Americans wished to compel the Japanese to supply American ships in distress with wood, water, and provisions and to treat shipwrecked American sailors humanely until they could be repatriated. Second, they wanted the right to buy coal for steam vessels sailing between California and China. Third, they wished to bring Japan into the "family of nations" or "community of nations" by accepting the diplomatic practices and legal conventions followed by the "civilized nations" of the world, such as the exchange of diplomatic representatives. Fourth, they wanted "friendly commercial intercourse," the opening of Japanese ports to American trading vessels, and unrestricted access to the Japanese market. And fifth, they wanted Japan to lift its prohibition on Christianity and open its doors to American missionaries. Behind all these specific goals lay the unstated hope that Japan would eventually have to mold itself into a "civilized" society—that is, one that conformed to Western cultural ideas and values.

What made Perry's efforts at negotiation more successful than earlier Western attempts was his mastery of cultural theater. From the outset Perry staged his encounter to overwhelm the Japanese not merely with the military and technological superiority of the Americans but with their cultural and moral superiority as well. Perry realized that *how* he negotiated was as important as *what* he negotiated. The right gestures were necessary to impress the Japanese with the importance of his mission. Aware that the Japanese elite laid great store on proper formality and protocol, he insisted that due respect be paid to him as the representative of a great country (see Document 13). Absolutely refusing to accept the validity of Japanese customs where they contradicted what he regarded as the "universal principles" of law and intercourse among nations, he positioned himself as a representative of a higher civilization. And by stubbornly refusing to leave until he had delivered his letter from President Fillmore, he backed the Tokugawa authorities into a corner. What strengthened his hand in this game of gestures was an unshakable conviction that Japan would benefit from "opening" as much as the Americans and the rest of the world.

When Perry returned to Edo Bay in early 1854, he persisted in his demands despite continuing efforts by the bakufu officials to put him off. The treaty finally signed at Kanagawa met the basic American demands: It allowed American ships to put into the ports of Shimoda and Matsumae; it assured that they would be supplied with wood, water, provisions, and coal as they required; and it gave the United States the right to station a consul or agent in Shimoda. During the negotiations, however, the bakufu representatives were firm in their refusal to permit trade with the Americans. Confident that sooner or later the Japanese would have to open the country, Perry chose not to press the issue. For him the treaty simply was the first step toward the eventual incorporation of Japan into the "community of nations." In a parting letter to the Japanese, he said that he had accepted continued restrictions on American access to Japan in the belief that once the Japanese understood the vast changes that had taken place in the world, they would open more ports.

The task of negotiating a trade treaty was undertaken by Townsend Harris, the first American consul, who arrived in Japan in late 1856. Unlike Perry, who negotiated from the deck of his gunboat in Edo Bay, Harris was tucked away in the remote port of Shimoda, where he sat simmering with frustration over the delaying tactics of the Japanese officials. It was nearly a year and a half before he was finally able to begin talks about a commercial treaty. Although Harris was convinced that the Japanese yielded nothing except from fear, he was unable to brandish American naval power as a threat. Instead, he cannily warned Hotta Masayoshi, the chief of the shogun's council of state, that a refusal to open the country would anger the British and the French, at the time engaged in a military expedition against China to secure enforcement of the treaties there. To "yield to a fleet what had been refused to an ambassador," he suggested, would weaken the bakufu by humiliating it (see Document 22).

The signing of the treaty with Harris in the summer of 1858 finally "opened" Japan on terms satisfactory to the United States. For the first time the Japanese agreed to allow the Americans to station a diplomatic representative in the capital at Edo. The treaty also opened four additional ports to the Americans (Yokohama [Kanagawa], Nagasaki, Niigata, and Kōbe [Hyōgo]), and it permitted them to trade and reside in these ports, where they would be subject to their own country's laws and tried by their own consular officials if they committed criminal offenses. The devout Harris, who prided himself on holding the first Protestant religious service ever conducted in Edo, made sure that the treaty included a provision allowing the Americans to practice their religion and to erect suitable places of worship in the treaty ports. It is little wonder that the antiforeign activist Yoshida Shōin feared that the treaty would pave the way for foreign subversion from within (see Document 24). In one sense, he was wrong: The Americans, having accomplished their agenda with the signing of the Harris treaty, were not interested in turning Japan into a colony; in another sense, he was right, for the opening of the country set in motion a process of cultural subversion that undermined Japanese confidence in their own superiority and led to a new assessment of what constituted "civilization" and what did not.

THE AMERICANS AS BARBARIANS

However benign the Americans thought their demands, the Japanese saw them as quite ominous. In the Chinese historical classics that the samurai elite devoured with the same attentiveness that men like Townsend Harris read the Bible, the fall of a dynasty was often signaled by "troubles within" and "threats from without," the confluence of domestic rebellion and "barbarian" invasion. It was precisely such a historical confluence that many feared Japan was facing on the eve of Perry's arrival (see Document 16). In the 1830s a series of bad harvests and widespread famine had provoked a sudden burst of peasant uprisings and urban riots, culminating in an abortive rebellion led by Ōshio Heihachirō, a low-ranking retainer of the bakufu, that left much of the great commercial center of Ōsaka in ashes. With mixed success the bakufu and many domains embarked on reform programs to contain the social dislocations created by rural distress and economic change. But signs of growing outside pressure intensified deep anxiety over the country's future. Even if reform could address troubles within, the only way to ward off threats from without was to reaffirm and intensify the policy of national isolation.

Despite growing interest in Western science and growing knowledge about the West, fear of the Western barbarians—called by terms such as "red hairs" (kōmōjin) or "hairy barbarians" (ketōjin) to distinguish them from Asians—remained strong. Indeed, as the foreigners came closer and closer to Japan, a visceral xenophobia gained ground among the samurai and educated commoners. Everything about the foreigners, from their big noses to their peculiar writing system, was outlandish, grotesque, or disgusting to some Japanese. The patriotic poet and historian Rai San'yō (1781–1832) could even turn the peaceful arrival of a Dutch ship in Nagasaki into a sinister or menacing event by suggesting the underlying bestiality of the foreigners (see Document 3). Such protoracist rhetoric, however, was less significant than the construction of an image of the Westerner as a barbarian in a cultural sense, bereft of proper morality, uncultivated in manners, and given to wild or violent behavior.

This new and virulent antiforeign sentiment drew heavily on the Confucian view that humankind could be divided between the "cultured" *(ka)* and the "barbarian" *(i)*. To be "cultured" meant to have the ability to understand and follow the "Way," moral principles such as loyalty and filial piety, revealed in the basic Confucian canon and embodied in the very structure of the natural world. In the realm of politics, it was thought appropriate that the "cultivated man" or the "superior man," who had mastered the Way through a tireless process of study and contemplation, should govern his moral inferior, the "ordinary or small man" who thought only of his personal profit or interest (see Documents 4 and 30). The category of "cultured" distinguished societies where the Way was widely understood from "barbarian" peoples, who did not understand it at all. In China, this distinction had licensed the expansion of Chinese culture among the nomadic peoples of central and inner Asia and the establishment of a loose hegemony over neighboring states like Tibet, Vietnam, and Korea.

In Japan the same concept was brought to the support of an intense ethnocentrism. Traditionally, the Japanese had used the term "barbarian" *(i)* to refer to ethnically different peoples living on the archipelago, such as the Emishi and the Ezo, who were thought to be morally, culturally, and materially inferior to the Japanese. It was simple enough to apply the term to the Westerners as well. But Japanese ethnocentrism extended to the country's Asian neighbors as well. Drawing on a tradition of cultural nativism that gathered force in the eighteenth century, many educated samurai and commoners had come to believe that the Way was truly practiced only in Japan. Unlike Chinese rulers, who were constantly overthrown and replaced by new ones, the Japanese imperial family, descended from the Sun Goddess, Amaterasu, had reigned since the beginning of history, venerated by subjects imbued with the virtues of loyalty and filial piety. This made the Japanese view themselves as morally superior not only to the "loathsome barbarians" from the West but to the Chinese. Indeed, Japanese antiforeign activists habitually referred to their own country rather than China as the "Middle Kingdom" at the moral center of the civilized world.

Among the exponents of the new ideology of isolation was Aizawa Seishisai (1781–1863), a Confucian scholar from the domain of Mito, who called for a program of military rearmament and spiritual mobilization to fend off the predatory foreigners. In his *Shinron (New Theses)* (1825), an influential polemic defending the policy of isolation, Aizawa gave strident voice to this new nativist ethnocentrism (see Document 4). Not only did he rail against the subversiveness of the Western religion, but he voiced a paranoid conception of Japan, surrounded by enemies who had little on their minds but how to take advantage of the country. Every move of the Russians and the English seemed to him part of an "international conspiracy" against Japan. Like most defenders of the "hallowed ancestral policy of isolation," he pointed to the economic and financial disadvantages of trade with the foreigners, but he was even more concerned about its cultural impact. Propelled as it was by the pursuit of private profit or gain, the expansion of foreign trade, he feared, would corrupt popular morals and propagate profligacy and luxuriousness among the "ignorant people" [*gumin*].

Few but the shrillest antiforeign scholars were mindless xenophobes, determined to shut out all knowledge from the outside world. Fear of the foreigners did not necessarily entail rejection of foreign knowledge. Indeed, as we have already seen, Takahashi Kageyasu, the bakufu official who had urged the promulgation of the 1825 decree, was a Dutch Studies scholar, familiar with Western-style astronomy and mathematics. Most antiforeign scholars and officials understood the advice of Sun Tzu, the classic Chinese military strategist, who said that the first requirement of defense was to "Know the enemy." This meant learning not only about the enemy's weapons and fighting techniques but gathering intelligence about its wealth, laws, customs, and institutions as well in order to evaluate their strengths and weaknesses. Indeed, the growing sense of foreign threat gave a boost to the spread of Dutch Studies and a new interest in Western technology. Men like Aizawa urged the shogun and the daimyo to manufacture Western-style guns and to train their retainers to use them.

The outbreak of the Opium War in China in 1839 increased the anxieties of antiforeign scholars and officials. The defeat of the Ch'ing army and naval forces at the hands of the English raised fears that Japan would be next on the agenda of barbarian aggression. As the Dutch Studies

scholar Sakuma Shōzan (1811–1864) argued, it would be a simple matter for the British to use forces already in the region against Japan at
little extra cost. Like Aizawa he found sinister motives behind all their
moves. To prepare for the eventuality of foreign invasion, Sakuma out-
lined a program of military readiness and institutional reform, including
the development of Western-style military technology (see Document 6).
The bakufu, on the other hand, responded more cautiously to news of
the English victory over the Ch'ing. In 1842 it eased the 1825 edict that
called for repelling foreign ships by force, and it made halting efforts to
improve the military fortification at the mouth of Edo Bay.

By the time of Perry's arrival, the Japanese elite embraced contradictory attitudes toward the Americans: On the one hand, they fitted the
Americans into the xenophobic stereotype of the greedy, wily, and
aggressive barbarian, intent on subverting the foundations of Japanese
society with their religion and their relentless pursuit of profit; on the
other hand, since knowing the enemy was the first step toward defense,
they wanted to learn more about the Americans and the land they came
from.[23] These contradictory attitudes toward the American "barbarians"
reverberated through the debate on how to respond to Perry's demands.

Traditionally the bakufu, which acted as the overlord of the local
daimyo, had monopolized the country's dealings with foreigners, but the
American challenge to the policy of isolation was so formidable that the
bakufu's leaders decided to seek out the daimyos' advice.[24] Should the
encounter with Perry escalate into a confrontation like the Opium War,
the bakufu would have to rely on their military and financial support. It
is not known how all the daimyo responded, but the extant replies suggest that their views ranged from adamant opposition to any change in
the isolation policy to expedient willingness to make temporary concessions to Perry. At one extreme, Tokugawa Nariaki, the influential daimyo
of Mito who echoed the views of antiforeign scholars and officials, urged
the bakufu to reject all of Perry's demands: Better to fight the Americans,
he argued, than capitulate to their pressure (see Document 16). Most
daimyo agreed that the bakufu should maintain the "ancestral policy" of
isolation, but since they were aware of the country's limited military capa-
bilities and apprehensive about the costs of war, they advised against such
a military confrontation with Perry.

Just how isolation was to be maintained without giving affront to the
Americans was not very clear. A few daimyo like Ii Naosuke suggested
that the bakufu should accede to some American demands temporarily
until the country was able to master new knowledge from the West in
order to develop the technology of steam power, build up its naval forces,

and strengthen coastal defenses (see Document 15). Ii recognized the superiority of Western military and naval technology, but he did not think them invincible. The Americans and the Russians, he pointed out, had only recently become skilled in the art of navigation, and eventually a newly strengthened Japan might be able to restore the policy of isolation. It was perhaps this strategy the bakufu had in mind when it signed the first treaty with the Americans.

By the time of the Harris negotiations, the consensus had moved in favor of opening of the country. Hotta Masayoshi, the chief bakufu minister, who took a stand in favor of signing a commercial treaty, warned that the alternative was probably war with all of the foreign countries (see Document 23). Except for a few firmly xenophobic daimyo, the majority had come to agree. Even Tokugawa Nariaki changed his mind, though he urged that the Japanese try to maintain control over trade with the foreigners by setting up a trade mission abroad. The only dissent came from the imperial court, ironically casting itself in a role as the chief defender of the bakufu's "ancestral policy" of isolation. In doing so, it not only cited the American affront to "national honor" but reiterated fears that the barbarian intrusion would upset internal peace and order.[25]

The final "opening" of the country in 1859, however, shifted the grounds of the debate over the "barbarian" problem. With its prestige weakened by the concessions made to the foreigners, the bakufu found itself faced with rising calls for reform. A fundamental shift in cultural consciousness was slowly taking place as more and more members of the samurai and educated commoner class came to feel that many outworn ideas, policies, and practices were no longer appropriate. Radical activists, including Yoshida Shōin and his students, called for "expulsion of the barbarians" *(jōi)*, but it was clear to many that the only realistic way to resist further foreign intrusion or control was to probe the secrets of their "wealth and power" *(fukoku kyōhei)*. Indeed, a handful of scholars, many trained in Dutch Studies, such as Yokoi Shōnan (1809–1869), began to suggest that Japan could learn not only from Western technology but from Western laws and institutions as well (see Documents 29 and 30). Such ideas were to pave the way for the final overthrow of the bakufu in 1868.

OBSERVING THE AMERICANS

Before the arrival of the Perry expedition, very few Japanese had ever laid eyes on an American, or any other Westerner for that matter, except perhaps a Dutch kapitan on his way to or from the capital at Edo (see Document 36). In that respect the policy of isolation had been enormously successful. Most Japanese remained in complete ignorance about Westerners. Popular media—books, woodblock prints, and maps—often portrayed the outside world as a frightening place, populated by strange people and fantastic beings. As one of the castaways on the *Morrison* told his American benefactors, he had been taught that in some Western countries "men were covered with hair and lived in trees" (see Document 7). That knowledge may well have come from one of the fantastic world maps that circulated in the early nineteenth century, depicting a globe populated by giants, pygmies, women warriors, and other semihuman creatures; or it may have come from the widely circulated illustrated books of the woodblock artist Hokusai, who drew curious pictures of humans with no eyes, holes in their chests, no heads, or improbably long (or short) arms and legs.

Yet isolation was unable to quench the palpable curiosity that ordinary Japanese, overcoming fears of official reprisal, demonstrated whenever a foreign vessel made its way to Japanese shores. When the *Morrison* weighed anchor in Edo Bay in 1837, its decks were soon aswarm with inquisitive local fishermen, marveling at the height of its masts or scrutinizing the goats and pigs on board, and the same thing happened when other American vessels reached Japan. After Perry's arrival opportunities to satisfy curiosity about the Americans multiplied swiftly. New and closer contact with the foreigners did not necessarily diminish distrust or hostility, but it did break down the demonic caricatures and stereotypes constructed by the antiforeign ideologues, leading to a much more complicated and much more puzzling image of the Americans.

Observers were not necessarily any more reliable than the xenophobes. Often what were purported to be eyewitness depictions of the Americans turned out to be secondhand or even totally imaginary reports, but even those who met the Americans face to face or who visited the United States could convey only limited fragments of what they had seen or experienced. Invariably what they saw in the United States was filtered through lenses of status, age, and gender or was shaped by what they were doing there. A high-ranking samurai on a diplomatic mission was likely to see an America very different from the one a castaway fisherman saw, and both observers had to translate their impressions into familiar terms. Nevertheless, within a few years of Perry's arrival, familiarity with the Americans and the United States grew as new reports, travel accounts, and other information accumulated.

The arrival of the first Perry expedition, which plunged the city of Edo into a panic,[26] aroused intense popular curiosity about the Americans. News of the "black ships" spread quickly, reaching the ends of the archipelago within days. While there were no modern communications like telegraph lines or telephones, nor even a very extensive postal system, travelers between the capital and the remoter domains exchanged gossip and rumor along the way at tea shops and inns, and cargo boats plying the sea coast carried with them news as well as goods. Many domains sent samurai observers to bring back reports of the Americans and their ships and artists to record what they saw. The official expedition report noted the "inordinate curiosity" of the Japanese officials who visited. But curiosity was also shown by commoners, who went to see the Americans with their own eyes. Sugano Hachirō, a wealthy peasant farmer from Fukushima who made his way to Kanagawa in early February 1854, recorded in his diary that he saw "foreign ships like mountains" and heard cannon salutes that made children cover their ears and sent old people scurrying under the covers. The contents of the Perry treaty soon became known to the wealthier and better educated farmers, even in the more remote mountain villages, and by the late 1850s copies of the treaties with the Americans were being sold all over the country at a modest price.

Many commoners (and samurai) came to know of Perry's visit through popular woodblock prints and broadsides, the functional equivalent of our supermarket tabloid papers (see Documents 17–19). These pictorial representations of the Americans and their ships probably had more credibility for the commoners than reports by word of mouth. Many prints and broadsides simply presented information about the Americans—the size and number of their ships, how fast they could travel, where they came from and what their country's population was—but others fed the public appetite for the fantastic and catered to its fear of the "red hairs." Widely circulated woodblock portraits of Perry, executed by artists who had never laid eyes on him, were caricatures in the antiforeign tradition, portraying him less as a human than as a frightful or ferocious barbarian beast. Many broadsides reported news of events that never happened, such as the capture and humiliation of Americans who attacked an island off the coast of Kyūshū (see Document 18). Other popular art works spoofed the odd and sometimes cunning behavior of the Americans (see Document 20).

The market for news about the Americans was robust, and the more startling the news, the better it would sell. Many prints reassured their viewers that the Americans were nothing to be afraid of. Often the Americans were portrayed as being overwhelmed by traditional Japanese deities, who smote them with bolts of lightning or other supernatural forces. Another popular scene, based on actual events, showed sumo wrestlers delivering heavy bales of rice to the Americans as a parting gift from the bakufu, as puny little American sailors looked on in awe or struggled unsuccessfully to lift the bales themselves (see Document 17). (The sumo wrestler triumphing in a brawl with an American sailor was a popular theme in many prints of the late 1850s as well.) The message was clear: The Americans might have steamships and heavy guns, but as individuals they were not so formidable at all. The bakufu authorities, anxious to bolster popular confidence that the Americans were under control, were doubtless happy to see such a message circulated.

With the opening of the treaty ports in 1859 came opportunities for more firsthand observation of the Americans and other foreigners. It was as though a piece of the outside world had been transplanted to Japan, providing the Japanese with a small-scale model of what the West was like. In the treaty ports of Yokohama, Kōbe, and Nagasaki the Japanese could see with their very own eyes not only the steamships and cannons that made the West so powerful but the daily lifestyles, customs, and material culture of the Americans and other foreigners. As one American treaty port merchant noted, the port of Yokohama presented the "contrast of the civilization of the Nineteenth Century with the semibarbarism of the Fifteenth [i.e., Japan]" (see Document 26). The treaty ports, which lay outside legal writ of the bakufu, also offered access to foreign books, newspapers, magazines, and pictures, unrestricted by official censorship. Soon some of this information was finding its way into Japanese translation.[27]

During the early 1860s commercial artists and publishers produced "Yokohama prints" *(Yokohama-e)* that represented, sometimes quite fancifully, what life among the foreigners was like. The sexual habits of the foreigners were of continual interest to a Japanese audience, whose views on the matter were generally much more tolerant than those of a more puritanical America. Since the majority of the treaty port residents were young unmarried males liberated from conventions that might have restrained them at home, woodblock artists had ample reason to show rowdy, dissolute, and lascivious foreigners whiling away their idle hours drinking, gambling, and patronizing the licensed brothels set up by the Japanese on the outskirts of town. And scenes of carousing foreign sailors were common too.

But other prints showed peaceful domestic scenes, based not on actual observation but copied from foreign publications. Many depictions of the American life, for example, were gleaned from illustrations in *Frank Leslie's Illustrated Newspaper,* a popular American news weekly. Although the printmakers often did not get the details right, they were fascinated with the Americans' peculiar clothes and interesting gadgets—their top hats and crinoline skirts, their watches and sewing machines. Not too surprisingly, just as fashionably dressed geisha had been the subject of traditional woodblock prints, the Yokohama prints often depicted American women, few of whom were actually to be found at the port. For the first time too, the Americans and other foreigners were shown with wives and children. The Yokohama prints still exoticized the Americans but did not demonize them as prints of the Perry expedition sometimes did. Their homely details presented the Americans neither as dissolute nor deceitful but as a placid and plain people given to the simple pleasures of domesticity (see Document 27).

For the most part, the prints and publications that came out of the treaty ports, including guidebooks such as Hashimoto Sadahide's *Yokohama kaikō kenbun shi (A Record of Observations in the Open Port of Yokohama)*, offered vicarious knowledge of the Americans, but there were a growing number of Japanese who had seen the United States firsthand (see Document 28). The earliest were castaway Japanese sailors and fishermen repatriated by foreign vessels. Although many castaways were fearful of being executed on their return home, the death penalty was rarely carried out. Instead, the returnees were subject to intense interrogation by bakufu officials at Nagasaki and Matsumae, often lasting several months. The authorities were anxious to make sure that the castaways had not been converted to Christianity or subverted by their experiences abroad, but they also wanted to extract from them as much information about the outside world as they could. Since most castaways were ill educated or uneducated, their observations were of limited value, but the few who had learned English or some other foreign language, or who had lived among the foreigners for an extended period, were a useful source of information.

The most famous castaway was Nakahama Manjirō (1827–1898), a fisherman's son who returned to Japan in 1851 after several years of living in the United States, where he had been taken under the wing of an American whaling captain in New Bedford, Massachusetts. The record of his interrogation, much of which seems quite bizarre to an American reader, shows how hungry the bakufu authorities were for firsthand information about the Americans and how difficult it was to assimilate that information (see Document 11). Manjirō's recollections may well have been accurate, but his interrogators were forced to translate his experience into terms comprehensible to themselves, finding vocabulary to describe things, from churches to privies, that did not exist in Japan. The report, compiled at a time when the bakufu was expecting the arrival of an American expedition, was kept secret from the public. Indeed, Manjirō's account of life in the United States was so sympathetic that Tokugawa Nariaki opposed using him as the official interpreter for the Perry negotiations for fear that he might work for the advantage of the Americans rather than the Japanese.

After the signing of the treaties, much fuller accounts of life in the United States were published by other former castaways. Few knew the country as well or had immersed themselves in its society as deeply or spoke its language as fluently as Hamada Hikozō (Joseph Heco), who returned to Japan in 1859 to settle in Yokohama. Hamada, who had the distinction of meeting three American presidents (Pierce, Buchanan, and Lincoln), was the first Japanese to be naturalized as an American citizen. As one might expect, his account of the United States was highly sympathetic, but it also demonstrated the difficulty of getting the Japanese to understand a society so radically alien from their own (see Document 12). Although baptized as a Christian, he wrote about American religion using terms more appropriate to Buddhism, and in describing the governmental system he had to strain to find vocabulary that might make sense to a Japanese reader. The more observers like Hamada moved beyond the material surface of life, the more difficult it was for them to explain exactly what American culture was.

The problem was all the more severe for members of the first diplomatic mission to the United States in 1860, the first samurai to glimpse American culture with all its complexities, unfamiliarities, and contradictions. The mission, dispatched to exchange ratification of the Harris treaty, was originally proposed by Iwase Tadanari (1818–1861), an astute bakufu official who hoped to see the American capital with his own eyes. The mission included several young "foreign experts" in the employ of the bakufu, like Fukuzawa Yukichi (1835–1901) and Katsu Kaishū (1823–1899), as well as a dozen or more young samurai from various domains who had wanted to see America for themselves. But most of the mission members were petty officials with no particular interest in the West.

What makes accounts of the mission so interesting is precisely the fact that its members were rather conventional, neither radically committed nor opposed to the opening of Japan. The cultural shock of confronting the odd customs and behavior of the Americans eroded their cultural certainties, loosening the hold of a narrow ethnocentrism in quite unexpected ways. The diaries and journals of the mission members are filled with expressions of astonishment and confusion, admiration and contempt that reveal the state of their cultural disorientation. They were navigating an unfamiliar social and cultural landscape, lacking in familiar markers and signposts, that confounded their conventional ways of evaluating, weighing, and judging the behavior of others. Sometimes their confusion led to simple faux pas, like drinking water from a finger bowl or mistaking a chamber pot for a washbasin, but often it ran deeper. As Muragaki Norimasa (1813–1880), the mission's second in command, noted in a poem: "So strange is everything, their language, their appearance / That I feel as if living in a dream-land" (see Document 32).

With few exceptions the mission members were impressed by the factories, hospitals, schools, museums, arsenals, and public buildings their proud American hosts were so eager to show them. But as their journals and reminiscences reveal, what confused them, and often evoked their contempt or criticism, were the social habits, customs, and manners of the Americans. The informality of the Americans, particularly of high officials, was unsettling to men who were used to calibrating the nuance of every gesture and move in official encounters. For example, Muragaki Norimasa, who had taken the trouble to dress in his most formal ceremonial kimono when he visited the White House, was surprised that the American president met the delegation in a "simple black costume of coat and trousers in the same fashion as any merchant" with neither sword nor decoration to mark his rank. He was also taken aback by the presence of women at official ceremonies, a thing unheard of at home. Such practices merely confirmed just how "barbarous" the Americans were. Equally puzzling were the institutions of the "republic," especially the Congress, whose members behaved like merchants at the Nihonbashi fish market at Edo.

The younger, lower-ranking members of the mission, however, were often attracted by what they saw in American society. The lack of official decorum that Muragaki deplored, for example, appealed to others. Even without the elaborate rituals and constraints regarded as necessary to maintain order in Japanese society, the Americans seemed to manage quite well. As Fukushima Yoshikoto (b. 1841), a minor attendant, noted: "The high officials of this country are not indecently scornful of their subordinates, nor do they show off their authority. For that reason ordinary people do not fawn upon high officials, and the country's wealth and the people's tranquility rest safe and steadfast."[28] Even Muragaki admitted that the reason the Americans paid so little attention to formalities was that "their country allows neither prudishness nor class discrimination, but is ruled by the principles of sincerity and friendship." While the Americans might act as boorishly as country bumpkins at times, that did not mean that they lacked a sense of "benevolence" or "propriety."

The mission's visit to the United States undermined any firm sense of Japan's cultural or moral superiority among many of its members, who returned home tinged by a new cultural relativism. As Fukushima reported:

> In Japan seven or eight out of ten people think of the Europeans as no different from dogs and horses [i.e., beasts]. There are even some who attack them with swords. . . . Well, the Westerners do not do this. They show benevolence to foreigners, and they treat them like members of their own family. Among [the foreign countries] America is a new country. The character of its people is temperate, and even though their real intentions are difficult to understand, they appear on the surface to be frank and honest. . . . Most of the seventy-seven members of the mission had been angry and hateful toward [the Americans], but nevertheless when they came to understand the truth [about them] all regretted their past error.[29]

Such views were still limited to a tiny minority among the samurai class, but that they existed at all demonstrates how thoroughly a direct encounter with American society could disturb the cultural moorings of the elite.

By the time of the Iwakura mission, dispatched by the new imperial government to tour the outside world in 1871, the political and cultural landscape in Japan had changed completely. The new imperial government in Tokyo (as the city of Edo was renamed) had plunged headlong into a program of reform. A flurry of government laws had banned "barbarous" customs like mixed bathing in public bathhouses and eroded old legal distinctions between commoner and samurai. With the help of foreign advisors, engineers, and workmen, telegraph lines were being strung along the old highway system, a railway line was being constructed to link Tokyo and Yokohama, and a modern mint was established at Ōsaka to produce a new national currency. Craftsmen at new government arsenals and naval yards were learning how to use Western machinery, and a few small modern mechanized cotton spinning or silk reeling operations were starting up. Most dramatically of all, shortly before the departure of the Iwakura mission, the old daimyo domains were finally abolished, replaced by a new prefectural system under the full control of the imperial government.

The members of the Iwakura mission, nearly all of them top-ranking government officials, arrived in the United States eager to learn all they could about the country. As Itō Hirobumi (1841–1909), one of its few English-speaking members, assured an audience in San Francisco: "Today it is the earnest wish of both our Government and our people to strive for the highest points of civilization enjoyed by more enlightened countries. . . . The red disk in the center of our national flag shall no longer appear like a wafer over a sealed empire, but henceforth be . . . the noble emblem of the rising sun, moving onward and upward amid the enlightened nations of the world."[30] Well aware that the treaties the bakufu signed with the Americans and the other foreign powers treated the Japanese as an "unenlightened" or "half-enlightened" people, the new imperial government was anxious to achieve parity with the treaty powers. Although the ostensible purpose of the mission was to seek a renegotiation of the treaties, its real purpose was to let the country's new leadership investigate conditions that had created "wealth and power" in the West.

The decision to visit the United States rather than Europe first was not entirely a matter of geography. Not only was America the country with which the Japanese had signed the first treaty, it was also the newest of the Western nations. In contrast to the bakufu mission of 1860, which spent most of its time in Washington and New York, the Iwakura mission traveled across the continent from California through the Rockies and the Great Plains to Chicago before heading toward the East Coast. From their railroad carriages they could see the country's vast expanse, and on their stops along the way they learned how quickly the country had grown. The question they must have asked themselves was: How had the United States, founded as an independent state only a century before, unified and developed itself so rapidly, while Japan, with a fraction of its territory but a population equal in size and a much longer history, was still so backward and poor? Although the mission visited twelve countries altogether, its final report, compiled by Kume Kunitake (1839–1931), devoted one-fifth of its pages to the United States (see Document 35). It concluded that the secret of America's success lay not simply in the enormous physical and natural wealth of the country but in the industriousness, vitality, and foresightedness of its people.

The Japanese visitors with the best opportunity to observe American life were the students who arrived in the late 1860s. A handful of venturesome young Japanese smuggled themselves out of Japan or were dispatched to study in the United States by their domains even before the Meiji Restoration. With the help of the American missionary Guido Verbeck, for example, two nephews of Yokoi Shōnan came to the United States in 1866 to study at a private academy in New Brunswick, New Jersey, before going on to the naval academy at Annapolis. By the early 1870s there were perhaps two hundred or so Japanese students in the United States, most of them on government scholarships, but a few supported by their own income or by their families. Nearly all came from samurai backgrounds, and nearly all returned home to occupy important positions as diplomats, high government officials, university professors, scientists, or engineers. Yet despite their ability to speak and read English — many nearly forgot their native Japanese during their years abroad — their impressions of American society were limited. Attending schools in the Northeast (New England, New York, and New Jersey), and often boarding in the households of their teachers or professors, it was the genteel life and values of the white Protestant North to which they were exposed. Had they lived and studied in a southern market town or a frontier village, their impressions of America would have been quite different.

By the mid-1870s the Japanese elite were coming more and more to identify America with the culture of the East Coast middle and upper classes. The undifferentiated America described by the castaways and the simple caricatures brushed by woodblock artists were fading, and in their place a more complicated picture of the American cultural hierarchy was emerging. The report of the Iwakura mission, for example, devoted much space to blacks, Indians, and others who lived on the margins of American society, but it also reflected distinctions made within the white population as well. The rough and ready port of San Francisco was their gateway to America, but it was to eastern cities like Boston and New York that the members of the Iwakura mission looked for the sources of American culture and values. In their eyes, the East Coast was more "civilized" than the rest of the country, and it was there that they sought to learn the most.

INTERPRETING THE AMERICANS

Observing the Americans was one thing; interpreting them was another. Occasionally, of course, observers had to interpret simply because they were trying to translate the unfamiliar into the familiar. Take the case of the Dutch Studies scholar Mitsukuri Shōgo (1821–1847), who wrote the first detailed account of the United States in his illustrated *World Atlas (Konyo zushiki)* (see Document 10). When he came across the puzzling word "republic" in one of his Dutch sources, he looked it up in a Dutch dictionary only to find that it meant a political system with no monarch, a complete anomaly in Japanese or Chinese historical experience. Ōtsuki Bankei (1801–1878), another Dutch Studies scholar, suggested that he translate the word as *kyōwa* ("cooperative harmony"), a term applied to a brief period in ancient Chinese history when two ministers ruled together without a monarch after a dissolute king had been driven from power. The connotation, of course, was quite different from that of "republic," which is derived from the Latin *res publica* (public affairs), but Mitsukuri, who did not know that, used it anyway.[31]

No doubt the suggestion that American government was based on "cooperation" and "harmony" tempted reform-minded scholars to see the United States as a kind of political utopia. Even though they understood the institutions of a "republic" only dimly, they were impressed by the firm political unity and high popular morale in the United States, a country so much vaster than their own. For example, in describing his plan for building "national wealth and strength," Yokoi Shōnan, an influential scholar from the domain of Saga, invoked George Washington as a model ruler who, like the Chinese sage kings Yao and Shun, had laid down enduring institutions for a prosperous society (see Document 29). Although his reform plans relied on traditional Japanese formulas, and although he remained hostile to Western religion, Yokoi was willing to present America as a new model for enlightened and benevolent rule.

Until the late 1860s the Japanese continued to struggle with the opacity of American institutions and customs. Although more and more familiar with the surface of American material life and daily behavior, from its gold watches to its sewing machines, the Japanese still had trouble grasping the "essence" of American culture. Fragments of cultural information gathered from direct contact with the Americans had yet to be assembled into an image of what might be called the core values of American society or fitted into new cultural paradigms to replace the old distinction between the "cultured" and the "barbarian"—those with the "Way" and those without it. Such new paradigms did not really take hold until the establishment of a new imperial government committed to importing the customs, institutions, and ideas of countries once considered barbarian. The process began with a redefinition of Japan's position in the world.

As knowledge of the West grew, the Japanese found themselves suddenly displaced from the cultural pinnacle on which late Tokugawa thinkers like Aizawa Seishisai had placed it. It was no longer possible to put Japan at the center of a moral universe, let alone at the center of the world. The traditional universalism embodied in the Confucian worldview was gradually supplanted by a new universalism imported from the West. The older hierarchy of humankind, which separated the cultured from the barbarian on the basis of Confucian moral values, was replaced by a new one rooted primarily in the criteria of visible wealth and strength, but linked to Christian and Enlightenment values as well. By the early 1870s the modernizing elite accepted the Western notion that human societies could be ranked along a continuum from "savagery" to "civilization," each representing different stages in the "progress" of humankind. And it became the goal of the new imperial government to escape from its "unenlightened" or "half-enlightened" past by acquiring the technology, institutions, and even the daily customs of the "civilized" nations.

The transformation of Japan's perception of itself as a local culture instead of as a "central kingdom" led the Japanese to identify themselves with the "Orient" or "East" *(tōyō)* as opposed to the "Occident" or "West" *(seiyō)*. These terms were not entirely new, but their meanings had changed. For example, the word for "Orient" (literally "Eastern Seas") had originally been used by the Chinese to refer to Japan, which was located to their east. But with the arrival of the Europeans and the Americans, cultural geography underwent a profound shift. Obviously, since every point on the same meridian is both east and west of every other, it made sense only for the Westerners to refer to Asia as the "Orient" because that was the direction voyagers from the early Portuguese to Perry had sailed to reach it. Conversely, although the seventeenth-century Japanese had thought of the Europeans as "southern barbarians" because that was direction from which they approached Japan, the nineteenth-century Japanese came to think of them as "Western barbarians" instead. Even more important, "Orient" came to signify not so much a place as a state of mind or a set of attitudes that marked a profound moral and cultural division in humankind.

Finally, as the Japanese absorbed the Western worldview, they discovered that they belonged to the "yellow race." Like most people, the Japanese had always been aware of physical differences between themselves and outsiders, but only in the late 1860s did they learn that humankind was divided into "five races"—the white, red, brown, black, and yellow.[32] Interestingly, however, since the old Confucian view that ultimately "All men are brothers" retained its force, the notion of race at first merely served as another marker of distinctions among humankind (see Document 38). It was only later, after the introduction of the theory of evolution to Japan, that the Japanese adopted the Western notion that race was linked to the cultural hierarchy of "civilization."

Fukuzawa Yukichi, whose widely read work *Seiyō jijō (Conditions in the West),* provided an encyclopedic survey of the major countries of the West, introduced many of these new concepts. The title itself, of course, assumed the contrast between "West" and "East," and the book's frontispiece displayed pictures of each of the "five races" (see Document 38). The basic paradigm behind Fukuzawa's work was a teleological model of history that sorted peoples and societies on the basis of their development toward "civilization" (see Document 39). It drew heavily on the works of Western historians like François Guizot (1787–1874) and Henry Thomas Buckle (1821–1862), who wrote grand narratives of human progress, chronicling the growth of an ever more bountiful, ever more enlightened, and ever more peaceful human society. Although this reading of history may seem naive to anyone living in the late twentieth century, it was revolutionary for men nurtured in a culture that conventionally looked to the past for its social ideals.

The model of civilization Fukuzawa presented was largely based on his observations of England and the United States, the two Western countries he had visited. In *Seiyō jijō,* he described civilization largely in terms of material culture, institutions, inventions, and social practices—from steam engines to national assemblies—but in his later writings he suggested that it involved attitudes or values such as openness, freedom, equality, rationality, and productivity as well. Fukuzawa and other writers in the early 1870s did not simply equate civilization with Western culture. Japanese visitors to the West, such as the members the Iwakura mission, were quick to observe that the countries of Eastern and Southern Europe were less "civilized" than those of Northern Europe, and from that it was easy to conclude that geography neither guaranteed progress nor hindered it. Any society, it seemed, whether in the "West" or in the "Orient," could become civilized if it had the will to do so. In this sense, civilization was universal.

By the early 1870s the Japanese political and intellectual elite realized that America represented a distinctive variant of civilization. There can be little doubt that the feature of American culture that the Japanese found most distinctive was its spirit of freedom, independence, and self-reliance. For Fukuzawa, whose early writings idealized the United States as a country where the laws were magnanimous, the people were unfettered, class distinctions were absent, and lineage and pedigree counted for little, what made America different was the "independence" *(jishu)* and "free choice" *(nin'i)* of its citizens. All the early Japanese visitors to the United States, from Joseph Heco onward, were also impressed by the openness of American society. Native or foreign, anyone could enter the White House unhindered by the guards or gates that kept the royal palaces of Europe blocked to ordinary folk, and the American president could stroll the streets of the capital without an entourage of guards and attendants.

But freedom meant more than a mere lack of hierarchy and ceremony; it was the wellspring of national development. As they passed through the Western frontier, the members of the Iwakura mission came to appreciate how much the United States was a self-made country, created by inhabitants who chose to live there and who brought with them a spirit of independence. As Kume Kunitake perceptively noted at the end of the report on the United States:

> Thus, this country is newly founded, its land is newly opened, and its people are immigrants. But withal it is a place where those Europeans most endowed with the spirit of independence and self-government have gathered and are in control, and moreover, since its vast land is fertile and its goods abundant, they have developed splendid sites of production and acting in a grand and bold manner have carried all things before them. This, we can say, is why America is America.[33]

In other words, the pursuit of liberty and freedom not only made the United States a "true republic" unrivaled in the world, it was responsible for the very construction of the nation.

To their surprise perhaps, many Japanese visitors and observers were also impressed by the centrality of religion in American culture. While the Japanese continued to find much that was absurd and illogical in Christian belief, they came to understand that American Christianity was quite different from the Christianity that the Japanese had encountered in the sixteenth and seventeenth centuries. The Iwakura mission report, for example, concluded that American Protestants held to a far deeper faith than the perfunctory devotions of Buddhist and Shintō believers in Japan, and that Protestantism's firm moral code provided the country's spiritual backbone. However odd the stories in the Bible might seem, this "sacred book" provided moral guidance for Americans just as the Confucian classics did for the Japanese. Indeed, some Japanese observers, no doubt reflecting the views of their American interlocutors, came to the conclusion that Protestantism was associated with "progress" and "civilization" in a way that other varieties of Christianity such as Roman Catholicism and Greek Orthodoxy were not. It was, after all, the Protestant countries that had succeeded in industrializing.[34]

Finally, the Japanese were also impressed by the social importance of education in the United States, where the number of schools, schoolchildren, and newspapers seemed to surpass that of other countries. In *Seiyō jijō,* Fukuzawa Yukichi pointed out that there was hardly a city, town, or village in the Western countries that did not boast a school. In Japan the daimyo domains had provided education for young samurai, but schools for commoner children were supported by private fees. By contrast, the American government regarded the support of elementary education for all children as one of its most important functions. From the ages of six or seven boys and girls alike were sent to school to learn history, geography, arithmetic, astronomy, elementary science, poetry, music, and so forth. The focus of education on such practical subjects meant that American schools served to spread knowledge rather than simply to shape character or morality.

Indeed, many Japanese leaders and intellectuals concluded that widespread elementary education was what produced the human resources that made America so rich and strong. After a visit to elementary schools in Washington, Kido Takayoshi, a top government leader in the Iwakura mission, noted in his diary that "it will be difficult indeed for us to promote the enlightenment of the common people and to develop their intellects in order to promote our national sovereignty and prevent any infringement on our independence" unless the government devoted itself to the building of a school system. One of the most radical advocates of educational reform was Mori Arinori, the first Japanese minister to the United States, who urged that Japan adopt an American-style educational system that would "provide universal learning and include all classes and kinds of persons without distinction and with perfect impartiality." By that he meant that education should not only cross class lines but cross gender lines as well. "Everyone," he wrote, "whether male or female should be its recipient."[35] Mori solicited the opinions of several dozen leading American scholars and educators on how Japan should reform its educational institutions and what the content of education should be, and in the early 1870s, the government carried out reforms with the help of American advisors, and translated American textbooks were in wide use in the new school system.

Even though the Japanese elite had always appreciated the value of education, especially moral education, the prosperity and productivity of American society clearly convinced them that basic universal education held the key to national strength; so did the wide diffusion of knowledge. In contrast to Japanese society, where higher learning usually focused on the scrutiny of historical and philosophical texts, the Americans were seen as constantly educating themselves in the rational, practical, scientific disciplines required in the new age of progress and steam power. As the Iwakura mission report observed, while the "Orient" pursued "the study of abstract principles *(mukei no rigaku)* " (i.e., metaphysics and philosophy), the Americans devoted themselves to the "study of material principles *(yūkei no rigaku)* " (i.e., science and technology), using their learning to make new discoveries in agriculture, commerce, and industry. Bakufu officials like Muragaki Norimasa had found the artifacts displayed at the Smithsonian Institution to be examples of American barbarism in 1860, but the Iwakura mission report praised the Americans for their public museums and botanical gardens (see Document 35). It was by such means, the mission believed, that common people were exposed to practical knowledge that gave the Americans and other Westerners their superior technology and guaranteed their "wealth and power."

REJECTING THE AMERICAN MODEL

The act of interpreting American culture was a process of self-discovery for the Japanese of the 1870s. As they reflected on how they differed from the Americans, they were learning to redefine themselves. The contrasts between the "Orient" and the "Occident," even when deployed to criticize their own institutions or behavior, served to underline what was essential and distinctive about Japanese culture. Interpretation was also a way of sorting out what elements of "civilization" constituted the irreducible requisites of "national wealth and power." It was through interpretation that the Japanese elite concluded that though much was to be admired in American culture, in the final analysis not all of it appeared relevant to the construction of a "New Japan." Weighing which aspects of the American model would work in Japan and which would not narrowed the choices that had to be made in their own pursuit of establishing parity with the "civilized" countries.

For example, most Japanese observers agreed that although the Americans were advanced in the arts of peace, the country was not impressive as a military power. The local militia who turned out for the parades and ceremonies greeting the Iwakura mission, for example, were not professional soldiers but part-time amateurs. Kido Takayoshi, a member of the Iwakura mission, was surprised to learn that the proprietor of a Washington, D.C., store where he fitted himself out with Western clothes was a colonel in command of the capital's militia. Even the arsenals and shipyards the Americans so proudly showed the mission were no match for those they saw in England and Europe. The mission's leaders were especially impressed by their visit to Berlin, where Helmuth von Moltke (1848–1916), the fabled chief of the German general staff, and Otto von Bismarck (1815–1898), the German chancellor, told them candidly that only if a country increased its military power would it be treated as an equal by other states. This advice so clearly suited the Japanese leaders' goals that, not surprisingly, they turned increasingly to Imperial Germany as a model.

For a time, to be sure, the new imperial government experimented with the American political model.[36] In June 1868 the government promulgated a basic constitutional document that echoed American political practices: it set up a bicameral legislature, provided that high officials be changed every four years, and asserted that the government's power be divided among executive, legislative, and judicial functions.[37] After only a year, however, the document was supplanted by a more conservative one, and gradually the government turned away from the American model. Leaders like Kido Takayoshi, who spent his days in Washington poring over a draft translation of the American Constitution, continued to be interested in the American political system, but they had no intention of turning Japan into an American-style republic. Like most former samurai, Kido harbored reservations about giving too much power to the ordinary people, and so did radical antigovernment activists like Itagaki Taisuke (1837–1919), who called for a popularly elected national assembly but wanted to limit suffrage to the ex-samurai, the well-to-do landlords, and the rich merchants. In the debate over whether and how to establish a constitutional system during the late 1870s, the American model was pushed aside in favor of the examples of the British and the German constitutional monarchies, which seemed more appropriate to Japan's circumstances. Even former U.S. President Ulysses S. Grant (1822–1885), when he visited Japan in 1879, warned the Meiji emperor and his ministers to proceed cautiously in establishing a representative body, since the rights of suffrage and representation were difficult to withdraw once they had been granted.

It was not merely the lack of a historical tradition of representation that made the American political model less appealing to the Japanese. As the Japanese became more and more familiar with the actual workings of American democracy, they discovered negative aspects of representative government that seemed to counterbalance its positive aspects. They found disturbing the demonstrable flaws of the democratic process—the arbitrariness of the majority rule, the dangers of demagoguery and mob rule, the sacrifice of public good to the interests of the few, and the corruption of officials and elected representatives. In 1875 even Fukuzawa Yukichi, an early admirer of the American political system, had come to the conclusion: "Popular government turns out to mean that the people unite and use force, and this use of force does not differ in severity from that of an absolute monarch; the only difference is that in one case it is initiated by the whim of one man and in the other case by the masses."[38] The idea of a "republic" seemed less enticing than it had been to Yokoi Shōnan.

Indeed, the Japanese were uncomfortable with much that flowed from the excess of freedom that the Americans enjoyed. For example, they found it difficult to understand or accept the American gender system. While women did not enjoy political equality with men in the United States, as Japanese visitors observed over and over again, women were given extraordinary freedom and precedence in ordinary social transactions. Not only were women present on social occasions where they would not be in Japan, they were also much bolder and more assertive than Japanese women. Men like Fukuzawa Yukichi, who spoke of the need for "male-female equality" or called for the introduction of greater equality in marriage relationships, found few supporters. Even though many American women thought that they were due more freedoms, the prevailing view in Japan was that American women were entirely too liberated (see Documents 35 and 36). In the United States and Europe men appeared to have become slaves to women and, to many, that appeared to contravene the natural order of things. To build the "national wealth and strength" of Japan it was less important that women be placed on an equal footing with men than they become "good mothers" able to educate their children for life in a "civilized" society.

Nor despite their admiration for Protestant pietism did the Japanese elite rush to embrace the foreign faith after the ban on Christianity was eased. Most Protestant missionaries who came to Japan in the 1860s and 1870s were Americans, often New Englanders whose erudition, puritanical ideals, and stiff moral standards persuaded many young men from the former samurai and educated commoner classes to become Christian converts. These missionaries also played an important role in the founding of new schools and colleges that introduced the "new knowledge" so avidly sought from the West. But by the late 1870s many Japanese intellectuals argued that the country should return to traditional values as the basis of a new national morality. The radical egalitarianism of the American-style Christianity, with its celebration of the human conscience and its distrust of hierarchy, seemed dangerous to a government anxious to consolidate its hold on the commoner populace. In a sense, the old fear that Christianity might undercut the moral foundations of Japanese society persisted.

By the end of the 1870s enthusiasm for American culture and institutions as a model was beginning to fade. If growing familiarity had not bred contempt for the United States, it certainly raised doubts about many aspects of American life. For the nation's new leadership America was less a "shining city upon a hill" than a useful source of practical advice on specific matters, such as how to build a new educational system, how to start up a new banking system, or how to develop the "frontier" in Hokkaidō. In the overall reconstruction of their society, however, the Japanese elite felt more comfortable with models provided by the older societies of Europe, especially of England and Germany, whose long histories and hierarchical societies more closely resembled their own. Instead of constructing a new "republic," they created a new monarchical state managed by a self-selecting bureaucracy.

As the Japanese contrasted their own success in building national wealth and power with the "decline" of their "semicivilized" neighbors in Korea and China, the cultural self-confidence forfeited in the humiliating first encounter with the Americans began to recover. The political and intellectual leaders of the "New Japan" were willing to acknowledge their debt to America, and they were gratified that the Americans were less predatory toward other countries than the European powers. Nevertheless, they were ready to chart their own course, certain that they could achieve a new cultural synthesis that buttressed lessons learned from the West with reinvigoration of Japan's own cultural traditions. By the 1880s a revival of Confucian ethics, if not the Confucian worldview, was well underway, and textbooks extolling loyalty and filial piety as patriotic virtues for the modern state had supplanted older ones based on American texts.

But even though the political and intellectual establishment looked less and less to the United States for inspiration, America remained a model for radicals, dissidents, and reformers who wanted to push Japan farther than its leaders were willing to. Members of the antigovernment "popular rights" movement that gathered strength in the late 1870s continued to idealize America as the "land of liberty" and to glorify democratic heroes like Patrick Henry and George Washington. *Kajin no kigu (Chance Meetings with Beautiful Women)*, an 1885 political novel written by the journalist and politician Shiba Shirō, a journalist who went to study in the United States in 1879, opens with a scene at Independence Hall in Philadelphia, where the protagonist waxes eloquent about the American Revolution. He offers an unrestrained encomium of American society:

> Americans have made it a rule to side with the weak and crush the strong; and within the country they have produced schools instead of arms, encouraged industry and commerce, fostered agriculture, and established this rich, strong, and civilized nation for themselves. They are thus now enjoying liberty and singing the praises of peace. . . . Our people are too myopic. . . . Out of personal grudges they ignore public duties, and out of personal friendship they employ mediocre persons.

When we compare them with Americans, who abandon personal feelings, follow public opinions, and serve their country, we see between the two a gap as vast as the gap between heaven and earth.[39]

Like the author, the protagonist saw the gap between the two countries as one to be bridged, not celebrated.

Although their efforts had only limited impact on Japanese society, a small but vocal minority continued to utopianize America. In the 1880s political radicals seeking the freedom to express their views sought refuge in the United States, especially in California, where a small group of exiles began publishing antigovernment newspapers. Social reformers, inspired by antiprostitution or temperance activists in the United States, advocated similar changes in Japan. And early Japanese feminists, inspired by the relative freedom of American women and the ideals of domesticity represented by the American middle class, tried to uproot the patterns of gender behavior that seemed so deeply embedded in their own society. But the practical effect of their efforts was limited. Only when the United States began to raise barriers against Japanese immigration in the early twentieth century did disillusion set in among admirers of America, who were forced to conclude that America was betraying its own ideals of freedom and equality.

THE AMERICAN DISCOVERY OF JAPAN

In the years after the Civil War, Americans were concerned less about the outside world than about what was going on at home—the reconstruction of the South, expansion into the wide-open spaces of the Far West, and the industrialization of the Northeast. To the extent Americans worried about the outside world at all, their gaze was usually turned across the Atlantic rather than the Pacific. Japan, however, was becoming less and less the terra incognita that it had been at the time of Perry's arrival at Uraga. A small but steady trickle of American diplomats, travelers, merchants, teachers, and missionaries in Japan sent back reports of how the country was changing, and a rising flow of exports from Japan was finding a ready market in the United States. For those interested in Asia, it was becoming clear that the "New Japan" was very different not only from the "Old Japan" but from its Asian neighbors too.

In the 1870s many Americans came to know Japan by what it produced. The Japanese goods exhibited at the 1876 Centennial Exposition in

Philadlephia, second in volume only to those exhibited by the British, attracted much public interest by their novelty. The tea pavilion, delicate porcelain plates, bronze statues, elegant lacquerware, jade artifacts, and rich silk brocades on display presented an entirely new and exotic aesthetic to the American middle-class audience, and some critics were even willing to concede that Japan had achieved a highly advanced sense of beauty that surpassed even that of the West. "We have been accustomed to regard [Japan] as uncivilized, or half-civilized at best," wrote one, "but we found here abundant evidences that it outshines the most cultivated nations of Europe in arts which are their pride and glory, and which are regarded as among the proudest tokens of their high civilization."[40] What Americans admired most, however, was not the restraint, harmony, or simplicity of Japanese art and crafts but their exuberant design, lavish adornment, and careful craftsmanship. By the late 1870s middle-class American parlors and living rooms, especially on the East Coast, began to fill with curios, carpets, carvings, and cabinets imported from Japan or designed "in the Japanese style."

If the Japanese exhibit in Philadelphia demonstrated that Japan could not be considered aesthetically "primitive," testimony by American witnesses of the imperial government's crash reform program confirmed that Japan could no longer be lumped among the "uncivilized" or "half-civilized" peoples of the world either. The astonishing speed with which the government had broken with the past in the early 1870s seemed nothing short of miraculous. To many American observers, it almost seemed as though the Japanese were making a sudden and successful leap from the middle ages into modern times. One American traveler to Japan breathlessly reported that the restoration of imperial rule was "one of the most remarkable events in history":

> This has taken Japan out of the ranks of the non-progressive nations, to place it, if not in the van of modern improvement, at least not very far in the rear. It has taken it out of the stagnant life of Asia, to infuse into its veins the life of Europe and America. In a word, it has, as it were, unmoored Japan from the coast of Asia, and towed it across the Pacific, to place it alongside of the New World, to have the same course of life and progress.[41]

At the end of the 1870s, the American minister John Bingham noted that seldom if ever in history "had any ruler done so much within so brief a period for the reformation and well being of a people" as the new Japanese leaders had.[42]

By contrast, the other major Asian countries—India, China, Korea, and Annam (modern Vietnam)—remained in the thrall of what most Americans regarded as harsh and despotic regimes or were slowly coming under the control of outside powers. Only Japan had been able to defend its independence by sloughing off its "Oriental torpor," and only Japan was likely to emerge someday as the new leader of Asia. Such a view was endorsed by American writers, including William E. Griffis, who did much to spread the image of an "awakening Japan" to the American audience. In 1876 Griffis, who had just returned from several years as a teacher in Japan, published *The Mikado's Empire,* a book that became a major source of information about Japan's history, geography, customs, folklore, and its "recent revolution" (see Document 43). The book underlined the strangeness of Japanese culture, but it also reminded readers that the Japanese were a "frank, honest, faithful, kind, gentle, courteous, confiding, affectionate, filial, and loyal" people who were "simply human, no better, nor worse than mankind outside." They were, he also stressed, perhaps the best suited of all the Asian peoples to receive the "highest form of civilization."

The easing of the anti-Christian policy in 1873 also raised American hopes that Japan was on the verge of a spiritual or religious awakening. Although Christianity was not formally legalized, the government's policy of de facto religious tolerance encouraged American missionary organizations to expand their activities in Japan. Conversions were still few and far between in the 1870s, but the American missionaries found themselves making unexpected headway with the young generation who flocked to the new government and missionary schools. Even American laymen like William S. Clark, who was hired to head the government's agricultural college in Hokkaidō, saw themselves as bearers of the Gospel to Japan. Clark, for example, mixed his science lectures with lessons on Christian ethics, and by the end of his brief stay all his students asked to be baptized. No wonder that many Americans predicted that Japan would experience the "leavening" of Christianity as it acquired "the fruits of Christian civilization."

With a congenital optimism that any people or any country could become "civilized" if they made the effort, American observers had little doubt that the Japanese had embarked on an irreversible course into a new future, thanks in no small measure to the positive influence of the United States. It was this sense of being benefactor to Japan, whether as the country that "opened" Japan to the outside world or as a schoolmaster to its eagerly striving people, that dominated American discourse on

Japan until the end of the century. But as the Japanese retreated from their early dalliance with American culture and turned instead to Old World models, many Americans experienced a twinge of disappointment. The determination of the Japanese to forge their own path into the future, whether that meant an independent foreign policy or independence from American mission societies, undercut the satisfaction of knowing that once the United States had been Japan's principal friend and helper. In the long run, such feelings paved the way for the deep alienation that was to emerge between the two countries after the turn of the century.

NOTES

[1] In theory, the shoguns' authority was delegated by the emperor, a semidivine monarch with no power; the shogun in turn served as the suzerain for the daiymo, regional territorial lords, who exercised direct control over most of the population.

[2] D. C. Greene, "Correspondence between William II of Holland and the Shogun of Japan, A.D. 1844," *Transactions of the Asiatic Society of Japan* 34 (1907): 112.

[3] Ronald Robinson and John Gallagher, "The Imperialism of Free Trade," in *Economic History Review,* 2nd ser., 1.1 (1953): 1–15.

[4] Cf. the so-called Charter Oath issued by the Meiji emperor in early 1868. A translation may be found in Ryusaku Tsunoda, William T. deBary, and Donald Keene (comps.), *Sources of Japanese Tradition* (New York and London: Columbia University Press, 1965), 643–44.

[5] As one Japanese intellectual commented in 1874, it was easier at first to learn from the Americans, whose culture was "rough and shallow," than from the "refined and deep" scholarship of the Europeans. *Meiroku zasshi: Journal of the Japanese Enlightenment,* translated and edited by William Reynolds Braisted with Adachi Yasushi and Kikuchi Yūji (Tokyo: University of Tokyo Press, 1976), 227.

[6] Jurgis Elisonas, "Christianity and the Daimyo," in *The Cambridge History of Japan, Vol. 4, Early Modern Japan,* ed. John Whitney Hall (Cambridge: Cambridge University Press, 1991), 367.

[7] Often local magistrates required commoners to demonstrate their religious orthodoxy by stepping on images *(fumi-e)* of Jesus Christ, the Virgin Mary, or the Cross. Since planting one's foot on something or someone was a sign of contempt, a true *Kirishitan* would expose his beliefs by refusing to do so.

[8] George Elison, *Deus Destroyed: The Image of Christianity in Early Modern Japan* (Cambridge, Mass.: Harvard University Press, 1973), 241.

[9] Engelbert Kaempfer, *The History of Japan,* Vol. 3 (Glasgow: James MacLehose and Sons, 1906), 313.

[10] Donald Keene, *The Japanese Discovery of Europe, 1720–1820* (Stanford, Calif.: Stanford University Press, 1969), 75–76.

[11] Cf. Bob Tadashi Wakabayashi, *Anti-Foreignism and Western Learning: The New Theses of 1825* (Cambridge, Mass.: Harvard University Press, 1986), 66–68.

[12] Sakamaki Shunzo, *Japan and the United States, 1790–1853* (Tokyo: Asiatic Society of Japan, 1940).

[13] As one popular school geography book noted, "Their [i.e., the Japanese] rejoicing color is black; and on the contrary, white is used for mourning. They place the beauty of the teeth in their being very yellow; they can not bear to drink anything cold, and they find all our

dainties detestable." D. L. C., *Geographic Compilation for the Use of Schools,* Vol. 1, (Baltimore: 1803), 25.

[14]*Manners and Customs of the Japanese in the Nineteenth Century* (New York: Harper and Brothers, 1841), iii.

[15]Kimura Ki, *Japanese Literature: Manners and Customs of Meiji-Taisho Era,* tr. Philip Yampolsky (Tokyo: Obunsha, 1957), 13.

[16]Michael Adas, *Machines as the Measure of Men: Science, Technology, and Ideologies of Western Dominance* (Ithaca, N.Y.: Cornell University Press, 1989).

[17]*New York Times,* August 3, 1873.

[18]Probably the first American attempt to open up trade was that of Captain Stewart, who arrived in Nagasaki in 1803 with a cargo of goods from Bengal and Canton. The local authorities granted his request for water but rejected his request for trade.

[19]The Opium War, or first Anglo-Chinese War, broke out in 1839, when local Chinese officials cracked down on the illegal import of opium by British and American merchants. The British used their military victory to extract trade and other concessions from the Ch'ing government.

[20]*The Merchant's Magazine and Commercial Review* 12 (1845): 30.

[21]Quoted in Norman Graebner, *Empires on the Pacific: A Study in Continental Expansion* (New York: Ronald Press Company, 1955), 225.

[22]Herman Melville, *Moby Dick,* ch. 24.

[23]No one embodied this contradiction more strikingly than Yoshida Shōin, a young samurai scholar from Chōshū, who eventually became an ardent advocate of "expelling the barbarians." When Perry's fleet put in at Shimoda in April 1854, Yoshida attempted to smuggle himself aboard one of the ships. As he wrote in a letter handed over to the American interpreter, Samuel Wells Williams, "When a lame man sees others walking, he wishes to walk too; but how shall the pedestrian gratify his desires when he sees another one riding. . . . [W]hen we see how you sail on the tempests and cleave the huge billows, going lightning speed thousands and myriads of miles, scurrying along the five great continents, can it not be likened to the lame finding a plan for walking, and the pedestrian seeking a mode by which he can ride." Francis L. Hawks, *Narrative of the Expedition of an American Squadron to the China Seas and Japan Performed in the Years 1852, 1853, and 1854* (Washington, D.C., 1856), 420.

[24]The Tokugawa shogun's formal title was *sei-i-tai-shōgun* ("great barbarian quelling general"), implying a grandiose claim that was to haunt the bakufu until its overthrow in 1868.

[25]Cf. William G. Beasley, *Select Documents on Japanese Foreign Policy, 1853–1868* (London: Oxford University Press, 1955), 180–81, 193–94.

[26]It is not surprising that when Perry's fleet sailed into Edo Bay in 1853, rumors quickly spread that war was imminent. City officials issued regulations calling for inhabitants on the coastline to move inland, and constables and fire stations were put on alert in case of emergency. The streets began to fill with panic-stricken residents, young and old, hauling furniture, household belongings, and clothing as they sought safe haven with friends or relatives in the city's rural outskirts. One popular verse, punning on the similarity between the words for "steamship" and "teacup," poked fun at the panic: "Only four cups of tea / And it is impossible to sleep peacefully." (A second pun on the similarity between the words for "night" and "world" would make the second line read, "And the peace of the world is upset.") When Perry returned with a larger fleet in the winter of 1854, however, the local authorities managed to restore calm.

[27]In 1864 several Japanese, including a former castaway, Hamada Hikozō (Joseph Heco), began publication of the *Kaigai shinbun,* the first Japanese language newspaper, which contained articles translated from foreign newspapers brought into the port. For example, it kept its readers up to date on the latest political developments in Washington, and reported in much detail the progress of the Civil War.

[28]Kamei Shunsuke, *Jiyū no seichi: Nihonjin no Amerika* (Tokyo: Kenkyusha, 1978), 26–27.

[29]Ibid.

[30]Charles Lanman, *The Japanese in America* (New York: University Publishing Co., 1872), 13–14.

[31]Kamei Shunsuke, *Jiyū no seichi.* The term *kyōwa* is still used to mean "republic" today.

[32]In the mid-nineteenth century, both scholarly and popular discourse in the United States often referred to the five races as the Caucasian, the American, the Mongolian, the Malay, and the Ethiopian. The Japanese found it simpler to use a color code.

[33]Kume Kunitake, *Tokumei zenken taishi Bei-Ō kairan jikki,* Vol. 1 (Tokyo: Hakubun-shu, 1877), 402.

[34]This reevaluation of the social role and cultural importance of Christianity may have hastened a decision to ease the ban on the religion within Japan. The Iwakura mission, for example, was struck by the extent of religious toleration in the United States, where one could find every sort of religion practiced, even Buddhism. The Japanese minister in Washington, Mori Arinori, argued for the establishment of religious freedom at home, and in early 1873, even before the mission returned home, the government took down public signboards prohibiting Christianity. Cf. T. W. Burkman, "The Urakami Incidents and the Struggle for Religious Toleration in Early Meiji Japan," *Japanese Journal of Religious Studies* 1:2 (June–Sept. 1974).

[35]Arinori Mori, *Religious Freedom in Japan: A Memorial and Draft of Charter* (Washington, D.C., 1872), 11–12.

[36]In the final days of the bakufu, the former castaway Hamada Hikozō (Joseph Heco) helped to draft a private "Plan for the National Polity" based on a partial translation of the American Constitution. The document proposed a new federal union of daimyo domains with the shogun as chief of state and a tricameral national assembly that included a separate house for the daimyo. It also gave political rights to ordinary peasants and urban commoners, including protection of their civil rights. As one might expect, the bakufu did not accept such a radical document—nor did anyone else for that matter. But in his autobiography Hamada later recalled a visit from Itō Hirobumi and Kido Takayoshi, who were to become key officials in the new imperial government less than a year later. Joseph Heco [Hamada Hikozō], *The Narrative of a Japanese: What He Has Seen and the People He Has Met in the Course of the Last Forty Years,* Vol. 2, ed. James Murdoch (Yokohama: Yokohama Printing Company, n.d.), 90.

[37]See *Japanese Government Documents of the Meiji Era,* Vol. 1, reprint ed. (Washington, D.C.: University Publications of America, 1979), 7–15.

[38]Fukuzawa Yukichi, *An Outline of a Theory of Civilization* (Tokyo: Sophia University Press, 1973), 42–43.

[39]Quoted in Shunsuke Kamei, "The Sacred Land of Liberty: Images of America in Nineteenth Century Japan," in Akira Iriye (ed.), *Mutual Images: Essays in American-Japanese Relations* (Cambridge, Mass.: Harvard University Press, 1975), 67.

[40]Neil Harris, "All the World a Melting Pot? Japan at American Affairs," ibid., 30.

[41]Henry M. Field, quoted in Akira Iriye, *Across the Pacific: An Inner History of American–East Asian Relations* (New York: Harcourt Brace, 1967), 26.

[42]Quoted in Charles E. Neu, *The Troubled Encounter: The United States and Japan* (New York: John Wiley and Sons, 1975), 19.

PART TWO

The Documents

1

The Policy of Isolation

1

From *Kirishitan Monogatari* (*Tales of the Christians*)

1639

This anonymous anti-Christian tract was written at the time Portuguese ships were prohibited from entering Japanese ports. While the work purported to give an account of the spread of Christianity in Japan, its real purpose was to refute or ridicule basic elements in Christian doctrine as the author understood them and to discredit the motives of the missionaries and their followers. Works like this, describing the wickedness of the foreign missionaries and the outlandishness of the foreign religion, shaped the Japanese image of Christianity until the nineteenth century.

How a Man Appeared to Accuse the Kirishitans of Desiring to Subject Japan to South Barbary

Some time about the Genna Period (1615–1623) a monk came up from Higo Province and presented himself at Suruga.[1] Received before the Council of Elders, he reported as follows: . . .

"The King of South Barbary plans to subjugate Japan. His means is the diffusion of his brand of Buddhism. To that end he has sent a great many Bateren [priests] over here, and has diverted the income of five or ten

---

[1] In the interest of simplicity, original footnotes in this and other documents have been eliminated. All notes are the editor's.

George Elison, *Deus Destroyed: The Image of Christianity in Early Modern Japan* (Cambridge, Mass.: Harvard University Press, 1973), 355–56, 361–62, 374.

provinces of his country toward the needs of his Japanese undertaking. Under the pretext of annual trading vessels he ships over all sort and manner of articles to entangle Japan in his web. Each of the Kirishitans' temples in the Capital and in the countryside gets its share, so that they do not lack the wherewithal. Moreover, annually they compile a great list of the people (so many hundreds, so many thousands) whom they have that year persuaded to join their religion, and they send this list from Japan to South Barbary. This is a plot to take over the country without even a battle fought with bow and arrow. Right before our eyes, in Luzon and Nova Hispania, the King of South Barbary has installed his own governors, and has new officials sent over every three years. In sum, the plot consists of the design to spread religion.

"Quickly, dispatch someone to Higo to summon forth my adversaries, so we can have a confrontation before the August Presence. Naturally, if it proves that I have spoken but idle lies, then please dispose of me as you wish, though I be ripped apart by oxen or carriages. Until my adversaries appear I must, of course, be kept in prison." . . .

All this was brought to the attention of His Highness, who favored the report with much apparent satisfaction, being heard to comment, "A loyal individual!" Orders were transmitted to Katō Lord Higo, who thereupon had the suitor's adversaries brought up to court. A confrontation between the two sides now took place. The Kirishitans made a confession in all particulars, and it was determined that they had, in fact, been steeped in the plot to take over the country. From that point on His Highness grew to hate them deeply and had their temples destroyed. And he gave strict notice as follows: "Those among the followers of this religion who choose to fall away upon this occasion shall remain further unmolested; but should there be any who persist, they shall meet with immediate chastisement."

How the Kirishitan Religion Was Subjugated

This first time the ruler thought it quite pitiable that poor illiterates upon hearing the teachings of this devilish heresy should take them for the truth, and bestowing his grace upon them he granted pardon to those who would fall away. This news did not remain unheard in South Barbary. Forthwith the doctrinal standpoint was changed, to state that one was free to renounce the faith any number of times, as long as his internal devotion remained unchanged. This was transmitted to Japan, along with a bit of gold for each Kirishitan, which was secretly distributed. In this case also there appeared an informer. More and more, their plans to subvert the country came out into the open.

The ruler's hate for them now grew deep indeed. Orders were sent . . .

to scour every last place in the country for Kirishitans: village by village, mountain hut upon mountain hut, island by island, fishers' cove upon fishers' cove—no place was to be omitted. Down to the last baby born yesterday or today, all were to be registered in the rolls of Buddhist parish temples. Pledges written in the most uncompromising terms had to be presented to the authorities: "I and my whole family, children and grandchildren, definitely declare ourselves to be parishioners of this temple. If even one among us should prove to be of the Kirishitan persuasion, then the temple shall be confiscated and the priest subjected to any applicable punishment." To make sure that none who reneged escaped undetected, these pledges had to be repeated once a year: by townsmen to the ward elders and their assistants on monthly rotation, by villagers to the village headman and chief peasant, by samurai to their group leader. Moreover, notice boards offering rewards for information about Kirishitans were erected in settlements throughout every province. All too often, some ten or twenty were discovered here and there and were put to the fire, or crucified upside down, or subjected to the ordeal by water. And despite these various punishments more are being discovered even these days. How strange it is! . . .

During this reign the Kirishitan religion has been cut down at its root and cast out of our land. Such must indeed have been the judgment of the Buddhas, Gods, and Bodhisattvas — and it is a blessing deserving universal gratitude, of proportion to render Mount Sumeru low and the blue ocean shallow in comparison. How can mere words and similes do justice to this favor!

But why was the outcome so fortunate? Japan is called the Land of the Gods. But it is also terrain where Buddha's Law is widely spread. It is traditional in the Three Countries that the Royal Sway, the Way of the Gods, and the Path of Buddha are like unto a tripod's legs: if one of them be broken off, then the sun and moon are fallen from the sky and the lantern is lost which lights up the gloomy night.

Barbarians from foreign lands came here, to spread their cursed doctrine and, despising the Buddhas and the Gods, to destroy them and do away with them, determined thereby to make of Japan a domain of devils. How wretched it was, how lamentable! Men of wisdom spent their days and nights in grief and sorrow over this. But then the Kirishitans were exterminated, without being allowed to grasp an inch of our soil, to stand on a foot of our land. And all the major and minor deities of our sixty and more provinces, all the Buddhas of the Three Worlds rejoiced thereat, extending their protection for ten thousand eternities and a myriad years.

The Empire is at peace, the land in tranquillity, the reign of longevity.

The people partake of the virtue of the ruler and his subject princes. Verily, our age can be called another sainted reign of Engi, a golden age indeed.

2

HONDA TOSHIAKI

From *Keisei hisaku*
(A Secret Strategy for Ruling the Country)
1798

Honda Toshiaki (1744–1821), a Dutch Studies scholar who had traveled widely throughout Japan recording his impressions of local conditions, was one of the first Japanese to argue that Japan ought to follow European models in order to strengthen itself and overcome internal economic difficulties. In 1798 he wrote a tract, Keisei hisaku (A Secret Strategy for Ruling the Country), *outlining the country's "four imperative needs": manufacturing gunpowder, producing metals, building up a merchant marine, and developing colonies overseas. The program, inspired by the example of England, aimed at building up the country's "wealth and power." This excerpt, describing the Russian peril in the north, suggests the strategic as well as economic advantages of colonizing the northern island of Ezo (Hokkaidō) (see Document 4).*

Some years ago a complaint was directed to the Matsumae [domain] about the activities of the Russians in the area of the trading stations, and officials were accordingly dispatched to investigate. They were told by the Russians: "We were cast ashore on this island two or three years ago. Our ship was wrecked, and we have been unable to return to our country. If you would be so kind as to take us back to Japan and send us on to Nagasaki, it will be the best place from which to return, since there are Europeans there. Grant us this favor and save our lives." Thus they pleaded to the accompaniment of tears.

On first hearing their story, one might think that these were unfortu-

Donald Keene, *The Japanese Discovery of Europe, 1720–1830,* rev. ed. (Stanford, Calif.: Stanford University Press, 1969), 187–89.

nate men deserving of help, but they were Europeans, whose nature it is to be very cunning. One should never take what a European says for the simple truth. To give an idea how skilled they are in deception, let me relate the story of a Russian named Simeon Dorofeivitch Ishuyo, who spent eight years in the islands from Etorofu to Kunashiri. Officials were sent from Matsumae who ordered him on several occasions to return to his country, but Ishuyo replied each time, "I fled here because I was convicted of a crime in Russia, and I cannot return. Even now, if I were caught by a Russian official I would be executed. It is only natural in such circumstances that I have no desire to go back to my country. Rather than be driven from here, I would prefer that you cut off my head." In so saying, he stuck out his head and did not withdraw it an inch.

The officials were at a loss what to do. They delayed deciding his case from day to day, but in May of the same year that Kōdayū, the sailor from Shirako-machi in Ise,[1] was returned to Japan, a Russian envoy came for Ishuyo and they went back to Russia together. The story that he was a criminal and therefore could not return was thus so much deception and cunning.

This Ishuyo showed in his daily behavior that he was no ordinary man. He is reported to have been not only courageous but learned and accomplished. I imagine that he was a Russian spy who had been selected for his heroism, conspicuous even in Russia, to keep watch on the government and people of Japan. Since such persons as Ishuyo exist, it seems highly improbable that the Russians at present on Karafuto just happen to have been shipwrecked there. . . . There are grounds for suspicion already in the religious teachings being given to the natives of Etorofu and Kunashiri by Russian officials. Crosses over ten feet high have been erected in front of the thrones of the tribal chiefs and are worshiped morning and night. (The cross is called *kurusu*.) There are also three types of images—paintings, wooden statues, and metal statues—in twelve aspects. . . . I imagine that they are connected with the heretical sect [i.e., Christianity] that was proscribed at the end of the sixteenth century. It is especially noteworthy that the tribal chiefs of Etorofu and Kunashiri have been taken by ship to Okhotsk, where they have met high Russian officials and been given lavish presents. Many similar instances could be cited. For Japan such incidents at present constitute a minor disgrace, but I need not go into what may happen if things continue in this manner.

It is clear that when the Ezo islands are colonized they will yield several

---

[1]Southwest of modern Tokyo.

times as much produce as Japan does today. Although there are other islands to the east and west that should also be Japanese possessions, I shall not discuss them for the moment. At this crucial time when the Ezo islands are being seized by Russia, we are faced with an emergency within an emergency. When, as now, Japan does not have any system for colonizing her island possessions, there is no way of telling whether they will be seized by foreign countries or remain safe. This is not the moment for neglect; such actions by foreign powers may lead to the destruction of our national defense. With the establishment of a system of colonization, a knowledge of navigation will naturally develop among Japanese, but if navigation, shipping, and trade continue to be considered the occupation of merchants, the natives of our island possessions are doomed to an eternal want of civilization. The fact that the Ainu[2] are living in a state of barbarity has been regarded by Russia as affording a fine opportunity for devoting her energies to the colonization of the islands, a timely undertaking. The lack of a colonization system has kept Japanese rule from the island, and has meant that the natives are unaware of the goodness of the ruler of Japan. Because of this ignorance they have been quick to become subject to Russia.

So important is colonization that I have termed it the fourth imperative need.

[2]Indigenous ethnic group living in Ezo.

3

RAI SAN'YŌ

Dutch Ship (Poem)

1818

Rai San'yō (1781–1832), a Confucian scholar from the domain of Aki, is best known for his Nihon gaishi (An Unofficial History of Japan), *completed in 1827 and published in 1844. This widely read work, which recounted Japanese history as a narrative of the recurring downfall of suc-*

Burton Watson, *Japanese Literature in Chinese, Vol. 2, Poetry and Prose in Chinese by Japanese Writers in the Later Period* (New York: Columbia University Press, 1976), 129–30, 146–47.

*cessive shogunal regimes, was infused with regret that the emperor was
no longer the undisputed ruler of the country. Not surprisingly, Rai's history became a bible for the antiforeign activists in the 1850s. A restless
and rebellious personality, he was disinherited by his father after he fled
his domain as a youth. He eventually settled in Kyōto, where he scraped
together a living as a private scholar, but continued to travel about the
country. This poem, reflecting his ardent xenophobia, was written during
a sojourn in western Japan, where he spent three months in the port of
Nagasaki.*

In Nagasaki Bay, southwest where sky and water meet,
suddenly at heaven's edge a tiny dot appears.
The cannon of the lookout tower gives one roar
and in twenty-five watch stations bows are bared.
Through the streets on four sides the cry breaks forth:
"The redhaired Westerners are coming!"
Launches set out to meet them, we hear the drum echo,
in the distance signal flags are raised to stay alarm.
The ship enters the harbor like a ponderous turtle,
so huge that in the shallows it seems certain to ground.
Our little launches, so many strings of pearls,
tow it forward amid a clamorous din.
The barbarian hull rises a hundred feet from the surface,
sea winds sighing, flapping its pennants of felt.
Three sails stretched among ten thousand lines,
fixed to engines moving up and down like wellsweeps.
Blackskinned slaves nimble as monkeys
scale the masts, haul the lines, keeping them from tangling.
The anchor drops with shouts from the crew,
giant cannon bellow forth roar after roar.
Barbarian hearts are hard to fathom; the Throne ponders,
aware that defenses are far from complete.
Ah, the wretches, why do they come to vex our eyes,
pursuing ten thousand miles their greed for gain,
their ships pitiful leaves upon the monstrous waves,
drawn like giant ants to rancid meat?
Do we not bear ox-knives to kill a mere chicken,
trade our most precious jewels for thorns?

4

AIZAWA SEISHISAI

From *Shinron (New Theses)*

1825

Aizawa Seishisai (1782–1863), son of a low-ranking samurai in the domain of Mito, was one of the leading figures in the so-called Mito School, a highly nationalistic brand of Confucianism. When crew members of an English whaling vessel put ashore on the coast of Mito in 1824, Aizawa became deeply alarmed at what he regarded as an unwelcome foreign intrusion. The following year, he wrote his Shinron (New Theses), *a long memorial (i.e., an opinion paper) on how to deal with the barbarian threat. While this document was not published until much later, it had an enormous influence on members of the antiforeign movement in the 1850s and 1860s.*

Our Divine Realm is where the sun emerges. It is the source of the primordial vital force sustaining all life and order. Our Emperors, descendents of the Sun Goddess, Amaterasu, have acceded to the Imperial Throne in each and every generation, a unique fact that will never change. Our Divine Realm rightly constitutes the head and shoulders of the world and controls all nations. It is only proper that our Divine Realm illuminates the entire universe and that our dynasty's sphere of moral suasion knows no bounds. But recently the loathsome Western barbarians, unmindful of their base position as the lower extremities of the world, have been scurrying impudently across the Four Seas, trampling other nations underfoot. Now they are audacious enough to challenge our exalted position in the world. What manner of insolence is this?

> (Gloss: The earth lies amid the heavenly firmament, is round in shape, and has no edges. All things exist as nature dictates. Thus, our Divine Realm is at the top of the world. Though not a very large country, it

---

Bob Tadashi Wakabayashi, *Anti-Foreignism and Western Learning in Early Modern Japan: The New Theses of 1825* (Cambridge, Mass.: Harvard University Press, 1985), 149–50, 200–09, 211.

reigns over the Four Quarters because its Imperial Line has never known dynastic change. The Western barbarians represent the thighs, legs, and feet of the universe. This is why they sail hither and yon, indifferent to the distances involved. Moreover, the country they call America is located at the rear end of the world, so its inhabitants are stupid and incompetent. All of this is as nature dictates.)

These barbarians court ultimate ruin by ignoring the moral laws of nature and refusing to accept the lowliness of their status.

. . . Unless a Great Hero bestirs himself to assist Heaven's normative processes, all creation will fall prey to the wily, meat-eating barbarians. . . .

The Barbarians' Nature

For close to three hundred years now the Western barbarians have rampaged on the high seas. Why are they able to enlarge their territories and fulfill their every desire? Does their wisdom and courage exceed that of ordinary men? Is their government so benevolent that they win popular support? Are their rites, music, laws, and political institutions superb in all respects? Do they possess some superhuman, divine powers? Hardly. Christianity is the sole key to their success. It is a truly evil and base religion, barely worth discussing. But its main doctrines are simple to grasp and well-contrived; they can easily deceive stupid commoners with it. Using clever words and subtle phrases, they would have commoners believe that to deceive Heaven is to revere it, and that to destroy the Way is needed for ethical understanding.

They win a reputation for benevolence by performing small acts of kindness temporarily to peoples they seek to conquer. After they capture a people's hearts and minds, they propagate their doctrines. Their gross falsehoods and misrepresentations deceive many, particularly those who yearn for things foreign. Such dupes, with their smattering of secondhand Western knowledge, write books with an air of scholarly authority; so even daimyo or high-ranking officials at times cannot escape infection from barbarian ways. Once beguiled by Christianity, they cannot be brought back to their senses. Herein lies the secret of the barbarians' success.

Whenever they seek to take over a country, they employ the same method. By trading with that nation, they learn about its geography and defenses. If these be weak, they dispatch troops to invade the nation; if strong, they propagate Christianity to subvert it from within. Once our people's hearts and minds are captivated by Christianity, they will greet the barbarian host with open arms, and we would be powerless to stop them. Our people would consider it an honor and a privilege to die for this foreign god, and this willingness to die, this fearlessness, would make them fit for battle. Our people would gladly cast their riches into the sacrificial coffers of this foreign god, and those riches would finance barbarian campaigns. The barbarians believe it their god's will that they seduce other peoples into subverting their respective homelands; they borrow the slogan "universal love" to achieve their desired ends. Barbarian armies seek only plunder, but do so in the name of their god. They employ this tactic in all lands they annex or conquer. . . .

. . . Russia has expanded tremendously of late. It utilized Christianity to seduce the Ezo tribes into submission and to capture island after island [to our north]. Now Russia has turned its predatory eyes on Japan proper. The English also appear at frequent intervals, furtively trying to beguile our commoners and peoples in outlying areas. . . .

The peoples of Europe happen to be at war with each other now. But they all revere the same god. When the opportunity for a quick kill presents itself, they combine forces, and [after attaining victory,] divide the spoils. On the other hand, when they encounter difficulties, each withdraws to its own territory. This explains why we enjoy peace here in the east whenever there is strife in the west, and why there is peace in Europe whenever they venture to the east seeking plunder and territory. Russia, after subduing the lesser barbarians to the west, has turned its attention to the east. It has captured Siberia, and wants to infiltrate the Amur River area. But the Ch'ing empire, as strong as ever, is frustrating Russian designs there. As a countermove, Russia now is invading our Ezo territories. . . .

First, the Russians confined themselves to drawing sketches and maps of our terrain and coastline and to studying our moves and countermoves. Then they began to seduce our commoners into their fold and politely requested permission to trade. But when we denied this request, they ravaged Ezo, seized our weapons, and set fire to our outposts there. Then they requested permission to trade once more. In other words, after slowly and methodically reconnoitering our position, they make their requests, sometimes under the cloak of politeness and correct protocol, sometimes accompanied by armed violence. They use every conceivable technique to achieve their ulterior motives, ulterior motives that are clear to any thinking man.

But our temporizing, gloss-it-over officials say, "They only come for provisions of rice; there is no cause for alarm." What simpletons! Unlike us, the barbarians eat flesh, not rice: A lack of rice should not bother them. . . .

But the Russians have been strangely quiet of late, and in their place, the English have suddenly appeared. First they perpetrated violence in Nagasaki. Then they forced their way into Edo Bay. In short, the Russians, who have harbored designs on us for over one hundred years, suddenly disappear without a trace, and the English, who have rarely ventured to our coasts, just as suddenly zoom in to reconnoiter and probe. Can this be mere coincidence? Vicious birds of prey always pounce on their victims from dark shadows: The Russians are now hiding in wait for the kill. To facilitate their sly stratagem, they have English underlings do their reconnaisance work. . . .

The bakufu once made it plain to Russia that Japanese law requires us to destroy on sight any barbarian ship approaching our coasts. But now the English regularly appear and anchor off our shores, and we do not lift a finger to drive them away. [Quite the contrary], . . . when they have the gall to land, we go out of our way to provide for their needs and send them merrily along. Will the barbarians have any respect for our laws after they hear about this? The English come and go as they please, draw maps and sketch our terrain, disrupt our inter-island transport system, and win over our commoners with their occult religion and the lure of profit. If smuggling increases and we fail to stop commoners from aiding and abetting the barbarians, who knows what future conspiracies may hatch?

But our temporizing, gloss-it-over officials reply, "The foreigners are just fishermen and merchants doing nothing out of the ordinary; there is no cause for alarm." What simpletons! The barbarians live ten thousand miles across the sea; when they set off on foreign conquests, "they must procure supplies and provisions from the enemy." That is why they trade and fish. Their men-of-war are self-sufficient away from home. If their only motive for harpooning whales was to obtain whale meat, they could do so in their own waters. Why should they risk long, difficult voyages just to harpoon whales in eastern seas? . . .

. . . The English barbarians come and anchor off our shores whenever they please; they learn all about convenient approaches to our islands, about the location of bays and inlets along our coastline, and about our climate and our people's spiritual make-up. Should we let them occupy the small islands off to our southeast, . . . and establish bases on

Hachijōjima, Yaskushima, and Tanegashima,[1] they would be in a perfect strategic position to invade our Middle Kingdom. This would be another case of two birds with one stone. It is easy to see why the English conspire with the Russians and spy on our coastal fortifications: They are eager to combine forces and obtain spoils.

But those ignorant of the bakufu's astute reasoning and farsightedness argue, "If we treat the barbarians with kindness, they will comply docilely; to intimidate them only invites reprisals." Such men cling to out-dated, erroneous views with unbelievable tenacity. They would have the bakufu issue injunctions when in fact the barbarians understand nothing but force.

For hundreds of years the barbarians have desired and resolved to subvert enemy nations through their occult religion and thus conquer the whole world. They will not be deterred by occasional acts of kindness or displays of force. When they wreak vengeance against us, they intimidate us into backing down; when they submit meekly before us, they lull us into a false sense of security. They employ these two tactics "to probe for strengths and weaknesses." Those spied on can never fully fathom the thoughts and feelings of the spies: The barbarians "assume different guises and employ a variety of feints." This forces us to commit ourselves one way or the other on each occasion and throws us off balance; so we often commit blunders in spite of ourselves. This should explain the acuity and astuteness behind the policy of armed expulsion. . . .

Again the dimwits argue, "The barbarians' religion is a set of shallow, base doctrines. They may deceive stupid commoners with it, but they will never beguile our superior men *(chūn tzu)*. There is no cause for alarm." But the great majority of people in the realm are stupid commoners; superior men are very few in number. Once the hearts and minds of the stupid commoners have been captivated, we will lose control of the realm. The ancient sage kings enforced harsh penalties for seditious and subversive activities . . . ; such was their hatred for those who incited stupid commoners to rebel. The barbarians' religion infiltrated Kyūshū once before, and spread like the plague among stupid commoners. Within less than a hundred years, two hundred eighty thousand converts were discovered and brought to justice. This indicates how fast the contagion can spread. . . . It is of no avail for a few superior men to remain untouched by the pollution spreading around them. The immunity of superior men to Christianity does not permit complacence.

[1] Islands off the coast of Japan.

5

A Bakufu Expulsion Edict
1825

The bakufu issued this edict, sometimes called the "no second thought"
(ninen naku) edict, in 1825 in response to the increasing intrusions of
Western whaling vessels into Japanese waters. Much stronger in tone than
a similar edict issued at the time of the Russian mission under Adam Lax-
man in the 1790s, it represented the most extreme and severe official
expression of the policy of isolation. When Western ships made unautho-
rized probes into Japanese waters, as the Morrison *did in 1837, officials*
repelled them with cannon fire (see Document 7). The edict remained
in force until 1842, when it was canceled in the wake of the Opium War
in China.

We have issued instructions on how to deal with foreign ships on numerous occasions up to the present. In the Bunka era [1804–17], we issued
new edicts to deal with Russian ships. But a few years ago, a British ship
wreaked havoc in Nagasaki [the *Phaeton* Incident of 1808], and more
recently their rowboats have been landing to procure firewood, water, and
provisions. Two years ago they forced their way ashore [in Satsuma
domain], stole livestock and extorted rice. Thus they have become
steadily more unruly, and moreover, seem to be propagating their wicked
religion among our people. This situation plainly cannot be left to itself.

All Southern Barbarians and Westerners, not only the English, worship Christianity, that wicked cult prohibited in our land. Henceforth,
whenever a foreign ship is sighted approaching any point on our coast,
all persons on hand should fire on and drive it off. If the vessel heads for
the open sea, you need not pursue it; allow it to escape. If the foreigners
force their way ashore, you may capture and incarcerate them, and if their
mother ship approaches, you may destroy it as circumstances dictate.

Note that Chinese, Koreans, and Ryukyuans can be differentiated
[from Westerners] by physiognomy and ship design, but Dutch ships are
indistinguishable [from those of other Westerners]. Even so, have no

---

Bob Tadashi Wakabayashi, *Anti-Foreignism and Western Learning in Early Modern Japan:
The New Theses of 1825* (Cambridge, Mass.: Harvard University Press, 1985), 60.

compunctions about firing on [the Dutch] by mistake; when in doubt, drive the ship away without hesitation. Never be caught offguard.

6

SAKUMA SHŌZAN

Kaibōsaku (A Plan for Coastal Defense)
1842

Sakuma Shōzan (1811–1864), a samurai from the domain of Matsushiro in central Japan, became one of the foremost students of "Western learning" (yōgaku) in the 1850s. After receiving a traditional education in Confucian studies, first under his father, then at the bakufu academy (Shōheikō) in Edo, he turned his interests to the study of Western military tactics, gunnery, and applied science. What prompted this change in direction was news of the Opium War in China. Like many of his contemporaries, he thought that the best way to deal with the "barbarians" was to learn the secrets of their strength. In 1842, hoping to acquire knowledge needed to defend Japan against foreign encroachments, he became a student of Ezawa Tarōzaemon, a leading expert on Western gunnery. While studying Western military methods he wrote Kaibōsaku (A Plan for Coastal Defense), *a memorial to his daimyo, who had been put in charge of coastal defenses.*

Of late the bakufu has begun to give due care to the defense of our country's territory, and your excellency has been placed in charge of coastal defense. Since the situation between China and England has turned more and more unfavorable beginning in the tenth year of Tempō [1839], and there often has been news of conflict between them, preparations have been made so that Japan will remain unperturbed in case the worst should happen.

According to historical records, in ancient times, during the Tempyō-Shōhō era (749–756), when the An Lu-shan rebellion occurred in China, military defenses were strengthened in the Kyūshū region. The An Lu-

---

Nihon no meicho: Sakuma Shōzan/Yokoi Shōnan, ed. Matsuura Rei (Tokyo: Chūō kōron-sha, 1970), 116–22.

shan rebellion was no more than a disturbance within the court of the T'ang dynasty, but rigorous [military] preparations were carried out [in Japan] since it was not clear what its consequences might be. We can only be struck with awe by the farsightedness and prudence of the statesmen in those ancient times.

The present actions of the English, however, are not to be compared with the rebellion of An Lu-shan. This is clear from the circumstances. The English, who have been rampaging willfully and arbitrarily in countries far across the sea, have begun a war with China as their enemy. At this juncture if we do not take full measure of the enemy, assess our own strengths, and make adequate preparations, the danger will be great indeed.

I have recently heard of the contents of a letter that the Dutch presented to the bakufu in the second month of this year. According to this letter the Chinese forces are extremely weak, and the English have already occupied the area around Fukien and Ningpo.

Some years ago an incident occurred in which an English ship[1] approached the Sagami coast to repatriate seven Japanese castaways. The bakufu turned the ship away, and the castaways were compelled to return to the port of Macao in Kuantung Province. One of them died, and two joined the English military forces that invaded China, but the other four remain at Macao. Those four, moved by concern for their home country, wrote a letter about the true state of affairs with respect to England and sent it to Nagasaki. According to this letter, after England concludes the war with China, it intends to demand trade with Japan, and if Japan refuses, the English will take a closer look at the unlawfulness [of the Japanese] who earlier fired on the ship that brought back the castaways.

Furthermore, according to what I have heard the Dutch underlings are saying, once it finishes war with China, England will send warships to three places: Nagasaki, Satsuma, and Edo.

I think that there are many other reports of this sort, but if we consider just these three, there can be no doubt that the English harbor sinister designs on Japan.

According to the interpretation of some, the castaways wrote and sent the aforesaid letter because they were sincerely worried about their ancestral land, but in my view this is an intrigue of the barbarians. To make the Japanese government open trade under threat of force, the

---

[1]This refers to the *Morrison,* an American trading vessel, which visited Japan in 1837 (see Document 7). Like other Japanese, Sakuma assumed the ship was English because it bore the name of Robert Morrison, a Protestant missionary in China.

English have used the castaways, making them write the letter, then relied on the Dutch to deliver it to Nagasaki. . . .

It is in the national character of the English to attach great importance to profit and loss. Even if they bear some deep grudge toward Japan, for example, they will never spend huge sums of money, dispatch warships, and take violent action simply to settle such a grudge. At the moment, however, the English have already sent troops to China. With both weapons and men close at hand, it would be quite simple [for them] to cross a single ocean and advance their forces toward Japan. From their point of view, the English will have made gains if they secure their demands for trade simply by threatening and menacing [Japan], brandishing as their pretext the incident when their ship was fired upon off the Sagami coast several years ago. And since they have already made military preparations, it will be easy for them simply to rely on military force and open trade under more favorable conditions. [England] is a country that by nature has little to do with morality and justice, so if it thinks that it can turn a profit, undoubtedly it will make unreasonable demands on Japan even though it bears no special grudge toward it. No matter how much we insist that there is no cause for war, the other side will not accept our view.

Moreover, from England's point of view, if they start a war with Japan, it will naturally involve no great cost since troops have already been sent to China. It will be of great profit to them simply to control the seas surrounding Japan. By stationing warships in the seas around Japan, they can interrupt Japan's maritime shipping and pursue at their leisure the whaling activity that has been so profitable to England in recent years or carry on trade with the various islands near Japan. [If they do so] after several months and years, there will be no need for them to bring in special funds from their home country. Thus, England will suffer no loss, and only Japan will pay dearly. . . .

. . . At the present moment no goods are especially wanting in Japan. On the contrary, just as knowledgeable men in the past worried that copper was flowing out of the country as the result of trade with Holland, I fear that useful goods will leave [if trade with England is opened]. If we begin trade with England, the tendency to exchange the useful commodities of Japan for the useless commodities of foreign countries will grow stronger, and this will invite extreme peril for Japan in the future. Furthermore, if we permit the English to trade, Russia will not sit by quietly. During the Bunka era (1804–17) the bakufu handed the Russian envoy Rezanov a letter saying that Japan had a national prohibition on trade. If now we permit trade with England, the Russians will be angered at this betrayal. In addition, if the Russians see that Japan has given in to the English despite previous prohibitions on trade, they will conclude that the national strength of Japan has declined and they will make particularly unreasonable demands. I think there will be no way we can respond to them. At that time, does the bakufu then intend to open trade with Russia as well?

It is for these reasons that I think that trade with England absolutely must not be permitted.

However, if the bakufu were simply to refuse to permit trade, there can be no doubt that war would come. If Japan were certain to win, there would be no need to worry deeply about going to war, but in its present state the Japanese side has no prospect of victory. At this moment, I humbly implore the bakufu to adopt the best possible measures and devote itself with all its power to solidifying military preparedness, thereby making the barbarians respect Japan in their hearts and letting the people live in peace. . . .

Eight Policies for Coastal Defense

First, build gun batteries at strategic points along the coastline of the whole country in order to be able to return fire against the aggression of foreign enemies.

Second, bring a complete halt to the export of copper to Holland, using the copper to cast hundreds and thousands of Western-style cannon and distribute them to the various daimyo domains.

Third, build large Western-style ships and assure that vessels carrying food supplies into Edo are not shipwrecked nor meet with accidents.

Fourth, exercise care in the appointment of officials responsible for maritime shipping and take stern measures to assure that no improprieties arise concerning intercourse with foreign countries and other problems in connection with maritime traffic.

Fifth, build Western-style warships and thoroughly practice Western-style naval strategy.

Sixth, build schools and promote education in every part of the country and assure that all the common people follow the Way of Loyalty and Filial Piety and maintain proper principles.

Seventh, unify the minds of the people by clarifying the system of rewards and punishments and carrying on government with justice and mercy.

Eighth, establish institutions so that men of talent will be promoted on the basis of ability.

2

American Views of Japan

7

SAMUEL WELLS WILLIAMS

From *"Narrative of a Voyage of the Ship* Morrison"
1837

This eyewitness report of the voyage of an American merchant ship, the
Morrison, *to Japan in the summer of 1837 appeared in* The Chinese
Repository, *a journal published in Macao on the China coast. The author,*
Samuel Wells Williams (1812–1884), a Protestant missionary who
arrived in China in 1833, was one of the few Americans with even a rudi-
mentary knowledge of Japanese. Using the few grammar books and dic-
tionaries available, and tutored by Japanese castaways, he managed labo-
riously to acquire a working knowledge of the language. He even prepared
a Japanese translation of the Gospel of Matthew, probably the first attempt
at translating the Bible from English into Japanese. Because of his knowl-
edge of Japanese, he was later invited to join the Perry expedition
(1853–54) as an interpreter and assisted in the negotiation of a treaty
with the Japanese.

July 30th.   The morning light found us not far south of Mi-saki or cape
Sagami, the southern point of the principality of the same name, and
which also forms the western point of the entrance to the bay of Yedo
[Edo], more properly speaking. The bay . . . is a large estuary, between

Samuel Wells Williams, "Narrative of a Voyage of the Ship *Morrison,* Captain Ingersoll, to
Lewchew and Japan, in the Months of July and August, 1837," *The Chinese Repository,* vol.
vi, no. 8 (December 1837): 356–57, 361–63, and 376–78.

thirty and forty miles wide at its entrance, and extending thirty miles north at nearly a uniform width up to Mi-saki. . . .

The banks of the bay are abrupt, but not high and as we approached either side in our zigzag course, the shores offered an agreeable variety of hill and dale, covered with vegetation. Trees of many sizes and kinds skirted the tops of the hills, and a low growth of bushes their sides, both of a lively green, giving the scenery a cheerful aspect, very different from the ruggedness of the mountains of Izu.

About twelve o'clock, we first heard the distant report of guns, though it was some time before the fact could be distinctly ascertained, on account of the haziness, and the noise attendant on working the ship. The reports were heard at considerable intervals, and we assigned different reasons for so unexpected a proceeding; nor could the Japanese give us a satisfactory clue to operations so opposed to all their experience; and they suggested hoisting the ensign. Some thought that the guns were to report to the court our progress; others surmised that the officers near the harbor of Uragawa did not feel at liberty to allow a foreign vessel to pass into the anchorage without orders from their superiors, and some suggested they were saluting the ship: but all our doubts concerning their designs were removed, as soon as the weather cleared up and we saw the balls falling towards the ship half a mile ahead. . . .

We anchored about 3 P.M., and soon after boats began to approach the ship; but the few first could not be induced to come alongside, and returned to the shore, satisfied with gazing at the ship and masts. An old man first ventured up the sides, who as he crossed the gangway took a survey of the deck, and then stepped down. When fairly aboard, he saluted us by slowly bending his body and suspending his arms, until his fingers nearly touched the deck. He then proceeded to examine the objects about him, slowly passing from one to another, but was speedily interrupted and recalled by his companions; but on his favorable report, all immediately clambered on board. Other boats now arrived, and the decks were soon covered with Japanese, who went over the ship, making their remarks on what they saw to each other, without paying much heed to the foreigners. . . . The height of the masts and rigging were also sources of unceasing wonder, and the boats often stopped a little distance from the ship, while the inmates, to whom a foreign vessel would naturally be an object of interest, gazed upwards. . . .

All manifested friendly feelings, partaking of the refreshments offered them, inquiring our business, scrutinizing the ship and all on board, and inviting us to go on shore and ramble. Some of them promised to inform the officers of our request, but this promise was given in such an odd manner, as if from persons utterly unused to magisterial dignitaries, and whose line of life had been at a great remove from the precincts of a court, that we could hardly know what to predicate. They appeared much surprised that not any one of us was able to converse with them; some would seize the arm, enter in to earnest discourse, and then, after a few unsuccessful sentences, leave us, seemingly amazed at our doltishness and the ill success of their eloquence.

July 31st. . . . Towards four o'clock, three or four boats were seen coming down in shore from the upper point, which stopped near the fishing huts, and the men in them landed, and assembled on a low hummock near the beach. No particular notice was taken of their movements, until we were saluted by a cannon-ball, whistling over the ship, succeeded by three others, fired from four guns planted on the hillock where the party was assembled. This movement was so unexpected that we were for a moment nonplussed as to their intentions; and hoisted the colors, and soon after a white flag, in order to induce some one to come on board to explain the reason for such proceedings. No heed was given to our signals, and the fire continuing, we began to weigh anchor, and make sail. To show them that we were leaving, the spanker was hoisted; but the firing rather increased, and one ball struck the bulwarks, ploughing up the deck in its progress, but doing no other damage. . . .

It now became a serious question, what course it was best to pursue; two presented themselves: either to remain longer in the bay of Yedo, anchoring in the stream, or near the shore lower down; or to leave the port, and gain another port on the southern coast as quickly as possible. The latter commended itself, inasmuch as it was thought the officers here would not be favorable to our object, after committing themselves, by thus unceremoniously driving us away. . . .

The arguments against leaving the capital without opening a communication were strong and fully felt, especially when we had to do with a government so feudal as the Japanese, where every petty prince is amenable to his liege for his every action, suspicious of his peers, and cautious that what he does be not reported at court to his discredit. Some perhaps would have advised us to renew the attempt at the entrance of the bay, excusing ourselves to whoever came on board, for going up to Uragawa, by pleading ignorance of the regulations, and our desire to be as near Yedo as possible. However, . . . it was concluded to leave the bay for Toba in the principality of Sima, about 150 miles southwest of Yedo, from whence Iwakitchi and his two companions embarked, when they were shipwrecked.

If another attempt were made it was important to do it immediately, lest information of our repulsion should be sent along the coast, and orders given to all the officers to drive us away. Moreover, it was very unlikely that the court of Yedo knew our nation, object, or character, and on many accounts it was very desirable to declare all these points fully, even if the other objects of the voyage should not be gained. The indignation and disappointment of our men were as great as their previous hopes had been high; they were warm in their denunciations against the petty officers at Uragawa for so unprovoked an attack. . . .

In summing up the circumstances attendant upon both our attempts, and comparing them with what we could learn of previous trials, it was instructive to observe how gradually the Japanese government has gone on in perfecting its system of seclusion, and how the mere lapse of time has indurated, instead of disintegrating, the wall of prejudice and misanthropy which surrounds their policy. . . . When we approached the bay of Yedo, immediate intimation was given to the officers, and we were fired upon when the report of the guns was just audible, and the thick mist entirely hid us from view. This treatment any vessel in a starving condition would probably receive, and it is important to inquire what causes have been operating to produce it, and how far foreigners themselves may have increased it. It would not be amiss to make investigations, at the proper sources, into the conduct of the whalers that frequent the eastern coasts of Nipon [Nippon] and Yesso [Ezo], to learn whether in their dealings with the people and the vessels which they have met, there has not recently been conduct, unworthy of Christians, which will not bear being brought to light. . . . A people, who show the decision of character of the Japanese, silently erecting their batteries to drive away their enemies by force of arms, and bringing their cannon several miles to plant in a favorable position, are not to be lightly despised, or insulted with impunity. . . .

What course of conduct would have been pursued by the Japanese, if ours had been an armed vessel, it is impossible to say; but I am more than ever rejoiced, now the experiment has been made, that no cannon were carried. However; towards a people who thus manifest decision of counsels and reliance upon their own resources, although exerted in a barbarous and savage manner, and on an occasion when kindness was meant, a degree of respect and deference is paid. The believer in the promises of God's word looks forward to the time, when the same energetic qualities of mind, changed and enlightened by education, shall be directed toward better and nobler objects. Although cruel and prejudiced, they manifest a character, which can be moulded, by God's grace, into something more efficient, than that of their vacillating and edict-making neighbors, the Chinese and [K]oreans. Whatever purposes of mercy or of judgment may be towards this people in the counsels of their high Governor, it is not for us to inquire, but we hope that the day of their admittance into the family of nations is not far distant; when the preacher of peace and truth shall be allowed access to their hamlets and towns, when the arts of western lands shall be known, and commerce, knowledge, and Christianity, with their multiplied blessings, shall have full scope. Then will that ancient saying, *Luz ex oriente,* have its accomplishment; and the land of the Rising Sun will be the one to begin to shed the beams of civilization over the earth. But before this can be done, those who now enjoy these inestimable privileges have a great work to do; and who shall begin?

Let us look at this people a little longer. For more than two hundred years they have been separated from their fellow men, and when the tie was severed, at the expulsion of Catholicism and the Portuguese, it was done under great excitement, and in the flush of victory over those whom they supposed were undermining their liberties. What were the grounds for the allegations against the Jesuits, we will not stop to inquire; but the feeling manifested by the Japanese, when they challenged even the God of the Christians to touch their shores at his peril, shows how confident they then were of their own power and resources, and how determined to exclude foreigners. And they have excluded them; and, since that time, the only representatives of all Christendom whom they have seen, have been a few individuals at Desima, whose own historians give ample evidence that gain has always been their chief object. The Japanese, from what they know and have heard of European nations — of their wars, their deadly battles, their opposing interests, and their great power, must congratulate themselves on their seclusion from such contests. Not that they have enjoyed peace within their own borders, since they have built their wall of separation, but that, by repairing the breaches which interest and ignorance have from time to time made in it, they have not subjected themselves to the visits of fleets and armies. And if such are their feelings and ideas regarding us, can it be wondered at, that they look upon all foreign intercourse as a thing to be deprecated, and opposed in all possible ways? What might at first have been conjecture or slander regarding other countries, has probably now become, by repetition and the authority of books, received truth; at least, it is always the course of error to strengthen by time. One of our men says, he was taught, that in some western countries the men were covered with hair and lived upon trees. And in a Japanese work, we have seen representations of people, with arms so long, that the owner of one pair is engaged in fishing with them, and has mercilessly clutched a carp in his hands; and of others, whose legs enable the man elevated on them to pluck the fruit from palm trees; and in another place are two tribes of men drawn, one of which is so small, and the other so large, that the latter is figured as carefully holding one of the little men in the palm of his hand; Gulliver's heroes in Lilliput and Brobdingnag were proportionate compared to them.

And what are all these chimeras but painful illustrations of their ignorance and pride? But before they will lose them, juster and more correct notions must be imbibed. They now regard foreigners as ready to pounce upon their country the moment it should be opened ... and, before they will consent to receive them, they must be assured that those who seek their ports are peaceable friends. They can derive no just ideas of other nations, nor of their enterprise, commerce, and philanthropy, from what they see of foreign trade, cabined and reduced as it is by their laws; and who expects them to come with open arms, and request free intercourse, before they are acquainted with the benefits they would derive from it? Their ideas of Christianity are, every one knows, of the most erroneous sort, considering it as another name for intrigue and lust of power; and a thing to be kept out of the empire at all risks, as one would drive a viper from a nursery of children. Now there is no innate power in the Japanese, more than in other people, to teach and reform themselves; and do we expect that a miracle is to be worked, and that they are suddenly to become enlightened and inquiring? Let us not be weary in well-doing; but let us do all we can to give to the Japanese the knowledge of true Christianity, which seeketh not its own; let us present before them the Bible in their own tongue; and, with this pure river of life we know that civilization, commerce, and knowledge will flow through their land.

8

AARON HAIGHT PALMER

An American Businessman's View of Japan

1849

Aaron Haight Palmer, author of this pamphlet urging increased trade with Asia, was a New York businessman. He bombarded President Polk and Congress with petitions to send a special trade mission not only to Japan but to Persia, Burma, Cochin China, the Moro Islands, and India. While his views may have been idiosyncratic, he did represent an important strand of opinion in the East Coast business world.

Aaron Haight Palmer, *Letter to the Hon. John Clayton, Secretary of State, Enclosing a Paper, Geographical, Political, and Commercial on the Independent Oriental Nations; and Submitting a Plan for Opening, Extending, and Protecting American Commerce in the East &c.* (Washington, D.C.: Gideon and Co., Printers, 1849) 5, 12, 14–16, 17–20.

In its rapid career of national aggrandizement, this magnificent and mighty American empire republic is justly entitled to rank with the most enterprising and powerful maritime and commercial nations of the world. The time has arrived when it is imperatively incumbent on American statesmen to be conversant with the productive resources, and the geographical, political, and commercial statistics of foreign countries, so as to be enabled intelligently to foster, extend, and protect our own external commerce, and conduct advantageously our foreign relations.

It is eminently the policy of our Government to adopt early measures for opening friendly intercourse and trade with all the Oriental nations, in accordance with the views and suggestions of the memorialists, to make our star-spangled banner known and respected from the Arctic to the Antarctic oceans as the national ægis of "free trade and sailors' rights," and extend its protection over American citizens and their lawful commerce in every sea, "from the Orient to the setting sun."

With respect to the Oriental countries before mentioned, they all present favorable fields for American commercial enterprise. . . .

Japan

The isolated and mysterious empire of Japan, which has been, since 1637, hermetically sealed to all foreign intercourse and trade, except with the Chinese and Dutch, will be compelled, by force of circumstances, to succumb to the progressive commercial spirit of the age; and the Japanese Islands will eventually become in the east what the British Islands are in the west. . . .

The Japanese are a vigorous energetic people, and assimilate in their bodily and mental powers much nearer to Europeans than Asiatics. They are eager of novelty; open to strangers, extremely curious and inquisitive concerning the manners and habits of other countries; take great interest in learning the course of events and progress of the useful arts and sciences among the Western nations; are frugal, ingenious, sober, just, and of a friendly disposition; warm in their attachments, but proud, distrustful, and implacable in their resentments. In courtesy and submission to their superiors few nations can compare with them; and they are distinguished from all other Orientals by a lofty, chivalrous sense of honor. Instead of that mean, artful, and truckling disposition, so general among Asiatics, their manners are distinguished by a manly frankness, and all their proceedings by honor and good faith. . . . They have existed 2,500 years as a homogeneous race and independent nation, under the same form of government and system of laws, speaking the same language, professing the same national religion, owe no allegiance to China, and have never been conquered or colonized by any foreign Power. . . .

In the same proportion that the external commerce of Japan is circumscribed, its internal trade is active and flourishing. No imposts check its operations; and although its ports are sealed against foreigners, they are constantly crowded with coasting vessels, both great and small. At Sinagawa [Shinagawa], the suburb and port of Yedo [Edo], several thousands of vessels are sometimes collected, bearing tribute, merchandise, provisions, or fish, for the capital, which is said to contain a population of more than 2,000,000. Shops and markets overflow with every description of agricultural produce and manufacturing industry; and large fairs attract a prodigious number of people to the seaports and trading towns which are scattered throughout the empire. . . .

As the Dutch find an excellent market for the very limited quantity of merchandise they are allowed to offer for sale, there can be no doubt that, were the country opened to foreign commerce, the demand for the chief articles of import would be very extensive. With regard to exports, it is a matter of question whether the Japanese copper mines would be able to compete with those in other parts of the world, especially of Lake Superior, Cuba, Chili, Peru, Siberia, New Zealand, and the enormous Burra-Burra mines recently discovered in Australia; but that a very extensive and lucrative trade might be carried on with Japan, there cannot be the least doubt. . . .

American whaling ships commenced cruising last year in the inner seas, bays, and harbors of Japan, and its northern dependencies, the Kurile Islands, in the pursuit of their gigantic game. The great success which most of them have met with, will probably attract thither a large whaling fleet in the course of the present year. From want of reliable charts and accurate hydrographical information respecting those remote and comparatively unknown seas, several shipwrecks have already occurred. . . .

Lack of provisions and water, or stress of weather, will occasionally compel our whalers and merchantmen to put into Japanese ports, or seek refuge there from shipwreck. With the exception of the Chinese and Dutch, at their privileged factories in the harbor of Nangasaki [Nagasaki], all foreigners landing in Japan, no matter under what circumstances of distress or peril, are immediately arrested, and sent under military escort to that port, where they are detained in close confinement; kept on a short allowance of rice, fish, and water; are frequently severely beaten, exposed to many indignities, and compelled to trample and spit upon a picture of the Crucifixion. Such barbarous treatment of our distressed countrymen, who may have the misfortune to be driven upon those inhospitable shores, ought no longer to be tolerated by a nation of freemen.

In this untoward state of things our Government should address, without delay, a national missive to the Siogoon [shogun] of Japan, specially commending to the protection of his Imperial Majesty's Government and provincial authorities such of our mariners, employed in whaling, the naval or merchant service, as may be compelled by stress of weather, in want of repair and assistance, to put into any of the ports of the empire, that they may be aided and provided with necessaries to refit, at the current prices of the country; and, in case of shipwreck, that they receive kind and hospitable treatment, and be forwarded as soon as practicable to the care of the United States Consul, Batavia, who should be instructed promptly to reimburse all incidental expenses.

In the event of the Siogoon's declining to comply with so reasonable and just a request, our Government would be justified in taking such ulterior measures, as humanity and the national honor may require, to enforce its immediate and effectual observance by the imperial and provincial authorities of Japan. A strict blockade of [Edo Bay] and port of [Matsumae], for which two frigates are amply adequate, would soon compel that imperious Government to accede to our demands. . . .

There seems nothing to prevent the success of a mission properly managed, if the Siogoon, Council of State, and the Mikado can be made thoroughly to understand that we have no design upon their religion or government; that we seek a peaceful and mutually beneficial commercial intercourse with their Empire, and ask for neither lands, forts, factories, nor exclusive privileges therein; that we have no desire for *conquest* or *colonization,* and will engage that our citizens, who may be permitted to visit Japan on commercial business, shall strictly conform to its laws, pay the customary imposts and dues, scrupulously abstain from any interference in matters of religion and government, and yield due deference and respect to the established authorities, usages, and customs of the country; that so soon as the Imperial Government shall accord permission, a special envoy or commissioner of the United States be sent to Yedo to obtain an authentic record of such concession, privilege, or treaty as that Government might be induced to make to the freedom and security of American commerce in its ports, and which shall, at the same time, guaranty on our part full reciprocity of trade and protection of Japanese subjects in our ports, and lay the foundation of a lasting peace between Japan and the United States. . . .

9

Report of Japanese Cruelty to American Sailors

1852

By the 1850s allegations that local Japanese authorities treated American castaways badly were common in the American press. As the Morrison *episode demonstrated (see Document 7), local officials even refused to treat Japanese castaways with kindness. Many Americans regarded this behavior, which was dictated by bakufu policy, as a violation of the "law of nations" requiring "civilized" governments to give aid to foreign nationals forced to land on their shores by bad weather or shipwreck. As the Navy Department's instructions to Perry put it, a nation that treated castaways like "the most atrocious criminals" should be considered "the common enemy of mankind." In fact, the castaways described in this* New York Times *report were not the victims of nature but mutineers who had sought refuge on the Japanese coast.*

By the bark *Eureka,* arrived from Canton, this morning, we have the following statement of cruel treatment by the Japanese toward shipwrecked American seamen, and the murder of one of the unfortunate men taken at St. Helena some months ago:

"Murphy Wells, an American citizen, born in the State of New-York, late carpenter on board the American whaling ship *Lawrence,* of Poughkeepsie, Capt. Baker, states that the said vessel *(Lawrence)* was wrecked on the 28th of May, 1846, by running on a reef of rocks, in the dead of the night, about 300 miles off the coast of Japan, during very thick weather. All hands remained by the vessel till daylight, when three boats were manned, by the whole of the ship's company, who took with them all of their clothing, &c., that could possibly be got at, as the vessel was fast going to pieces, the sea making a breach over her. They then made the best of their way for the Island of Japan. During the night the boats separated, and two of them have never been seen since.

"Our boat (Wells's) arrived in safety, after seven days' passage. On the moment of arrival, the natives took possession of all of us, our boat and effects, and we were thrust into a prison cage, made similar to those in which wild beasts are kept for exhibition, where we were confined and half starved for *eleven months and a half,* after which we were transported to a Dutch settlement down the coast, where we were again put in prison by the Japanese for two months more.

"At the expiration of this confinement, we were brought before the chiefs and tried for daring to approach their land. We told them we were shipwrecked, which they would not listen to, and upon no terms would they grant us our liberation. They threatened to cut off our heads, because they thought we were English, whom they hate; but when we told them we were Americans, they said nothing more, except to ask us of what religion we were. Upon our telling them we worshipped God, and believed in Jesus Christ, they brought a cross bearing the image of our Saviour, and had we not trampled upon it at their request, they would have massacred us on the spot. We were then detained on shore, in prison, for a couple of days more, when they sent us board a Dutch ship, bound to Batavia, where we arrived in December, 1847 — each of us doing the best we could for ourselves to get a passage home.

"While we were in Japan, in prison, one of our comrades, Thos. Williams, endeavored to make his escape, but was caught and taken back to prison in a dying state, owing to wounds inflicted on him with some deadly weapon; there was a gash over his forehead which bled profusely. The poor fellow lived about six hours. The natives brought a coffin, into which they compelled us to place the corpse, when they took it away. What was done with it, we could never ascertain. . . .

"We heard of several English seamen being there in confinement similar to ourselves.

"It is anxiously hoped the American Government will not suffer this treatment, but more particularly so sanguinary an act towards hapless shipwrecked American seamen to pass without ample retribution."

3

Japanese Reports about America

<hr style="border-top: 3px solid;" />

10

MITSUKURI SHŌGO

From *Konyo zushiki (A World Atlas)*

1845–1846

Mitsukuri Shōgo (1821–1846), a Dutch Studies scholar who produced numerous works on Western geography, left his hometown at the age of sixteen to travel to Edo, Kyōto, and other parts of western Japan. After returning home, he studied Dutch medicine with a local physician, then returned to Edo to become the disciple of Mitsukuri Gempo, a well-known scholar of Dutch Studies. Relying on Dutch-language works, Mitsukuri compiled or wrote many reference works about the outside world, including his Konyo zushiki (A World Atlas), *from which this account of the United States is taken.*

The books that have been consulted in writing this work fall into a number of categories. They were all written by Hollanders during our *Tempō* period [1830–44], but, as they are based on divers sources of information, their contents have many discrepancies, as to the history and boundaries of the various nations. I have had to use my own judgment in selecting my materials, and the reader is cautioned against arriving at any conclusion as to the merits of this book merely by comparing it with some other one book. . . .

There is something new to record, every day, about the national customs, history, geography, and products of Western countries. The source-

---

Sakamaki Shunzo, *Japan and the United States, 1790–1853* (Tokyo: The Asiatic Society of Japan, 1940), 130, 132–34, 138–42.

books that I am using, although written only seven or eight years ago, and in some cases fifteen or sixteen years ago, are concerned with matters dating no later than fifty or sixty years ago. They are thus lacking in contemporary information, for which we must await the appearance of newer books. . . .

General Account of the American Continent

In a certain work, America is said to mean New World in some European tongue. According to one opinion, America was discovered by a subject of the King of Portugal, called Americus, from whom the name was derived. According to another opinion, this land was first discovered by a man of Genoa, Italy, named Columbus; hence, this land should be called Columbia. . . .

A General Account of the
Republican Government States
(The United States)

The inhabitants are of several races, and customs differ according to locality; but they all make no distinction of class [literally, between noble and mean]. In the southern part of that land, the people live by tilling the soil. In the north, the people manufacture divers sorts of things. Some of them carry on trade in all directions, going most frequently to Europe, to the East and West Indies, and to China, it is said. . . .

Although this country is merely a part of America, it is so large in area, its people are so numerous, and its vigor is so pronounced, that it is commonly referred to simply as North America. It was formerly just a vast wilderness, without even having a name. About the year 1683, Englishmen colonized Carolina, in the southern part of this land. Then, in the year 1734, they sent several hundred thousand colonists to New York and Connecticut, it is said. At that time, however, it was still a rather bleak and lonely wilderness, with nothing worthy of taking note. Some years later, several tens of thousands of Englishmen, who refused to subscribe to the tenets of the Anglican Church, were arrested and sent to this distant country. These people lacked sufficient food and clothing, at that time, but they privately rejoiced because there were no rulers in this land. They began, energetically, to clear the land and till the soil. Some of them fished, for a livelihood. A number of years later, their descendants came to number over 300,000, and the products of the land became extremely bountiful. So Englishmen finally came to that country to trade.

During our *Hōreki* period [1751–63], England was at war for some years. The people became sorely enfeebled, and the loss in foreign trade was not at all inconsiderable. The English sought, therefore, to employ the people of this land [America], and use them for their own ends. The people of this land, however, resented their abusive language and scorned their cheap wages, and refused to obey their orders. They even seized and threw into the sea some 342 boxes of tea that had been brought from India by the English. In great wrath, the English dispatched a number of warships, and blockaded the most important port of this land, thus stopping the transit of provisions into the country. The people found themselves in most desperate straits, and officials of the thirteen states assembled to ponder the situation. A military official named Washington, and a civil official named Franklin, promptly stood up and declared, "We must not lose this heaven-given opportunity. We must sever relations with the English forever." The assembly decided to adopt this proposal.

The English then realized that they could not attain their ends, and that their words had been unreasonable, so they lifted the blockade and departed. In 1780, a certain official of this land reached an agreement with the English that this should forever be a free and independent nation. Since then, the nation's strength has steadily increased, and its territory has expanded tremendously. . . .

A Short Biography of George Washington

George Washington died on December 14, 1800. He was a North American burgher (a term applied to puissant folk living in towns and combining the three professions of war, agriculture, and commerce) who became a general. That age produced many heroes, of whom he was the greatest. He was born in Fairfax, Virginia (one of the republican states,) in the year 1734. His father was a big farmer in this town. His grandfather was a man of England who, sixty years previously, had fled civil war in his native land, and had come to this country to live. As a child, he observed the rules of his family. He entered a school at Williamsburg (the name of a place). That place was formerly the capital of Virginia. He was by nature sagacious, and progressed rapidly in his studies, becoming particularly well versed in mathematics. After a time, he left the city school and returned to his homestead, where he worked at farming. In his spare moments, he studied battle tactics.

In the year 1752, France built a fort in Ohio (the name of a place in North America), and England, becoming angry, attacked it, but no decisive result was obtained. An English governor-general, who had come to

Virginia, now ordered Washington to negotiate peace terms with the French general. This was not accomplished, but he ascertained in great detail the exact situation of the enemy.

The English general made Washington a major, and ordered him to proceed to Ohio at the head of 800 troops from Virginia. With his few troops he fought bravely against the strong foe. An English official, named Braddock, arrived in Virginia with troops, in the year 1755, and Washington joined his forces as the leader of a detachment, with the rank of adjutant (an officer who supervises everything in a military camp). Washington commanded a band of troops whose duty it was to loot enemy provisions, and his spirited fighting greatly enhanced his fame, and caused all his associates to respect him.

In the year [1759], Washington resigned from his command. He married a woman of high birth, and returned to his homestead. There he devoted himself to his regular calling as a burgher. He studied most sedulously.

Events occurred in the year 1776 that caused the colonists in North America to hate their mother-country (England), and Washington voluntarily used his wealth to equip troops. He drilled these soldiers himself. On April 19, 1778, at the battle of Lexington (the name of a place), his side suffered many casualties. On May 10, that year, a meeting was held in Philadelphia (the name of a place), and troops were raised in the various states.

Washington was chosen commander-in-chief by common acclaim, and he devoted himself to affairs of state, in this time of national difficulty. Military supplies were not ample, and troops had been acting as they pleased, without obeying any rules. But he was extremely strict toward the army, and impartial. As opportunities arose, he led his troops in attacks on the enemy, and gradually saved the country from its peril, and established peace and order. But he undertook no unorthodox scheme, nor did he hazard any project that depended on good for successful fruition.

In the spring of that year [1778], an English general named Howe was defeated by Washington. He fled from Boston, but with many troops and administered severe defeats on various armies. Washington, however, being very cautious, left that place quickly, and was the only one to preserve his army intact. He adopted the good tactics of avoiding a frontal clash with the enemy, preferring to wait for some favorable opportunity. Later, his plans working out well, he crushed the Hessian troops at Trenton, and defeated an English general at Princeton.

The aggressive power of the American forces became greatly enhanced, bringing fear to the English, and winning renown throughout the world. In the year 1780, they captured an English army at Saratoga. France came to the assistance of the Americans, and the affair became greater. In the year 1781, seven thousand English soldiers were taken prisoner at Yorktown, and final victory was achieved. All this was due to Washington's great ability.

The English now realized that it was impossible to win the submission of the Americans, and peace negotiations were started. A peace conference was held in Paris. (Paris is the capital of France, and the conference was held there, probably, because the French had helped the Americans.) The home-country finally became an independent nation.

Washington now resigned from his command. His associates, appreciating his great services, and esteeming his virtues, tried hard to keep him from leaving, but he was adamant and returned to his homestead in Virginia. Here he lived in quiet solitude, for a year or two.

Peace had been secured, but no system of government had been established, and there was no unanimity of public opinion. Owing to the gravity of the situation, a general meeting was held in Philadelphia. Everyone asked that Washington become High Official. Hence, unable to help it, he again looked after the affairs of government. He established institutions and issued laws which were so well designed that they are still in force to-day. The next year, another assembly was convened, and Washington was named Highest Official [*Saijōkan*], for a term of four years. When this term came to an end, he was asked to serve for yet another period of four years. He was resourceful and conscientious in his administration. In the country there was a person called Hamilton, who was sagacious, eloquent, and well versed in political matters. So he was chosen by Washington to assist the latter in governing.

Burisutetto (the name of a Westerner) says that, when the republican government was established in that country, the people were greatly exhausted, but that Washington was in office for eight years, and managed the affairs of state so well, that there was excellent military preparedness, the nation prospered, the people enjoyed peace, and the country's renown encompassed the earth.

This is quite true. The nation's good reputation was reestablished, its trade was revived, and a dilapidated country was reborn as a newly risen nation. The national debt was no longer regarded as unpayable, every family prospered, men worked diligently, production greatly increased, and the government's revenue grew and grew. The people were governed by law and not by individuals, their customs were benevolent, and they behaved like persons of high birth.

Europeans all marvelled at the excellence of the governmental organization. *Burrisutetto,* commenting on him, says, "Washington was circumspect and discreet in managing matters, so his achievements are not so well known as Hamilton's, in the realm of government." Washington's name will be esteemed in history forever. Yet, in his day, there were some people who made slanderous charges against him. He was deeply hurt by this, and, when his term had been fulfilled, in the year 1798, he returned with relief to his homestead. There he lived in simplicity, after the manner of the sages, apart from the world.

Washington died at the age of sixty-seven. There was none among the people of this republican nation who did not mourn his death, and even people of other lands showed great sorrow. His name was therefore given to the capital, to perpetuate the memory of his achievements. When about to die, he prepared a will, freeing his slaves, giving a large sum of gold to the government, establishing a college in Columbia (a place-name differing from Colombia, in South America), and founding a school for the poor, in a certain place. His mausoleum is in Mount Vernon, his villa. The people have not yet put up any monument to this great man, nor even a tombstone, with an inscription recording his achievements. His name, however, has an imperishable place in history, obviating the necessity of a tombstone. Nothing more could one ask!

Washington had a dignified bearing. He was an able official, and a manly burgher. He was circumspect in his actions, and undaunted in the face of great difficulties. His devotion to his country was indomitable. His guiding principle was the preservation of national honor. He cherished his country, gave prosperity to its people, and was ever ready to serve others. He always had a sound basis for his views, but never sought to force those views on others. In managing affairs, he was strict, but benignant. This was his heaven-endowed nature, truly worthy of respect and adulation. He was an exceptional man, born to do great things, and to achieve success and distinction.

11

The Interrogation of a Castaway

ca. 1851

In 1841 fourteen-year-old Nakahama Manjirō (1827–1898), born in a fishing village on the island of Shikoku, was shipwrecked with four fellow villagers. William Whitfield, the captain of the American whaling vessel that rescued them, was impressed by Manjirō's intelligence and offered to take

Ishii Kendo, ed., *Ikoku hyōryū kikenshū* (Tokyo: Shinjimbutsu ōraisha, 1971), 256–58, 260–68.

him back to New England. After studying at a school near the captain's hometown of New Bedford, Massachusetts, Manjirō worked as a barrel maker and as a whaling ship's hand. Eventually he made his way to California during the gold rush. With the money he earned there he bought passage on an American vessel to return to Japan in 1851. His arrival coincided with rumors of an expected American expedition, so bakufu officials eagerly interrogated him to find out as much as they could about the United States. This document records his answers. In 1853 the bakufu recruited Manjirō as an official interpreter, and in 1860 he accompanied the first bakufu mission to the United States.

Manjirō's Education

After Manjirō's ship arrived in the country of America, with the help of Captain Whitfield he studied in a building that looked like a Japanese Buddhist temple. Afterward, he paid the teacher's fee, bought books, and covered his other expenses by running errands. Captain Whitfield provided him with meals. During that time he studied for about six months with a teacher named "Chihita." . . .

Conditions in America

Item: The government of America is generally the same as in Japan. There is a law code of twelve articles, and there is nothing complicated about it.

Item: There are seven kings.[1] The country [*kuni*] of North America is divided into thirty-six countries [*kuni*].[2] As for the climate, there are four seasons, as there are in Japan. Customs are similar to those in Hawaii. The kings are selected from among the wise men of the country, and they serve for four years. It is said that those who are especially wise serve for eight years. When they travel, each is attended by only one servant. . . .

Item: America is a country that has developed in recent years with assistance from Holland, and everything resembles things in Holland.

---

[1]This probably refers to the American cabinet: the president, the vice president, and five departmental secretaries.

[2]The word *kuni* (country) could refer either to the whole polity or its parts. It was common to refer both to Japan as a whole and to individual provinces as *kuni*. Another way to read the sentence would be: "The country of North America is divided into thirty-six provinces."

Since the country developed there has been only one era name [*nengo*],[3] ... [but] as in Japan there are twelve months in one year. However, there is no New Year's ceremony.

Item: When [Americans] travel, they ride in carriages. Usually seventeen or eighteen people are aboard. The [carriage] wheels are driven by fire as steamships are. There are also steamships but airships are forbidden and there are none to be had at this time.

Item: There are twenty-six letters. Abacuses are made in a square shape, unlike those in Japan. They are convenient for adding up large numbers.

Item: The people are upright and kind, and they do nothing that is bad. There are no murders or robberies or the like. It is said that if such things unexpectedly occur, there are laws to control them and [offenders] are immediately apprehended.

Item: At their wedding ceremonies, they do not make special offerings such as the *hikiawabi*[4] as they do at marriages in Japan but simply become husband and wife by giving notice to the *kami* [gods]. When that has been done, it is customary to take the woman on a sight-seeing excursion. By nature they are quite lustful, but otherwise they behave quite properly. . . .

Item: Those who are refined do not drink *sake,* and if they do they take only a little bit. Those who are vulgar drink like the Japanese. Drunkards are disliked and detested. The quality of the *sake* is worse than in Japan.

Item: Feelings between husband and wife are deep. Such intimacy within the family is to be found in no other country. . . .

Item: Training in the civil and military arts flourishes. [The Americans] know how to use swords and spears, and naturally they practice riding fast horses. They have a kind of donkey, but they use horses like those in Japan for mounted riding. . . .

Item: There are not yet many physicians. Of course, there are physicians who come from Holland. Something called the "Japan disease," accompanied by a high fever, has been spreading. To treat it the sick person is put in a tub filled with water or else buried in the ground so as to

---

[3]Like the Chinese, the Japanese did not number their years as Western countries did (e.g., 1854, 1855, 1860) but used era names (e.g., *Ansei,* or "Peaceful Rule," or *Man'en,* "Great Longevity") selected for their combination of felicitious characters. For example, in Japan the year 1853 was the year Ansei 1 and 1854 was Ansei 2 but 1860 was Man'en 1. Even today the Japanese use era names coinciding with the reign of the emperor. The year 1996 is Heisei 8, the eighth year of the reign of the Heisei Emperor.

[4]The reference is obscure; it may refer to the use of an abalone [*awabi*] which clings tightly to its rock, as the symbol of an enduring union.

cool him off and dampen the fever. For that reason very few people survive if they get sick. . . .

Item: The birds and beasts [in America] are generally like those in Japan. One finds tigers and elephants but no lions.

Item: Even in that country, I understand that they have a strong aversion to the likes of the *Kirishitan.*[5] . . .

The True Intentions of the Americans

Item: The large vessels that arrived earlier at Uraga[6] were not warships but ships that came to carry out surveys and so forth. They [came to] survey Japanese territory or they were whaling ships blown off course. They came only to request the provision of water and firewood. When the Japanese turned down their requests even though the Americans said that they were willing to leave hostages, the Americans were taken aback that the Japanese made such an outrageous fuss. [The Americans] say that the Japanese are short-tempered. The Americans are not only kind and benevolent, but since their country still is in the midst of development, they do not plot to spy on other countries. . . .

Item: The American king[s] live in low-roofed house[s] and do not construct great castles like our daimyo do.

Item: On top of the king's place of government there is placed a huge mirror, and [looking at] reflections from hundreds of leagues [*ri*] is like looking at the palm of one's hand.

Item: After those who serve as king retire, they receive a retirement fee and can live in comfort for the rest of their lives.

Item: Officials do not flaunt their authority during their comings and goings.

Item: The elegance of a person is judged by the color of his upper and lower garb.

Item: Depending on their education, even peasants are appointed [to office].

Item: Educated persons are permitted to wear refined clothing even if they are not high officials. . . .

Item: Among the various tools carried on Americans ships, there is a device that measures how many hundreds of leagues [*ri*] the ship has traveled. . . .

---

[5]In this case, the *Kirishitan* religion is probably identified with Roman Catholicism, which was looked down upon by many Protestant Americans in the mid–nineteenth century.

[6]See Document 7.

Item: The *Kirishitan* sect[7] is not to be found [in America]. Images resembling Buddhist statues are to be found in the temples of this sect, but since the people's minds are righteous, they are not bewitched by such strange things.

Item: When one goes to visit someone's house, one takes off one's hat [literally, straw hat] and enters. The master of the house sits on a chair. If he extends his right hand, the guest extends his right hand, and they grasp each other in greeting. [The guest] then sits down, states his business, and leaves.

Item: In their privies, they raise the opening, drop their buttocks in, and take care of their needs. They take books and the like inside to read. There are no buckets or boxes to hold the offal, and they defecate or urinate into a pit dug out in the ground. When they simply urinate they store it in a small jar[8] that they empty into the privy. Of course, if many people use [the privy], they throw away the offal after accumulating it in a bucket. Since the main fertilizer is fish, they do not use human dung very much.[9] When they do use it, they smear it on the ground, dry it out, then spread it on their fields. . . .

Item: To enter into marriage, [a man] looks for a woman by himself, then proposes to the woman he has set his heart on. If she consents, he announces this to her parents and his own as well. [The couple] then goes with their parents to the temple, where they ask for the priest, who calls the couple in. First, the priest faces the groom and asks him, "Do you take this maiden as your wife?" He replies, "Yes, I do." Then, [the priest] faces the bride and asks, "Do you have any objection to becoming the wife of this person?" She replies, "I have no objection." . . . After they make pledges to one another, they return home. There is nothing especially joyful about the wedding ceremony. . . .

Item: Under ordinary circumstances, they keep their watches and pocket pistols close to themselves. If they go to a place a little distant, they carry a staff. This staff is light, but if some danger arises, it is designed so that a knife pops out of its middle. . . .

Item: A fire is kindled in the hold of a steamship. When the smoke rises it turns gears, and the momentum of the wheels on both sides moves the ship as though it were flying. . . . There are also boats called *reirouta* [railroads] that travel on land. They pull along several boxes built like houses,

---

[7]The reference is probably to Roman Catholicism.

[8]The reference is to a chamber pot.

[9]Human waste was used a fertilizer in Japan. Indeed, dealers sold waste collected from urban privies to farmers in the neighboring countryside.

about three *kan* [18 feet] in length to carry freight. . . . The road they traverse is a path for the wheels laid down in iron. . . . These boats are about 20 to 50 *kan* [120–50 feet] in length.

12

HAMADA HIKOZŌ

From *Hyōryūki (The Record of a Castaway)*
1863

Hamada Hikozō (1837–1897), also known as Joseph Heco or Amerika Hikozō, became a castaway in 1850 when his cargo ship was blown off course. After serving on several American vessels, he and his companions attempted to repatriate themselves to Japan in 1852. Having failed to do so, he returned to San Francisco, where he became the protégé of B. C. Sanders, an influential banker with political connections, who served as the port's collector of customs. Sanders took Hamada to Washington, D.C., paid for his education at a Catholic school, and eventually found employment for him as a clerk in a San Francisco trading firm. After being offered the chance to serve on an American surveying vessel in 1859, Hamada took American citizenship. While in Hong Kong he met Townsend Harris, who offered him a job as interpreter at the new American consulate in Yokohama. Eventually Hamada went into business there, setting up his own trading firm and publishing the first newspaper in the Japanese language. In 1863 he published Hyōryūki (The Record of a Castaway)*, an account of his experiences in America.*

In Europe about 378 years ago, at a place called *Jinowa* [Genoa] (now in the territory of France), there lived a man named Columbus, who loved to make sea voyages. While making several trips to India, where he carried on trade, he heard that there was a country called Japan farther to the East and he set his heart on traveling there. Thinking to himself that the earth was round, he decided that if he sailed west from Europe, instead of crossing the mountains of China, he could reach Japan. He

Arakawa Hidetoshi, *Ikoku hyōryūkishū* (Tokyo: Yoshikawa kobunkan, 1962), 228–31.

explained his ideas to the king of *Hispania* [Spain], who listened to them with sympathy and provided him with three ships. [Columbus], much excited, sailed west for many days and arrived, as he expected, at a large country. It was America, however, not Japan, which he had set his sights on. Since Columbus unexpectedly discovered America while looking for Japan, and since people from America then came over to Japan to open its ports, we can say that this was destined and that Columbus finally achieved his goal.

When Columbus returned home with various treasures and curiosities to present to his king, the news spread. People from *Hispania,* of course, and all the other countries flocked to North and South America. The central part of North America, to which many Englishmen came, is the present United States. After many English settlers arrived there, the country developed, and trade prospered. The king of England raised taxes, making the [English settlers] suffer. As a consequence, many of them were embittered and wished to become an independent country by separating themselves from England, but all were merchants who knew nothing of military affairs. Having neither warships nor cannon, they had no choice at all but to follow the orders of the king.

By Heaven's grace, however, a great hero by the name of Washington was born. His own father, who had been born in England, had moved to America, where he sired Washington. In character Washington was a man full of benevolence, without selfish desires, obedient to the law, and willing to sacrifice his life for the sake of his country.

By dint of a fortuitous happenstance, [America] became an independent country. The reason was this: Before the English came to live in [America], there were native people who were called "Indians" [*Injin*]. While brave and strong in character they were lacking in wisdom. Even though overwhelmed by the English, [the Indians] behaved in a grand and lawless way, causing the English much trouble. To protect against the violence of the "Indians," the king of England appointed Englishmen living in America as generals. One of those generals was Washington. [The king] also appointed thirteen magistrates who were put in charge of government affairs.

From the outset, the inhabitants [of America] resented the cruel rule of these magistrates. The elders of the country, who gathered in an assembly to discuss [the matter], decided to separate from England. To accomplish that, there was nought to do but appoint generals and go to war. Calling on Washington to serve as commander-in-chief, they turned their backs on England. Thus, war broke out.

Since America is a large country, the [Americans] retreated into the mountains thirty or fifty leagues [*ri*] from the seacoast when the fighting turned against their advantage, but when they discovered carelessness by the English soldiers they sallied forth to fight again. With the fighting turning against them, [the English] had the French negotiate peace, and happily the war came to an end.

Since America was a country opened up by England, its political affairs, literature, and learning were similar [to those of England] but otherwise it was independent. The people gathered into assemblies, but since there was no leader in the country there was no one to rectify the laws and issue orders. By a unanimous decision, it was proposed to Washington that if he became [the country's] leader, his sons and grandsons would become the nation's kings in perpetuity.

After listening, Washington replied: "The recent war with England arose because of the king's harsh government. By gradually uniting the hearts of the people, [we] escaped from under such harsh government. Harsh government by a king which harms the people is worse than threats from without. If the people are united and live in amity, they will be able to resist any enemy, no matter how great. Even if my sons and grandsons were made king, inevitably some of them will be born without worthiness, causing the people grief. It is better to bring about peace in the land by laws that bring unity and amity to the country.

"That being so, all the inhabitants should be declared equal without respect to status; stipends and ranks should not be inherited over generations, and those with ability who will submit to the people should be selected to become officials; and the most outstanding among these should be made president [literally, "great chief" *(daitōryō)*], whose orders all the people will follow. Since men become haughty and extravagant if they remain in office for a long period, they should retire after four years to return to the people and other wise persons should be selected and appointed to office."

Those assembled, all putting aside selfish interests and truly serving the benefits of the people, decided to adopt these methods. Even today the president changes every four years. Moreover, all officials . . . , regardless of whether they were good or bad, resign from their positions and new ones are selected. The president decides on the officials who will serve as chiefs, then these chiefs choose lower officials and assistants who meet their wishes.

Government

In America the method for selecting [the government] is as follows. In all thirty-six parts of the country, that is to say, in all thirty-six provinces, the local inhabitants select the provincial governor by casting ballots *(nyūsatsu)*. In this case too, the people pass judgment on the affairs of the province every four years. . . .

[Two "senators" from each province] assemble in the seat of government at the capital city of Washington to discuss affairs and laws concerning the whole country, then await the decision of the President. For every 50,000 persons one is chosen as a delegate [*sōdai*] of the people. [These delegates] come to the seat of government, discuss affairs of state with the senators, and serve to assure that nothing inconveniences or causes distress to their provinces. These two officials [i.e., senator and delegate], who are the source of decisions about political affairs of America, are the most important offices.

By his own decision, the president chooses five persons of broad erudition and versatile talents, who are appointed to office if there is no objection after discussion with the senators. These five persons serve as advisors to the President: the first is in charge of the navy; the second is in charge of the army; the third is in charge of foreign countries and serves as prime minister; the fourth is in charge of the income and outgo of money [literally, "gold and silver"]; and the fifth is in charge of fields and forests. The granting and withdrawal of land depends on the judgment of these officials. [Their] duties are like those of the council of elders [*rōjū*] in Japan. When the president's term ends they resign along with him. Lower officials such as clerks and group leaders [*kumigashira*] are attached to important officials. These offices, which are held without a term of years, are occupied by persons accomplished at such tasks. . . .

The government pays for its needs by taxes. A magistrate is placed in every port to collect taxes. Taxes on land in forests, fields, or towns are delivered to the provincial governor or to the magistrate. These [taxes] are used to pay for local expenditures or are sent to Washington to pay what is due to the government. When the country is at peace and the government's coffers are full, the amount of taxes collected is reduced, but when the country's needs rise the amount collected increases. Since expenditures are very great at time of war, the government puts into circulation paper currency based on gold and silver, and when peace is achieved taxes return to normal and paper money is accepted in payment.

Prostitution

If adultery is discovered, . . . the adulterous woman is ostracized by her kinfolk and thrown out of the house. These women can not marry again so they make their living for the rest of their lives by selling sexual favors. In America prostitutes are all immoral and adulterous women who market themselves. [However,] one does not hear of parents selling their children.[1] If a parent were to sell a child, it would always be treated as a crime.

Religion

There are temples[2] everywhere, and the people are intensely devoted to their religious beliefs. The priests are always learned men. They preach to the people so that they will follow good and reject evil in accordance with religious teachings. In addition, [priests] are also teachers of reading, writing, arithmetic, and the like. Because they devote themselves to this calling, it is natural that they are respected by the ordinary people. The pope disciplines the priests, and those who violate the Way of Man [*jindō*] are corrected by the government.

There are many schools, hospitals, orphanages, and the like apart from those set up by the government so poor people do not have to pay entry fees. To help the people by providing medical treatment, school education, and child care, the priests all exert great efforts to raise money to set up such institutions. Schools and other institutions which uplift people are thought to serve the country. Many good people come from the studious poor, fewer from the rich. For that reason, religious persons work hard to set up academies [*in*] with the intention of spreading the eternal law.

Even though they seem to be most revered for single-mindedly devoting themselves to helping the people of the country, such religious persons as I have described can become obstinate as a result of their belief in religious teachings, and this can bring no small amount of trouble to the country. At the moment there has arisen a great rebellion in America [i.e., the Civil War], which had its origins in religious teachings.

In the West Indies there is a country under English control called "Jumeca" [Jamaica] that produces large quantities of sugar and tobacco. Because so few people lived there, [the English] bought black people in Africa and set them to work at farming. These people, called "slaves," had no freedom of life and limb. They were furnished only with food and clothing, and no provision was made to pay them wages. Learning from this example, people in the American South bought black people too. Since this part of the country was very hot, the local inhabitants were not able to work in the summer, but black people, who were born in a tropical country, did not mind the intense heat at all. As a result of their skill in

---

[1] In Japan poor parents often indentured their young daughters to brothels.
[2] *Tera* in Japanese (*tera* is the term used for Buddhist temples).

carrying on agriculture, cotton production in the American South grew year by year, yielding great profits. The American North shipped agricultural tools and other machinery to the South, so that both were able to mutually profit and flourish.

According to the view of certain religious persons in England, however, even though the country of "Africa" was not yet developed and black people were ignorant, buying and selling fellow human beings like implements was against the will of God and represented the height of inhumanity. Moved by this view, the king of England, and then all his ministers, bought the "slaves" in English territory using redemption money provided by the government and gave them freedom over their lives just like people in developed countries.

In the American North, there were those who adhered to this view as well, but even though they wished to put an end to [slavery] . . . the number of slaves in the American South was so enormous that they were unable to pay the redemption money [needed]. While this matter was being debated, people in the American South unanimously agreed at an assembly to split off from the North and make plans to set up a separate country. Eventually this led to war, the outcome of which is not yet decided.

Since ancient times, in all countries, civil wars have often arisen as the result of differences over doctrine or sectarian debates. It should be remembered that people who submit to religious schools can cause more harm to their country than those who are ignorant and unlearned.

Marriage

In America both men and women make up their minds to get married from the age of fourteen or fifteen. When they decide to become man and wife for their rest of their lives, they make a pledge to one another directly without a go-between, and [their engagement] can last as long as three to five years or as short as two to three years. During that period, . . . they inform their parents [of the engagement]. After that, seven close friends of the bride-to-be dress up in a similar fashion, with only the bride wearing a white silk garment, and the groom is accompanied by five to seven close friends.

Together with the parents and kinfolk from both sides, they go to the temple, where they inform the head of the temple of their intentions. The head of the temple changes his clothes, then both parties line up on either side of the altar. After [the couple] pledges . . . to maintain the Way of Husband and Wife for the rest of their lives and the scriptures [literally, sutras] are read, the man takes a ring from his purse and puts it on the woman's third finger. They use a ring that is undecorated and unblemished. Since the ring has neither beginning nor end, it symbolizes something that will never end.

If it is revealed that [the bride or groom] had committed adultery [i.e., had illicit sexual relations] before this ceremony, they can not become husband and wife. It is the custom to ostracize the offender. In America it is the rule that every man will have only one wife. It is strictly forbidden to have a mistress or, of course, to pay for prostitutes if one has already decided on a wife. If a man commits such an act, he is put in prison and charged with a crime. And even if one goes to a drinking place to make merry, one will find no barmaids nor geishas there.

4

The Arrival of the Americans

13

From *The Personal Journal of Commodore Matthew C. Perry*
1853–1854

At the time of his appointment to lead an expedition to Japan, Commodore Matthew C. Perry (1794–1858) could boast a long and distinguished naval career. After serving under his elder brother, Oliver Hazard Perry, in the War of 1812, he went on to help establish the colony of Liberia, fight pirates in the West Indies, cruise in the Mediterranean, and meet the Russian czar. His greatest contribution to the Navy, however, was his advocacy of a steam-powered naval force. In 1837 he took command of the Fulton, *one of the Navy's first steamships, and he organized the first naval engineer corps. After serving as commandant at the New York naval yard, he engaged in various "gunboat diplomacy" ventures, first along the West African coast in a campaign to suppress the slave trade, then as a commander in war with Mexico, where he led the squadron that captured the port of Vera Cruz. A certified naval hero known for his interest in expanding American naval power in the Pacific, he was a natural choice to head the expedition to Japan in 1852. The following journal entries describe his experiences in 1853–54.*

[*February 1854.*]   Parties of [Japanese] officials visited *Powhatan* [i.e., Perry's ship] on the 16th and 18th, ostensibly to enquire after my health and to bring me delicacies of fresh oysters, eggs, and confectionary, but

The Personal Journal of Commodore Matthew C. Perry, ed. Roger Pineau (Washington, D.C.: Smithsonian Institution Press, 1968), 159, 164, 168–69, 176–77, 182–83.

in reality to renew their arguments and persuasions for the ships to remove to Uraga, proposing as a sort of compromise that I should go there with one or two of my squadron, but I still resisted. I was convinced that if I receded in the least from the position first assumed by me, it would be considered by the Japanese an advantage gained. Finding that I could be induced to change a predetermined intention in one instance, they might rely on prevailing on me by dint of perseverance to waver in most other cases pending the negotiations. Therefore it seemed to be the true policy to hold out at all hazards, and rather to establish for myself a character of unreasonable obstinacy than that of a yielding disposition. I knew that upon the impression thus formed by them would in a measure hinge the tenor of our future negotiations, and the sequel will show that I was right in my conclusions. Indeed, in conducting all my business with these very sagacious and deceitful people, I have found it profitable to bring to my aid the experience gained in former and by no means limited intercourse with the inhabitants of strange lands—civilized and barbarian—and this experience has admonished me that with people of forms it is necessary either to set all ceremony aside, or to out-Herod Herod in assumed personal consequence and ostentation.

I have adopted the two extremes by an exhibition of great pomp when it could properly be displayed, and by avoiding it when such pomp would be inconsistent with the spirit of our institutions. I have never recognized on any occasion the slightest personal superiority, always meeting the Japanese officials, however exalted their rank, with perfect equality, whilst those of comparative distinction of their own nation were cringing and kneeling to them. For motives of policy, and to give greater importance to my own position, I have hitherto studiously kept myself aloof from intercourse with any of the subordinates of the court, making it known that I would communicate with none but the princes of the empire. Up to this time, I have succeeded far beyond my expectations in maintaining this extreme point of diplomacy, and as I believe to very great advantage. . . .

. . . It struck me that it was better to have no treaty than one that would in the least compromise the dignity of the American character. To agree to any arrangement that would recognize in the remotest degree the restrictions submitted to by the Dutch could not for a moment be thought of. . . .

It is probable that arrogance may be charged against me for persisting as I did; and, against the judgment of all about me, in changing the place of conference, and thus compelling four princes of the empire to follow the squadron, and subjecting the government to the trouble and expense of erecting another building [as a site for negotiation], but I was simply adhering to a course of policy determined on after mature reflection, and which had hitherto worked so well.

[*March 17, 1854.*]   It stormed on Thursday and consequently the meeting did not take place until the following day, 17 February. The commissioners arrived about noon from Kanagawa in a magnificent barge or rather galley covered with banners.

On landing I was conducted immediately to the private room set apart for the discussion, and we at once proceeded to business. A paper written in Dutch was now presented, similar in purport to one which had been previously sent me in the Chinese language. From the latter version Mr. [Samuel Wells] Williams had made an English translation, which being compared with the Dutch copy may be read, with the replies respectively submitted by me, as follows:

Propositions of Japanese Commissioners
with replies of Commodore Perry.

1st Japanese proposition.

From the first of next month, wood, water, provisions, coal and other things, the productions of this country that American ships may need, can be had at Nagasaki; and after five years from this, a port in another principality shall be opened for ships to go to.

Commodore Perry's reply.

Agreed to; but one or more ports must be substituted for Nagasaki, as that is out of the route of American commerce; and the time for the opening of the ports to be agreed upon must be immediate or within a space of sixty days. The manner of paying for articles received shall be arranged by treaty.

2nd Japanese proposition.

Upon whatever part of the coast people may be shipwrecked, those people and their property shall be sent to Nagasaki by sea.
Note. When after five years shall have expired, and another harbor shall be opened, those shipwrecked men will be sent either there or to Nagasaki, as may be most convenient.

Commodore Perry's reply.

Agreed to excepting as to the port to which the shipwrecked men are to be carried.

3rd Japanese proposition.

It being impossible for us to ascertain who are pirates and who are not, such men shall not be allowed to walk about wherever they please.

Commodore Perry's reply.

Shipwrecked men and others who may resort to the ports of Japan, are not to be confined, and shall enjoy all the freedom granted to Japanese, and be subject to no further restraints. They shall, however, be held amenable to just laws, or such as may be agreed upon by treaty.

It is altogether inconsistent with justice that persons thrown by the providence of God upon the shores of a friendly nation should be looked upon and treated as pirates before any proof shall be given of their being so, and the continuance of the treatment which has hitherto been visited upon strangers will no longer be tolerated by the government of the United States so far as Americans are concerned.

4th Japanese proposition.

At Nagasaki they shall have no intercourse with the Dutch and Chinese.

Commodore Perry's reply.

The Americans will never submit to the restrictions which have been imposed upon the Dutch and Chinese, and any further allusion to such restraints will be considered offensive.

5th Japanese proposition.

After the other port is opened, if there be any sort of articles wanted, or business which requires to be arranged, there shall be careful deliberation between the parties in order to settle them.

Commodore Perry's reply.

Agreed to, so far as it applies to ports other than Nagasaki.

6th Japanese proposition.

Lew Chew[1] is a very distant country, and the opening of its harbor cannot be discussed by us.

Commodore Perry's reply.

As there can be no good reason why the Americans should not communicate freely with Lew Chew, this point is insisted on.

[1]The Ryūkyū islands.

7th Japanese proposition.

Matsmai [Matsumae] is also a very distant country, and belongs to its prince; this cannot be settled now, but a definite answer on this subject shall be given when the ships are expected next spring.

Commodore Perry's reply.

The same with respect to the port of Matsumae, for our whaling ships, steamers, and other vessels.

These propositions and replies were consecutively discussed, the commissioners interposing all possible difficulties, contending that the laws of the empire were of such character as positively forbade the concessions I demanded. . . .

. . . During our stay in Edo Bay, all the officers and members of the crews had frequent opportunities of mingling freely with the people, both ashore and on board, as many of the natives visited the ships in the business of bringing water and provisions, and on official matters.

For the first few days after our arrival at Yokohama, Mr. Gay, the chief engineer of *Mississippi,* assisted by First Assistant Engineer Danby, with the requisite number of mechanics, was employed in unpacking and putting in working order the locomotive engine, whilst Messrs. Draper and Williams were equally busy in preparing to erect the telegraphic posts for the extension of the magnetic lines. Dr. Morrow was also engaged in unpacking and arranging the agricultural implements, all intended for presentation to the Emperor, after being first exhibited and explained.

The Japanese authorities offered every facility. Sheds were prepared for sheltering the various articles from the weather; a flat piece of ground was assigned to the engineers for laying down the track of the locomotive. Posts were brought and erected as directed by Messrs. Draper and Williams, and telegraphic wires of nearly a mile in a direct line were soon extended in as perfect a manner as could have been done in the United States. One end of the wire was at the treaty house, the other at a building allotted for the purpose, and communication was soon opened between the two operators in the English, Dutch, and Japanese languages, very much to the amazement of the spectators.

Meanwhile the implements of husbandry had been put together and exhibited, the track laid down, and the beautiful little engine with its tiny car set in motion. It could be seen from the ship, flying round its circular path exciting the utmost wonder in the minds of the Japanese. Although this perfect piece of machinery was with its car finished in the most tasteful manner, it was much smaller than I had expected it would have been, the car being incapable of admitting with any comfort even a child of six years. The Japanese therefore who rode upon it were seated upon the roof, whilst the engineer placed himself upon the tender.

These various exhibitions, with the singular groups of American officers, sailors and Marines, intermingled with the native mandarins, officials, and laborers presented an animated spectacle. . . .

. . . The Japanese are remarkable for their inordinate curiosity and, in the display of so many of the inventions of our ingenious countrymen, they had ample means of gratifying this propensity. They were not satisfied with the minutest examination of all these things, surpassingly strange as they must have been to them, but followed the officers and men about, seizing upon every occasion to examine every part of their garments, and showing the strongest desire to obtain one or more of their buttons. Those who were admitted on board the ships were equally inquisitive, peering into every nook and corner accessible to them, measuring this and that, and taking sketches after their manner of whatever they could lay their eyes upon, though it would be difficult to discover from their drawings what they were intended to represent.

Notwithstanding that the Japanese are themselves so fond of indulging their curiosity, they are by no means communicative when information is required of them, alleging as a reason that their laws forbid them to communicate to foreigners anything relating to their country or its institutions. We have had much better opportunities of picking up here and there, and from time to time, many interesting particulars respecting the laws, customs, and habits of these people than others who have preceded us. Yet a long time will elapse before any full and authentic account of their internal laws and regulations will be obtained; certainly not until we can establish men of intelligence in the country in the character of consular agents, merchants, or missionaries who, to enable them to make any progress, should acquire a knowledge of the language.

We found the common people more disposed to fraternize than were the mandarins or officials. It was evident that nothing but a fear of punishment deterred them from entering into free intercourse with us; but they were closely watched, and it may be inferred that the higher classes would be equally inclined to greater intimacy if they in their turn were not also watched. In truth every native has a spy set upon him in this country, as in Lew Chew. No one is entrusted with public business of any importance without having one or more associated with him, who are ever on the alert to detect and take note of the slightest suspicion of delinquency.

[*April 6, 1854.*] . . . At this time the squadron consisted of steam frigates *Powhatan* (flagship), *Susquehanna,* and *Mississippi,* and sail ships *Macedonian, Vandalia, Southampton,* and *Lexington.* This force was soon after joined by the *Saratoga* and *Supply,* making in all nine efficient vessels, a very respectable force, but much smaller than I had expected to have had.

It has often been said and written by me, that this force was quite sufficient for all purposes of defense, and for the chastisement of insult, but not large enough to make any great moral impression, especially after the ostentatious display at home of the intentions of the government with respect to the Japan expedition. I claim the greater credit, however, in effecting more than the government anticipated, with the reduced means placed at my disposal, and under all the discouraging circumstances under which I labored.

It is true, there has been no call for an exercise of force; and why? An interrogatory easily answered by replying that the Japanese government, without the slightest doubt in my mind, came to the conclusion after due deliberation not to bring about an issue of arms. Consequently from the moment of the passing of the flagship beyond Point Hope, all military show was studiously concealed. The great object of the commissioners was to induce me to return to Uraga and not to ascend higher up the bay to discover the defenseless condition of their capital. When they found that I could not be deceived by their misrepresentations, they at once and with apparent grace submitted to my ultimatum. From that time they discontinued a military work which had been commenced on Point Hope, and destroyed by fire in the night as if by accident the sheds which had been erected for the accommodation of the numerous workmen noticed to have been employed before the passing of the ships toward Edo.

This policy was easily seen through. They found that resistance would be useless, and very wisely determined to adopt peaceful measures and the exercise of a system of diplomacy peculiarly Japanese to evade by every possible means of falsehood and deceit the reasonable concessions demanded by my government. The result proved that they had at last to concede even more than was expected by the most sanguine of those through whose means the expedition was set on foot.

14

FRANCIS L. HAWKS

Official Report of the Perry Expedition
1856

In the hopes of persuading Nathaniel Hawthorne to write the official report of his expedition to Japan, Commodore Perry traveled to Liverpool, England, where the author was serving as American consul. Hawthorne declined, suggesting Herman Melville instead, but Perry ultimately chose the Reverend Francis L. Hawks, a well-known New York minister, who had published several works of history and biography. Much of the official report was based more or less verbatim on Perry's private journal, but Hawks also relied on journals and reports of other officers who accompanied the mission. The following passage explains why Perry did not press the Japanese for a commercial treaty.

From the circumstances of the case, there was novelty in the features of the mission on which Commodore Perry was sent. Little or no guidance was to be derived from our past diplomatic experience or action. The nearest approach to such guidance was to be found in our treaty with China, made in 1844. This, therefore, was carefully studied by the Commodore. It purports to be "a treaty or general convention of peace, amity, and commerce," and to settle the rules to "be mutually observed in the intercourse of the respective countries." . . .

It certainly was very desirable to obtain, if possible, similar privileges from Japan. The Commodore resolved that, if the Japanese would negotiate at all, his first efforts should be directed to that end. . . . He was not sanguine enough to hope that he could procure an entire adoption of the Chinese treaty[1] by the Japanese. He was not ignorant of the difference in national characteristics between the inhabitants of China and the more independent, self-reliant, and sturdy natives of the Japanese islands. He knew that the lat-

[1]The 1844 Treaty of Wanghsia giving Americans the right to trade.

Francis L. Hawks, D.D. LL.D., *Narrative of the Expedition of an American Squadron to the China Seas and Japan, Performed in the Years 1852, 1853, and 1854, Under the Command of Commodore M. C. Perry, etc.* (New York: D. Appleton and Company, 1856), 445–46, 447, 452–53.

ter held the former in some degree of contempt and treated them in the matter of trade very much as they did the Dutch. He was also aware that the
Chinese, when they made their treaty, did know something of the advantages that might result from an intercourse with the rest of the world. As to
the Japanese, in their long-continued isolation, either they neither knew nor
desired such advantages, or, if they knew them, feared they might be purchased at too high a price in the introduction of foreigners who, as in the
case of the Portuguese centuries before, might seek to overturn the empire.
It was too much, therefore, to expect that the Japanese would imitate the
Chinese in *all* the particulars of a treaty. Still, they might be disposed to adopt
some of its most important features when suggested to them by a knowledge of what other orientals had done. . . .

The Commodore, whose wish it was to do as far as possible everything
that might conciliate, of course made no objection to a request [to translate the treaty] so seemingly reasonable, though he knew it to be needless,
and was content to wait patiently for their reply. In one week that reply came
in writing, and was very explicit: "As to opening a trade, such as is now carried on by China with your country, we certainly cannot *yet* bring it about.
The feelings and manners of our people are very unlike those of outer
nations, and it will be exceedingly difficult, even if you wish it, to immediately change the old regulations for those of other countries. Moreover,
the Chinese have long had intercourse with western nations, while we have
had dealings at Nagasaki with only the people of Holland and China."

This answer was not entirely unexpected, and put an end to all prospect
of negotiating a "commercial treaty," in the European sense of that phrase.
It only remained, therefore, to secure, for the present, admission into the
kingdom, and so much of trade as Japanese jealousy could be brought to
concede. At length, after much and oft-repeated discussion, the point was
yielded that certain ports might be opened to our vessels. . . .

. . . [T]he whole treaty shows that the purpose of the Japanese was to
try the experiment of intercourse with us before they made it as extensive or as intimate as it is between us and the Chinese. It was all they
would do at the time, and much, very much, was obtained on the part of
our negotiator in procuring a concession even to this extent.

But, as he knew that our success would be but the forerunner of that
of other powers, as he believed that new relations of trade once commenced, not only with ourselves but with England, France, Holland, and
Russia, in the progress of events, could not fail effectually and forever
not only to break up the old restrictive policy and open Japan to the world,
but must also lead gradually to liberal commercial treaties, he wisely, in
the ninth article, without "consultation or delay," secured to the United

States and their citizens all privileges and advantages which Japan might hereafter "grant to any other nation or nations."

As far as we have yet learned, all other powers have been content to obtain just what we, as pioneers, have obtained. Their treaties are like ours. . . .

We respectfully submit, that all, and indeed more than all, under the circumstances, that could reasonably have been expected, has been accomplished. Japan has been opened to the nations of the west. It is not to be believed, that having once effected an entrance, the enlightened powers that have made treaties with her will *go backward,* and, by any indiscretion, lose what, after so many unavailing efforts for centuries, has at last been happily attained. It belongs to these nations to show Japan that her interests will be promoted by communication with them. As prejudice gradually vanishes, we may hope to see the future negotiation of more and more liberal commercial treaties, for the benefit, not of ourselves only, but of all the maritime powers of Europe, for the advancement of Japan, and for the upward progress of our common humanity. It would be a foul reproach to Christendom now to force Japan to relapse into her cheerless and unprogressive state of unnatural isolation. She is the youngest sister in the circle of commercial nations. Let those who are older kindly take her by the hand, and aid her tottering steps, until she has reached a vigor that will enable her to walk firmly in her own strength. Cautious and kindly treatment now will soon lead to commercial treaties as liberal as can be desired.

15

II NAOSUKE

Memorial on the American Demand for a Treaty

1853

The ancestors of Ii Naosuke (1815–1860), daimyo of the domain of Hikone, had traditionally served as advisors to the bakufu in times of crisis. When the Perry expedition arrived in Japan, Naosuke threw himself into the debate over how to respond to the American demands. As his memorial indi-

Select Documents on Japanese Foreign Policy, 1853–1868, tr. and ed. William G. Beasley (London: Oxford University Press, 1955), 117–19.

cates, he was strongly in favor of signing a treaty with Perry to avoid a military confrontation that was bound to end in disaster for Japan. Ii became a bitter political enemy of Tokugawa Nariaki, who firmly opposed any concessions to the Americans. When Hotta Masayoshi, the bakufu's chief minister, failed to secure imperial approval for the Harris treaty in 1858, Ii Naosuke was appointed "great elder" (tairō). After agreeing to sign the treaty, he dealt harshly with the daimyo who opposed him, including Tokugawa Nariaki, and he ordered the arrest or execution of samurai activists and scholars who opposed opening ports to trade. In 1860 he was assassinated by a band of disgruntled samurai, mainly from the domain of Mito.

Careful consideration of conditions as they are today . . . leads me to believe that despite the constant differences and debates into which men of patriotism and foresight have been led in recent years by their perception of the danger of foreign aggression, it is impossible in the crisis we now face to ensure the safety and tranquillity of our country merely by an insistence on the seclusion laws as we did in former times. Moreover, time is essential if we are to complete our coast defences. Since 1609, when warships of over 500 *koku*[1] were forbidden, we have had no warships capable of opposing foreign attack on our coasts with heavy guns. Thus I am much afraid that were the foreigners now to seize as bases such outlying islands as Hachijō-jima and Ōshima, it would be impossible for us to remain inactive, though without warships we should have no effective means of driving them off. There is a saying that when one is besieged in a castle, to raise the drawbridge is to imprison oneself and make it impossible to hold out indefinitely; and again, that when opposing forces face each other across a river, victory is obtained by that which crosses the river and attacks. It seems clear throughout history that he who takes action is in a position to advance, while he who remains inactive must retreat. Even though the Shōgun's ancestors set up seclusion laws, they left the Dutch and the Chinese to act as a bridge [to the outside world]. Might this bridge not now be of advantage to us in handling foreign affairs, providing us with the means whereby we may for a time avert the outbreak of hostilities and then, after some time has elapsed, gain a complete victory?

I understand that the coal for which the Americans have expressed a desire is to be found in quantity in Kyūshū. We should first tell them, as a matter of expediency, that we also have need of coal, but that should their

---

[1]One koku equals 10 cubic feet in measuring ship capacity.

need of it arise urgently and unexpectedly during a voyage, they may ask for coal at Nagasaki and if we have any to spare we will provide it. Nor will we grudge them wood and water. As for foodstuffs, the supply varies from province to province, but we can agree to provide food for the shipwrecked and unfortunate. Again, we can tell them, of recent years we have treated kindly those wrecked on our coasts and have sent them all home. There is no need for further discussion of this subject, and all requests concerning it should be made through the Dutch. Then, too, there is the question of trade. Although there is a national prohibition of it, conditions are not the same as they were. The exchange of goods is a universal practice. This we should explain to the spirits of our ancestors. And we should then tell the foreigners that we mean in future to send trading vessels to the Dutch company's factory at Batavia to engage in trade; that we will allocate some of our trading goods to America, some to Russia, and so on, using the Dutch to trade for us as our agents; but that there will be a delay of one or two years because we must [first] construct new ships for these voyages. By replying in this way we will take the Americans by surprise in offering to treat them generally in the same way as the Dutch.

We must revive the licensed trading vessels [system] . . . , ordering the rich merchants of such places as Ōsaka, Hyōgo, and Sakai to take shares in the enterprise. We must construct new steamships, especially powerful warships, and these we will load with goods not needed in Japan. For a time we will have to employ Dutchmen as masters and mariners, but we will put on board with them Japanese of ability and integrity who must study the use of large guns, the handling of ships, and the rules of navigation. Openly these will be called merchant vessels, but they will in fact have the secret purpose of training a navy. As we increase the number of ships and our mastery of technique, Japanese will be able to sail the oceans freely and gain direct knowledge of conditions abroad without relying on the secret reports of the Dutch. Thus we will eventually complete the organization of a navy. Moreover, we must shake off the panic and apprehensions that have beset us and abandon our habits of luxury and wasteful spending. Our defences thus strengthened, and all being arranged at home, we can act so as to make our courage and prestige resound beyond the seas. By so doing, we will not in the future be imprisoning ourselves; indeed, we will be able, I believe, so to accomplish matters at home and abroad as to achieve national security. Forestalling the foreigners in this way, I believe, is the best method of ensuring that the Bakufu will at some future time find opportunity to reimpose its ban and forbid foreigners to come to Japan, as was done in the Kanei period [1624–44]. Moreover, it would make possible the strictest prohibition of

Christianity. And since I understand that the Americans and Russians themselves have only recently become skilled in navigation, I do not see how the people of our country, who are clever and quick-witted, should prove inferior to Westerners if we begin training at once.

The national situation being what it is, if the Bakufu protects our coasts peacefully without bringing upon us permanent foreign difficulties, then even if that entails complete or partial change in the laws of our ancestors I do not believe such action could really be regarded as contrary to the wishes of those ancestors. However, I think it is essential to win the support of the country for Bakufu policy on this occasion, . . .

It is now no easy matter, by means of orders concerning the defence of the capital and the nearby coast, to ensure that all will be fully prepared for any sudden emergency, so not a moment must be wasted. However many iron walls we construct, they will certainly not be as effective as unity of mind if the unforeseen happens. The urgent task of the moment, therefore, is for the Bakufu to resolve on relieving the nation's anxieties and issue the appropriate orders.

16

TOKUGAWA NARIAKI

Memorial on the American Demand for a Treaty
1853

Tokugawa Nariaki (1800–1860) was appointed daimyo of Mito after a bitter dispute over the succession. Backed by reform-minded scholars like Fujita Toko and Aizawa Seishisai, he launched an aggressive program of domain reform, aimed at building up its military and economic strength. In the 1830s, as more and more foreign ships appeared in Japanese waters, he built new coastal defenses on the shores of his domain, melting down Buddhist temple bells to cast cannon. Fearing that an ominous conjunction of "threats from without" and "troubles within" might lead to the collapse of the country, he constantly pressed similar reform measures on the bakufu. Irritated by his pes-

Select Documents on Japanese Foreign Policy, 1853–1868, tr. and ed. William G. Beasley (London: Oxford University Press, 1955), 102–07.

tering memorials, the bakufu leadership forced him into retirement in the late 1840s, but he was released from house arrest in 1849. In 1853, as this memorial demonstrates, he became a leader of the forces opposing a treaty with Perry, and he remained associated with the antiforeign cause until his death.

Observations on coast defence

It is my belief that the first and most urgent of our tasks is for the Bakufu to make its choice between peace and war, and having determined its policy to pursue it unwaveringly thereafter. When we consider the respective advantages and disadvantages of war and peace, we find that if we put our trust in war the whole country's morale will be increased and even if we sustain an initial defeat we will in the end expel the foreigner; while if we put our trust in peace, even though things may seem tranquil for a time, the morale of the country will be greatly lowered and we will come in the end to complete collapse. This has been amply demonstrated in the history of China and is a fact that men of intelligence, both past and present, have always known. It is therefore unnecessary for me to speak of this in detail. However, I propose to give here in outline the ten reasons why in my view we must never choose the policy of peace.

1. Although our country's territory is not extensive, foreigners both fear and respect us. That, after all, is because our resoluteness and military prowess have been clearly demonstrated to the world outside. . . . Despite this, the Americans who arrived recently, though fully aware of the Bakufu's prohibition, entered Uraga displaying a white flag as a symbol of peace and insisted on presenting their written requests. Moreover they entered Edo Bay, fired heavy guns in salute and even went so far as to conduct surveys without permission. They were arrogant and discourteous, their actions an outrage. Indeed, this was the greatest disgrace we have suffered since the dawn of our history. The saying is that if the enemy dictates terms in one's own capital one's country is disgraced. . . . Should it happen not only that the Bakufu fails to expel them but also that it concludes an agreement in accordance with their requests, then I fear it would be impossible to maintain our national prestige [*kokutai*]. That is the first reason why we must never choose the policy of peace.

2. The prohibition of Christianity is the first rule of the Tokugawa house. Public notices concerning it are posted everywhere, even to the remotest corner of every province. . . . The Bakufu can never ignore or overlook the evils of Christianity. Yet if the Americans are allowed to come again this religion will inevitably raise its head once more, however strict the prohibition; and this, I fear, is something we could never justify

to the spirits of our ancestors. That is the second reason why we must never choose the policy of peace.

3. To exchange our valuable articles like gold, silver, copper, and iron for useless foreign goods like woollens and satin is to incur great loss while acquiring not the smallest benefit. The best course of all would be for the Bakufu to put a stop to the trade with Holland. By contrast, to open such valueless trade with others besides the Dutch would, I believe, inflict the greatest possible harm on our country. That is the third reason why we must never choose the policy of peace.

4. For some years Russia, England, and others have sought trade with us, but the Bakufu has not permitted it. Should permission be granted to the Americans, on what grounds would it be possible to refuse if Russia and the others [again] request it? That is the fourth reason why we must never choose the policy of peace.

5. It is widely stated that [apart from trade] the foreigners have no other evil designs and that if only the Bakufu will permit trade there will be no further difficulty. However, it is their practice first to seek a foothold by means of trade and then to go on to propagate Christianity and make other unreasonable demands. . . . That is the fifth reason why we must never choose the policy of peace.

6. Though the Rangakusha group may argue secretly that world conditions are much changed from what they were, Japan alone clinging to ideas of seclusion in isolation amidst the seas, that this is a constant source of danger to us and that our best course would therefore be to communicate with foreign countries and open an extensive trade; yet, to my mind, if the people of Japan stand firmly united, if we complete our military preparations and return to the state of society that existed before the middle ages, then we will even be able to go out against foreign countries and spread abroad our fame and prestige. But if we open trade at the demand of the foreigners, for no better reason than that, our habits today being those of peace and indolence, men have shown fear merely at the coming of a handful of foreign warships, then it would truly be a vain illusion to think of evolving any long-range plan for going out against foreign countries. That is the sixth reason why we must never choose the policy of peace. . . .

9. I hear that all, even though they be commoners, who have witnessed the recent actions of the foreigners, think them abominable; and if the Bakufu does not expel these insolent foreigners root and branch there may be some who will complain in secret, asking to what purpose have been all the preparations of gun-emplacements. . . . That, I believe, is because even the humblest are conscious of the debt they owe their country, and it is indeed a promising sign. Since even ignorant commoners are talking in this way, I fear that if the Bakufu does not decide

to carry out expulsion, if its handling of the matter shows nothing but excess of leniency and appeasement of the foreigners, then the lower orders may fail to understand its ideas and hence opposition might arise from evil men who had lost their respect for Bakufu authority. It might even be that Bakufu control of the great lords would itself be endangered. That is the ninth reason why we must never choose the policy of peace.

10. There are those who say that since the expulsion of foreigners is the ancient law of the Shōgun's ancestors, reissued and reaffirmed in the Bunsei period [1818–30], the Bakufu has in fact always been firmly resolved to fight, but that even so one must recognize that peace has now lasted so long our armaments are inadequate, and one cannot therefore tell what harm might be done if we too recklessly arouse the anger of the foreigners. In that event, they say, the Bakufu would be forced to conclude a peace settlement and so its prestige would suffer still further damage. Hence [it is argued], the Bakufu should show itself compliant at this time and should placate the foreigners, meanwhile exerting all its efforts in military preparations, so that when these preparations have been completed it can more strictly enforce the ancient laws. This argument sounds reasonable enough. However, to my mind the people here [in Edo] are temporizing and half-hearted; and even though the Shōgun exhort them day and night he cannot make them resolute. Now there is not the slightest chance that the feudal lords will complete military preparations, however many years may pass, unless they are set an example in military matters by the Bakufu. . . . On the arrival of the foreign ships recently, all fell into a panic. Some take matters very seriously while foreign ships are actually at anchor here, but once the ships leave and orders are given for them to revert to normal, they all relax once more into idleness and immediately disperse the military equipment which they had hurriedly assembled. It is just as if, regardless of a fire burning beneath the floor of one's house, one neglected all fire-fighting precautions. Indeed, it shows a shameful spirit. I therefore believe that if there be any sign of the Bakufu pursuing the policy of peace, morale will never rise though preparations be pressed forward daily; and the gun-batteries and other preparations made will accordingly be so much ornament, never put to effective use. But if the Bakufu, now and henceforward, shows itself resolute for expulsion, the immediate effect will be to increase ten-fold the morale of the country and to bring about the completion of military preparations without even the necessity for issuing orders. Hesitant as I am to say so, only by so doing will the Shōgun be able to fulfil his 'barbarian-expelling' duty and unite the men of every province in carrying out their proper military functions. That is the tenth reason why we must never choose the policy of peace, and it is by far the most urgent and important of them all. . . .

... In these feeble days men tend to cling to peace; they are not fond of defending their country by war. They slander those of us who are determined to fight, calling us lovers of war, men who enjoy conflict. If matters become desperate they might, in their enormous folly, try to overthrow those of us who are determined to fight, offering excuses to the enemy and concluding a peace agreement with him. They would thus in the end bring total destruction upon us. In view of our country's tradition of military courage, however, it is probable that once the Bakufu has taken a firm decision we shall find no such cowards among us. But good advice is as hard to accept as good medicine is unpleasing to the palate. A temporizing and time-serving policy is the one easiest for me to adopt. It is therefore my belief that in this question of coast defence it is of the first importance that the Bakufu pay due heed [to these matters] and that having once reached a decision it should never waver from it thereafter. . . .

17

Broadsheet of Sumo Wrestlers
Delivering Rice
1854

By the mid–nineteenth century, single-page news sheets (called kawara-ban) *circulated in Edo and other major cities in Japan. Sold at bookshops or hawked on the street by vendors, these broadsheets were filled with gossip about actors and entertainers, reports of natural anomalies and wonders, stories about vendettas and love suicides, or news about fires, earthquakes, and other natural disasters. Often the "news" reported was no more accurate than reports of space aliens found in today's supermarket tabloids. However, many broadsheets circulated at the time of the Perry expedition gave straightforward accounts of the American mission. For example, the one on page 107 describes a display of strength and acrobatics put on for the Americans by a group of sumo wrestlers. As the official report of the expedition noted, one carried a rice bale by his teeth and another held a bale while turning somersaults. However, the print doubtless exaggerates the contrast in size of the wrestlers and the American sailors.*

Kawaraban shinbun: Edo/Meiji sanbyaku jiken, Vol. 2 (Tokyo: Heibonsha, 1978), 19.

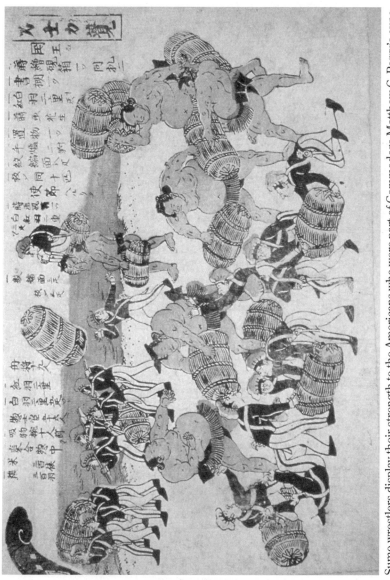

Sumo wrestlers display their strength to the Americans who were part of Commodore Matthew C. Perry's expedition.

18

Broadsheet on the "Capture" of the Americans
1854

In contrast to the broadsheet showing the performance of the sumo wrestlers (see Document 17), the broadsheet on the facing page reports on a completely fictitious event. Its caption reads as follows: "Our country is a land of military prowess and a land of righteousness, beyond compare with the foreign 'red hairs.' On the 12th day of the eighth month in 1854, an American steam vessel put in at a harbor in the Gotō Islands in the province of Hizen with the intention of making a night attack. On hearing this report, the authorities at the local castle immediately assembled a force of 1,500 men and fortified strong points all along the coast. Scouts were posted on the shore toward which the steam vessel was heading. When the red hairs arrived in the harbor, Japanese scouts sent back a report. Unaware of this, however, the enemy sent its small boats ashore at night. After landing they climbed the hill, attacked the local village and seized rice, saké, miso, firewood, and other things. When scouts posted on the coast reported to the castle, the 1,500 men assembled by the local authorities marched out in a single line. They destroyed the American vessel with their cannon, then they slaughtered 3,700 red hairs in a stroke, beginning with those on the vessel, then those who had come ashore here and there. Fifty-three [foreigners] who had attacked the villagers and their houses were captured, and five who had committed the heaviest offenses were sent to the capital at Edo. Truly, all who witnessed this affair were extraordinarily impressed by the great military prowess of the daimyo of the Gotō Islands."

Kawaraban shinbun: Edo/Meiji sanbyaku jiken, Vol. 2. (Tokyo: Heibonsha, 1978), 14.

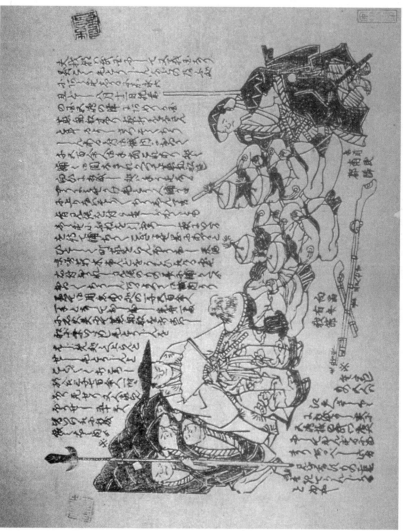

This broadsheet reports a fictitious event: the slaughter of 3,700 invading "red hairs" and the capture of 53 of them.

19

A Comic Dialogue

ca. 1855

In popular lore, the catfish was a powerful force of nature whose subterranean movements were thought to be the cause of earthquakes. In the fall of 1855, shortly before this broadsheet was published, a major earthquake struck the Edo area. The broadsheet on the facing page presents a comic dialogue between a catfish and an American, who are playing a children's game of tug-of-war with a cord around their necks. The earthquake-making catfish appears to represent antiforeign sentiments, while the American is extolling the virtues of his country. The plasterer refereeing their contest probably represents ordinary commoners who wanted to be rid of the problems brought both by the earthquake and the foreign demands for trade.

CATFISH: You stupid Americans have been making fun of us Japanese for the past two or three years. You have come and pushed us around too much. . . . Stop this useless talk of trade; we don't need it. We are sick of hearing the noisy calls of the candy sellers. Since we don't need you, hurry up and put your back to us. Fix your rudder and sail away at once.

AMERICA: What are you talking about, you stupid catfish! Mine is a country of benevolence and compassion. No matter what a person does, even if he is a laborer or a hunter, if he is benevolent he can become king. That's why many people want to come to my country. . . . But there is one thing which troubles us: we have too many people and not enough food to feed them. Therefore we have come to Japan to get rice, radishes and chickens; but you just say no, and have not given us anything. That's why we keep coming back.

CATFISH: Shut up, Perry. No matter how often you brag that your federation [*gasshū koku*] is a country of benevolence, if you don't have food you must be poor. If America had the buddha or the gods, then you would have a good harvest of the five grains. But since you don't, you

Kawaraban shibun: Edo/Meiji sanbyaku jiken, Vol. 2 (Tokyo: Heibonsha, 1978), 32. The translation of the caption may be found in Minami Kazuo, *Edo Commoners on the Eve of the Restoration: The Coming of the Black Ships,* tr. M. William Steele and Robert Eskildsen (Tokyo: International Christian University, 1989), 42–44.

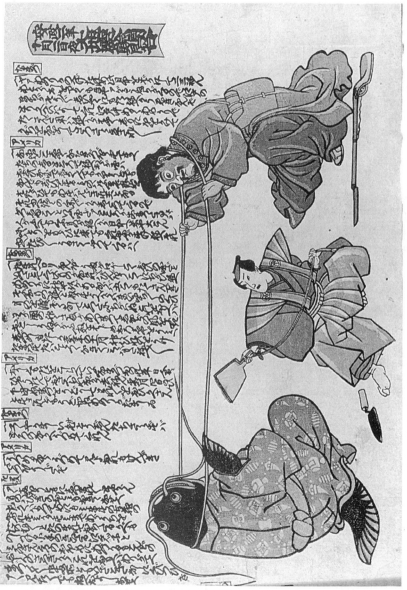

The catfish, representing antiforeign sentiments in Japan, wrestles with the American, who extolls the virtu[es] [of] his country.

have to depend upon piracy and steal your food. Knowing this, the gods of our country have gathered together and have caused a divine wind to blow to sink your ships and those of the Russians. For sure in the eleventh month of last year the gods struck out against your rudeness. I don't want to listen to any of your empty words.

AMERICA: You catfish! It is funny for your to speak like that, making up your own reasoning. Despite the fact that men can usually hold you down with a gourd, on the fourth day of the eleventh month you tried to send us away by shaking Shimazu and Numazu, but our American spirit remained unmoved.

CATFISH: You noisy[,] hairy barbarian! If you don't leave we'll bury you in mud!

AMERICA: Go ahead and try; I'll fight back with gun and bayonet.

PLASTERER: Both of you be quiet. If you are far away, listen carefully to my words; if you are close, look with your eyes and see the cracks in the warehouses. We are asked to patch up these cracks and holes, asked over and over again; we are asked to prop up the broken down walls; we are known for our fine work with the trowel. Everyone admires our work. We are thankful this time for the earthquake, but both of you try to resolve your differences without causing us any trouble. We don't want to see it; stop it!

20

A Black Ship Scroll with Dialogue

ca. 1854

When the Perry Expedition arrived in 1853–54, many domains sent officials to make reports and artists to draw pictures of the foreign vessels. Local artists also found the Americans a fascinating subject. The scroll from which the following section is taken was painted by an anonymous artist in Shimoda, where Perry's ships sailed after completing the treaty negotiations. It shows the Americans in a variety of situations: sketching the landscape; surveying the coastline; netting fish or shooting birds; taking pictures of a

Oliver Statler, *The Black Ship Scroll: An Account of the Perry Expedition at Shimoda in 1854 and the Lively Beginnings of People-to-People Relations between Japan and America* (San Francisco and New York: Japan Society, 1963), 60–61, 75–76.

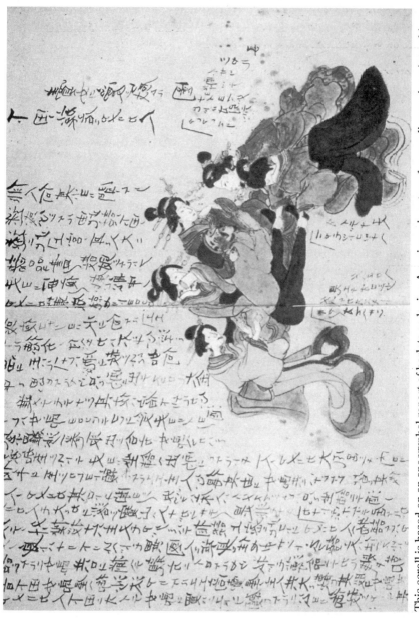

This scroll is based on an apocryphal report of harlots seducing Americans in return for supplies on American ships.

geisha; and pounding rice in a wooden mortar. The scene depicted in this section of the scroll was undoubtedly based on an apocryphal report. Intended to poke fun at the wiliness of the Americans, it shows that ordinary Japanese were not completely awed by the foreigners. contrary to perry's account

American with Harlots

The dialogue: " 'Hey, don't pull his leg so hard when he's still so high in his cups!' 'Oh, come a little closer to me!' 'I say, I say, it seems you've had too much and can't stand up!' "

The caption: "The Americans submitted a petition for permission to patronize the harlots in Shimoda. The authorities agreed and notified the brothel-operators of Shimoda, who were delighted at the prospect and passed this news on to the harlots. Unexpectedly, however, the harlots unanimously pleaded with their masters, saying, among other things: 'We are, to be sure, ill fated, engaged thus in an ignoble profession. Nevertheless, we have never made any contract saying we should go so far as to sleep with foreigners!' The surprised brothel-owners were greatly distressed at this and, after meeting in consultation, secretly reported the girls' complaint to the Americans.

"Needless to relate, the Americans were greatly crestfallen—just like, one might say, men returning empty-handed from a mountain loaded with treasure. In the midst of their desperation, however, one of the Americans, hearing this, exclaimed: 'All right, all right, we don't have to sleep with the girls. Only let us have the pleasure of drinking with them in the banquet room.' And when this proposition was explained to the brothel-keepers, they conveyed it to the harlots, who unanimously agreed.

"After that, when the harlots had come into the banquet room to serve saké, one of the Americans opened up a big parcel and, bringing out a bolt of fine purple woolen cloth, gave it to the harlot who was serving him. The harlot received this with great joy, and thereafter treated the man with special kindness and much saké until he returned to his quarters that evening. The harlot thereupon took the matter greatly to heart and the following idea popped into her mind: 'I get this precious treasure only for serving him drinks. If I gave him my body too, what limitless profits might be mine!'

"One night shortly afterwards, therefore, of her own volition she seduced the American. He, needless to say, was delighted, for his strategy had worked just as he had planned. Henceforth, each and every night the man had his pleasure thus, gradually depleting his ship of its supplies. Eventually, however, word of this reached his senior officer, who caused a great fuss about it.

"This story was told by a certain haiku poet of Shimoda."

21

Report of a Rape

1854

Not all encounters between the Americans and the Japanese in 1853–54 were diplomatic or cultural. While Commodore Perry's journal makes no mention of disciplinary problems, American sailors sometimes got into trouble with Japanese commoners. This official report records the consequences of a rape committed by an American sailor on a stopover in the Ryūkyū Islands. The Perry expedition report also makes a brief mention of the incident.

The Result of the Judicial Investigation of Mitu, of Higashi-mura, a female Aged Fifty

On the 12th of June she heard that some Americans, drunk with excess of liquor, were rambling about everywhere; she and her niece were alone and shut the doors of the house, when about 4 o'clock one of them came scrambling over the walls of the house and forced himself into the house. She was exceedingly alarmed, and in her fright ran out doors to get away, when the man seized her and drew a knife, threatening her, as he brandished it, into compliance with his desires. She cried out with a loud voice, but he held on to her; she was too weak to resist, and suffered his ravishment, losing all consciousness of herself. By this time, people hearing of it ran together, and giving her some stimulus, she anon came to herself.

The testimony of Jima, given on the trial.—"On the 12th of June, about 4 p.m., hearing a woman in the next house crying out, many persons came

Correspondence Relative to the Naval Expedition to Japan, 33 Cong., 2 Sess., Exec. Doc. 34, 172–73.

together, I also going to see what was the cause, and found that an American had violated a female of Kugusku, named Mitu, who was in truth a relative of mine. Unable to bear it patiently, I threw the man to the ground; but as she had fainted away entirely, I remained with her in the house to give her some remedies, and am therefore quite ignorant of what happened to this American afterwards."

The evidence of Tokisi.—"On the 12th of June, about four p.m., I heard that a woman of Kugusku, named Mitu, had been forced by an American, and as I ran quickly into the house I saw the man hastening out and running off. Irritated and greatly enraged, I threw a stone and hit him on the head and wounded him. Just then Konishi was at Tembe-chu (the temple of the Queen of Heaven) loitering about, and a great crowd came up from the Tenshikwan pursuing an American, which, when he had heard the circumstances, he joined in and threw two stones after him, which, however, did not hit to wound him. The American, ashamed to see people after such a deed, turned from the main road before him and passed aside towards the beach westward, directly towards San Chung Ching, where he fell into the water and was drowned. Konishi himself then went by a cross path to Hwashito, where he saw him drowned.

"Yara also was passing through the market at the time, and hearing the crowd speaking of the violence done to Mitu, and being near the Tenshikwan when the crowd was pursuing the man, threw stones at him twice, but not to wound him. When he passed the west beach and turned towards the San Chung Ching, there were many persons, unknown to the said Yara, who were likewise chasing the man, and saw him, some thirty or forty steps further on, fall in and drown. Chining, Arakaki, and Karagusku, hearing of the cause of the mob, joined it and cast stones at the man; yet not so as to wound him."

5

The Opening of Trade

22

From *The Complete Journal of Townsend Harris*

1857–1858

Townsend Harris (1804–1878), the American official who negotiated the commercial treaty of 1858, began his career as a clerk in a New York City dry goods store. A successful businessman active in the Democratic party, he was elected to the New York Board of Education in 1846. After his mother died, Harris took to drink. When his brother dissolved their business partnership, Harris acquired ownership of a trading vessel engaged in the Asian trade, but within a few years his venture failed. In 1853 he lobbied with political friends for a job as American consul in Hong Kong or Canton but was sent instead to the less significant treaty port of Ningpo. Using his ties to Senator William H. Seward and Secretary of State William L. Marcy, he finally managed to secure an appointment as the first American consul-general to Japan. En route to Japan, he negotiated a commercial treaty with the kingdom of Siam (now Thailand). Taught by his mother "to tell the truth, fear God, and hate the British," he had a chance to do all three after he arrived in Shimoda in 1856.

Monday, November 30, 1857. To-day I am to enter [Edo]. It will form an important epoch in my life, and a still more important one in the history of Japan. I am the first diplomatic representative that has ever been received in this city; and, whether I succeed or fail in my intended nego-

The Complete Journal of Townsend Harris, introduction and notes by Mario Emilio Cosenza (New York: Doubleday, 1930), 436–37, 440–41, 465–68, 484–87, 495–96, 537–39.

tiations, it is a *great fact* that will always remain, showing that at last I have forced this singular people to acknowledge the *rights of embassy*. I feel no little pride, too, in carrying the American Flag through that part of Japan, between the extremity of Cape Idsu [Izu] and into the very castle of the City of Yedo [Edo]. . . .

The authorities made their prostrations as before, but the people remained standing. As the authorities were changed every one hundred and twenty yards, there was a constant "knocking of heads" [i.e., deep bowing]. A large proportion of the assemblage wore two swords, showing they were of some rank, and almost all had on the . . . dress of ceremony. The number admitted into the streets through which I passed formed a rank of five deep on each side of the way. Every cross-street had its stockade closed to prevent too great a crowd; and, as I looked up and down those streets, they seemed a solid mass of men and women. The most perfect order was maintained from Sinagawa [Shinagawa] to my lodgings,—a distance of over seven miles. Not a shout or a cry was heard. The silence of such a vast multitude had something appalling [in] it. Lord Byron called a silent woman *sleeping thunder*.

I calculated the number of persons that lined the street from Sinagawa to my residence at one hundred and eighty-five thousand. I called the distance seven miles; that each person occupied two feet of front in his line, and that the lines were five feet deep on each side of the way. . . . In front of the lines of the spectators stood men about ten feet apart and armed with a long white stave like the marshals' staff in the courts at New York. . . . It easily appeared that they were the retainers of persons of rank, who "kept the ground" in the vicinity of his residence. The people all appeared clean, well clad and well fed; indeed, I have never seen a case of squalid misery since I have been in Japan. . . .

Sunday, December 6, 1857. This is the second Sunday in Advent. Assisted by Mr. Heusken [i.e., his interpreter] I read the full service in an audible voice, and with the paper doors of the houses here our voices could be heard in every part of the building.

This was beyond doubt the first time that the English version of the Bible was ever read, or the American Protestant Episcopal Service ever repeated in this city. What a host of thoughts rush upon me as I reflect on this event. Two hundred and thirty years ago a law was promulgated in Japan inflicting death on anyone who should use any of the rites of the Christian religion in Japan; that law is still unrepealed, and yet here have I boldly and openly done the very acts that the Japanese law punishes so severely!

What is my protection? The American name alone,—that name so powerful and potent now cannot be said to have had an existence then, for in all the wide lands that now form the United States there were not at that time five thousand men of Anglo-Saxon origin.

The first blow is now struck against the cruel persecution of Christianity by the Japanese; and, by the blessing of God, if I succeed in establishing negotiations at this time with the Japanese, I mean to boldly demand for Americans the free exercise of their religion in Japan with the right to build churches, and I will also demand the abolition of the custom of trampling on the cross or crucifix, which the Dutch have basely witnessed for two hundred and thirty years without a word of remonstrance. . . .

I shall be both proud and happy if I can be the humble means of once more opening Japan to the blessed rule of Christianity.

My Bible and Prayer Book are priceless mementos of this event, and when (after many or few years) Japan shall be once more opened to Christianity, the events of this day at Yedo will ever be of interest.

Saturday, December 12, 1857. Again visit the Minister for Foreign Affairs. Everything attending this visit was so exactly like my first visit that I have nothing to note except what relates to the conference I had with him. The Commissioners of my Voyage assisted the Minister on this occasion.

My private papers on "Japan" contain an exact copy of what I said on this occasion,—therefore, I do not copy it here.

It related to the changed condition of the world by the introduction of steam; that Japan would be forced to abandon her exclusive policy; that she might soon become a great and powerful nation by simply permitting her people to exercise their ingenuity and industry; that a moderate tax on commerce would soon give her a large revenue by which she might support a respectable navy; that the resources of Japan, when developed by the action of free trade, would show a vast amount of exchangeable values; that this production would not in any respect interfere with the production of the necessary food for the people, but would arise from the employment given to the actual surplus labor of Japan, etc., etc.; that foreign nations would, one after another, send powerful fleets to Japan to demand the opening of the country; that Japan must either yield or suffer the miseries of war; that, even if war did not ensue, the country would be kept in a constant state of excitement by the presence of these large foreign armaments; that to make a concession of any value it must be made in due season; and that the terms demanded by a fleet would never be as moderate as those asked by a person placed as I was; and that to yield to a fleet what was refused to an ambassador would humiliate the Government in the eyes of all the Japanese people, and thus actually weaken its power. This point was illustrated by the case of China, the war of 1839 to 1841, the events succeeding that war, and the present hostilities.

I told him that, by negotiating with me who had purposely come to Yedo alone and without the presence of even a single man-of-war, the honor of Japan would be saved; that each point would be carefully discussed, and that the country should be gradually opened.

I added that the three great points would be: 1st, the reception of foreign ministers to reside at Yedo; 2nd, the freedom of trade with the Japanese without the interference of Government officers; and 3rd, the opening of additional harbors.

I added that I did not ask any exclusive rights for the Americans, and that a treaty that would be satisfactory to the President would at once be accepted by all the great Western powers. I did not fail to point out the danger to Japan of having opium forced upon her, and said I would be willing to prohibit the bringing it to Japan.

I closed by saying that my mission was a friendly one in every respect; that I had no threats to use; that the President merely informed them of the dangers that threatened the country, and pointed out a way by which not only could those dangers be averted, but Japan made a prosperous, powerful and happy nation.

My discourse lasted over two hours and was listened to with the deepest attention and interest by the Minister. He asked some questions occasionally when he did not fully understand what was said.

When I had finished, the Minister thanked me for my communication, and said it should be communicated to the Tykoon [i.e., the shogun] and have that consideration which it merited, and that it was the most important matter ever brought before the Government.

He added that the Japanese never acted as promptly on business of importance as the Americans did, that many persons had to be consulted, and therefore I must give them sufficient time for those purposes. This was to prepare me for the usual delay of the Japanese in everything.

Saturday, January 9, 1858.   To-day the Prince of Shinano visited me for the first time in three days. I determined to bring about a crisis, and therefore began by saying that it was now twenty-nine days since I had made some very important communications to the Minister of Foreign Affairs, of which no official notice had since been taken; that they would not even name a period within which I should have a reply; that such treatment could not be submitted to; that the President had sent me to Yedo on a most friendly mission, having solely the benefit of Japan in view; that the United States asked nothing for themselves; that the trade of Japan was no object to us; that all we cared for was that our ships could make repairs and get supplies in their harbors, and that we had already got that point; that they must open their eyes and then they would see that I neither asked nor would I accept any favors from Japan; that ten days ago I offered to give them explanations on any points on which they needed information; and wound up by saying that their treatment of me showed that no negotiations could be carried on with them unless the plenipotentiary was backed by a fleet, and offered them cannon balls for arguments. I closed by saying that unless something was done I should return to Shimoda. Poor Shinano listened in evident trepidation. . . .

This was apparently a bold step on my part, but from my knowledge of this people I felt that I ran no kind of danger of breaking off my negotiations by what I did, and that the more I yielded and acquiesced, the more they would impose on me, while, by taking a bold attitude and assuming a threatening tone, I should at once bring them to terms.

Ash Wednesday, February 17, 1858. The Commissioners, instead of meeting me at noon, as they had appointed, did not arrive until near five P.M. They commenced by giving a history of my negotiations from the day of my audience up to the ninth inst. [Feb. 9], repeating many parts three or four times and constantly referring to the *Daimyō* and their opposition to any change in the ancient customs of the land, by permitting the residence of foreigners in Japan, etc., etc. This lasted for more than an hour, without their giving me any information as to what they desired. I plainly saw that there was a hitch somewhere. They then proceeded to say that on the eleventh inst. [Feb. 11] the Treaty, as it then stood, had been submitted to the *Daimyō* and instantly the whole Castle was in an uproar.

Some of the most violent declared that they would sacrifice their lives before they would permit such great changes to be made. The Council of State had labored incessantly to enlighten these men; had pointed out to them not only the policy, but necessity there was to make the Treaty if they would avert the ruin of the Kingdom, etc. They had brought over some, but others still remained obstinate; that the Government could not at once sign such a treaty, except at the expense of bloodshed; that they were sure the President did not wish to bring any such evil on Japan, etc., etc.

I at last discovered that they wished to delay the signing of the Treaty until a member of the Council of State could proceed as "Ambassador to the Spiritual Emperor" at Kyōto and get his approval; that the moment that approval was received the *Daimyō* must withdraw their opposition; that they were content to take the Treaty substantially as it stood, having only some slight verbal alterations to suggest, and solemnly pledged their faith that the Treaty should be executed as soon as the Ambassador returned from [Kyōto], which would require about two months. Having concluded this extraordinary conversation, I asked them what they would do if the Mikado refused his assent. They replied in a prompt and decided manner, that the Government had *determined not to receive any objections from the Mikado.* I asked what is the use then of delaying the Treaty for what appears to be a mere ceremony. They replied that it was this solemn ceremony that gave value to it; and, as I understood, it being known that the Mikado [had been] thus gravely appealed to, his decision would be final, and that all excitement would subside at once.

23

HOTTA MASAYOSHI

Memorial on the Harris Proposal

1857

Hotta Masayoshi (1810–1864), the daimyo of Sakura, was a patron of Dutch Studies. Known to be sympathetic to the cause of opening the country, he was appointed to succeed Abe Masahiro as the bakufu's chief minister in 1855. While negotiating a treaty to relax restrictions on the movement of Dutch merchants in Japan, he was warned by the Dutch representative that the British and other powers would soon put pressure on the bakufu to open the country fully to trade. As this memorial shows, Hotta himself seems to have realized that ending barriers to trade was inevitable. In 1858 Hotta negotiated a draft treaty with Townsend Harris, but he was unable to secure imperial approval for the document. His failure not only forced his resignation but triggered an intensified antiforeign agitation and opened a breach between the bakufu and the imperial court that was resolved only with the overthrow of the bakufu by proemperor forces.

Select Documents on Japanese Foreign Policy, 1853–1868, tr. and ed. William G. Beasley (London: Oxford University Press, 1955), 165–68.

As I informed you [the daimyo] some days ago, the American envoy recently made certain requests; and after consideration of the circumstances the Shōgun has come to the conclusion that he must make major changes in our long-standing laws. . . . Those who have views on the subject, therefore, are to report them without reserve. I shall first inform you in detail of my own views. If there are still points which are not clear, I will discuss them with you as often as may be necessary. . . .

There are at this time two views about the way in which the foreigners should be treated. According to the first, the peace our country has enjoyed for almost three hundred years has accustomed both high and low to indolence; what is more, our national strength has declined, our military preparations are inadequate, and we are in no position to eject the foreigners by means of war. Even if we were to open hostilities resolutely and without fear of the consequences, we have neither the warships nor the cannon adequate to match the foreigners if large numbers of their warships infest our coasts and begin to burn and plunder. The feudal lords and all their followers would be exhausted in ceaseless activity; resentment would grow among the whole people; and once our strength was exhausted we would have to sue for peace. We would then have no choice but to pay an indemnity, to cede coastal territories, and to consent to all the hundred other demands that they would make. Our country, which has been independent since the very dawn of its history, would on that account suffer disgrace a hundred times worse than any it could incur by its present policy. We are in imminent danger of suffering the same fate as China and have, indeed, no choice as to our policy. We must, say those who hold this view, ward off for a time the insistence of the foreigners. For the time being our duty lies in acting in accordance with their wishes in trade and other matters, postponing conflict year by year and meanwhile completing our military preparations so that the foreigners cannot use us with contempt. Now this view, when all is said, offers no more than that we should complete our military preparations and so ensure that the foreigners do not use us with contempt. Such a plan has no prospects of success, for in the meantime all kinds of incidents would arise and year by year we would lose ground. There is no knowing what the end of it would be.

There is another view held by some. They say that ever since the expulsion decree was rescinded in 1842 foreigners have vied with each other in voyages to Japan and more particularly since the Americans entered Edo Bay they have become extremely active here. Year by year they press upon us and there seems no limit to it. What is more, they say, that we should be intimidated by a handful of foreigners, reviving cere-

Townsend
and his
X-tianity

monies that have been forbidden for hundreds of years, bowing our knees to men no better than beasts and suffering their insults, is infuriating to the point of madness. That the ancient system of our State should now be sacrificed must at all costs be prevented. No matter how many thousands of warships the foreigners may send, by putting forth the whole strength of a united people it will not be impossible for us to effect our defence. Such an argument shows great resolution. But after all, even if everything was accomplished in accordance with its expectations we could still do no more than hold our own for a time in our own waters. The war would be ceaseless, unending. We would have no means of alleviating the [resulting] economic distress at home, nor does it seem that we could ever ease the burdens on our people.

Neither of these views is apt to the present state of affairs. Nor do they hold out any prospect of ultimate success. One inclines to procrastination, one relies on violence, and both alike would lead us astray in national affairs. Of recent times a change has come over world conditions in general. All countries are alike in concluding treaties by which they make friendly alliances, open trade, exchange their products, and help each other in difficulties. Should it happen that one of them breaks or repudiates an agreement, others form an alliance and open hostilities. When the war ends they resume friendly relations. Hence not to enter into friendly relations entails war and not to wage war entails entering into friendly relations; there is no other way, and there is not a single country which avoids both friendly relations and war, which spurns diplomacy and yet enjoys peace and maintains its independence. By behaving now as though the foreigners were our enemies, unreasonably rejecting offers of friendship and alliance, we are clearly making ourselves a hindrance to all countries; and it is certain that all the countries, which are now divided among themselves, will on that account unite their forces and one after another send warships to demand explanations and open hostilities. After incurring the enmity of all countries in the world, we could not long hold out in this remote and isolated island of the East. Such a policy would not only be to fold our arms and humble our spirit. It would be to inflict destitution on the innocent people of our country, and would leave us virtually no prospect of restoring our national strength.

Hence, although one can limit the essential tasks facing us at this time to two, namely to foster national strength and to raise morale, yet military power always springs from national wealth, and means of enriching the country are principally to be found in trade and commerce. I am therefore convinced that our policy should be to stake everything on the present opportunity, to conclude friendly alliances, to send ships to foreign countries everywhere and conduct trade, to copy the foreigners where they are at their best and so repair our own shortcomings, to foster our national strength and complete our armaments, and so gradually subject the foreigners to our influence until in the end all the countries of the world know the blessings of perfect tranquillity and our hegemony is acknowledged throughout the globe. . . . Although ours is a small country, its land is fertile, its population much denser than that of other countries, and it cherishes a spirit of resoluteness and valour. Once we have laid the foundations of national wealth and strength, therefore, it will be by no means impossible for us to accomplish thereafter the great task of uniting all the world. We must fix our eyes on that objective. . . .

24

YOSHIDA SHŌIN

From *Kyōfu no gen (Testimony of a Madman)*
Protest against Harris Treaty

1858

Yoshida Shōin (1830–1859), a lower ranking samurai from the domain of Chōshū, was one of the leading ideologues of the antiforeign movement of the 1850s. A brilliant student, at the age of eighteen he was appointed an instructor in the domain academy. In the early 1850s he traveled throughout the country, visiting Mito and briefly studying at Sakuma Shōzan's private academy. After he attempted to stow away on board Commodore Perry's flagship in 1854, he was imprisoned, then put under house arrest. During the next few years he wrote prolifically on how to deal with the intrusion of the foreigners. Young samurai like Itō Hirobumi and Yamagata Aritomo, who became leaders of the Meiji government, came under his influence at his small private academy. His Kyōfu no gen *(Testimony of a Madman), a memorial addressed to the Chōshū daimyo, was written in early 1858 at the time of the bakufu's negotiations with Townsend Harris. It reflects a deep distrust of the Americans, whose motives Yoshida likens to those of the "southern barbarians" [i.e., the Portuguese].*

Nihon no meicho: Yoshida Shōin, ed. Matsumoto Sannosuke (Tokyo: Chūō kōronsha, 1973), 313–15.

The great calamity of the realm is that we do not understand the cause of this calamity. If we understand that the source of this great calamity is the calamity itself, then at the very least could we not adopt a way of dealing with it? At the moment, the downfall of our country has reached a critical stage. Can there be any greater calamity than that?

The foreign countries that come to spy on the environs of our country are numberless. Among them America disports itself in the most willful fashion. It is said that the plan of the Americans is to open up trading houses manned by their officials in Kyōto andŌsaka as well as Kanagawa, Niigata, Nagasaki, and Hirado with the consul general [Townsend] Harris in charge of them all; and following their commercial laws, trade would be carried on freely between domestic merchants and foreign merchants with no government interference.

The signs are already clear that this [plan] violates and despoils our country. The American envoy, Townsend Harris, moreover, is trying to win his great gamble with one throw of the dice. If he defeats us, it will be to his great profit, but if we win he will lose all his remaining strength in the face of defeat. . . . If he is content with the position of consul, that tells us he is a man of no great caliber.

In his entreaties toward our country, [Harris] thinks of what suits him and jabbers glibly whatever he pleases, without reflecting deeply on matters. Our side, however, does not see through his lies and falsehoods and follows his lead in everything. In reality, once we follow his lead, the President *(daitōryō)* of America will continue pressing his demands. The profit he will accrue thereby is of a magnitude quite beyond imagination. But if at this time we refuse [the American demands] point blank, the President will not be able to do anything about it. Then, our side will realize that even America hesitates and retreats.

Ah, Kyōto, Ōsaka, Edo—the three great cities of the realm. Will we fold our arms and remain silent, or will we not, once the Americans have set up their trading posts and placed their consuls in these cities? Let me make various conjectures [about what will happen]. There are many beggars in our country, so [the Americans] will certainly set up poorhouses for them; there are also many abandoned children, so they will establish children's homes; and again, there are in our country many who are old and decrepit, crippled or unable to get medical care; they will probably build apothecaries and hospitals. If [the Americans] turn their hands in earnest to these projects, it will be easy enough to win the hearts of the ignorant people by such means.

Next, they will recruit a gang of people who can read and write their alphabet, and they will employ those who are erudite and expert in technology.

If that happens, rascals who think only of profit but know nothing of right-eousness and who know nothing of the Way, even though they command all kinds of knowledge, will follow along blindly, swarming like ants and flies. By then, the hearts of deeply ambitious bakufu officials will already be in America's clutches. Is there any greater calamity for the realm than that?

[Yoshida then devotes a passage to the dispute over the successor to the Shogun Iesada, a mediocre but hot-tempered person given to bizarre behavior, who had failed to produce an heir. After his death, two rival factions of daimyo backed different candidates to the succession. Since the country was facing a major crisis in its foreign affairs, the selection of a strong and competent leader was a matter of great urgency.]

The American officials who come to our country are certain to meddle in the question of shogunal succession. If that happens, the tale of how Shih Ching-t'ang[1] reached the imperial throne with the help of the Khitan barbarians[2] will not seem like some remote affair. But . . . if the daimyo do not yield to the Americans, our country will not be wrested from us. If worse comes to worst, however, overthrowing the daimyo will not be all that difficult [for the Americans].

What most troubles the daimyo today is the *sankin kōtai* system [which requires the daimyo to travel every other year to the shogunal capital at Edo]. The American officials will probably say to the daimyo, "Japan is a maritime country. The expenses are great if you go by land routes, traveling back or forth over hundreds and thousands of leagues. Therefore, you are best advised to use steamships."

When the daimyo reply that they can not do so because they have no ships, [the Americans] are certain to say, "There are many ships in America. If necessary we will provide you with money [to buy them]. If you pay us back over a period of five or ten years, that will be fine." The Americans will then take one county or one island as collateral, and during those five or ten years, they will build poorhouses, children's homes, apothecaries, and hospitals, cleverly winning the hearts of the people who live in those regions. Since the daimyo will find it useful to have the ships, they will not regard this seduction of the people with suspicion. If this is what the Americans are plotting, the downfall of our country is already clear as day. That indeed is what I mean by great calamity.

The foreigners, moreover, will use every means at hand to compete for profits from trade. If they compete for profit in this fashion, the nat-

---

[1] Founder of the Later Chin Dynasty in China.
[2] A nomadic tribal federation.

ural outcome will be to plunge the country into confusion. If the government does nothing at all to hold things in check as the competition for profit spurs confusion, the adverse consequences will be legion.

If the great calamity of the realm comes to this point, how shall we best deal with it? The ancients had a saying: "If a poisonous viper bites his hand, even the bravest man will quickly cut off his arm." Today when we consider what Japan should do, ordinary methods will not suffice to save the day. We must act with resolve like the bravado who cuts off his arm, turning disaster into good fortune and affliction into advantage. . . . Since the bakufu is far away and difficult to understand, I will outline what our domain should do for the moment. [Yoshida then lays out his own plans for reform to strengthen the domain.]

25

Two American Views on the Opening of the Treaty Ports
1858/1860

While the opening of trade was a major goal of American policy toward Japan, not everyone was sure that the benefits would be great. These two excerpts illustrate both an optimistic and a more skeptical view of the prospects for trade with Japan.

The Newly-Opened Trade with the East— Its Results upon our Pacific States and upon Mexico

FROM THE WASHINGTON UNION

Events are conspiring in every part of the world to give great importance to our possessions on the Pacific slope. Hitherto one-third of the entire population of the world have been shut in from intercourse with other nations, in China and Japan. The exclusive and seclusive policy of both

---

"The Newly-Opened Trade with the East—Its Results upon our Pacific States and Upon Mexico," *New York Times,* December 3, 1858. *Hunt's Merchants' Magazine,* "Japan: Its Resources, Trade, and Currency," 43, no. 1 (July 1860): 60, 62, 67.

these countries has now all at once been abandoned, and the western coasts of the Pacific Ocean are about to become as active with the hum of commerce as the northern coasts of the Atlantic. We doubt if the commercial activity of the United States, England, Holland and Sweden will hereafter at all compare with that of the Chinese and Japanese nations; now that scope has been given to the enterprise of these people, and a freer intercourse with European and American merchants has been legalized. The population of these countries vastly exceeds that of the commercial nations of Europe, and the trade carried on in their waters will probably exceed, in the course of a few years, that of all the American and European ports of the Atlantic, in as great a degree as the number of their people exceeds that of the populations of the commercial nations of Christendom.

It is impossible to over-estimate the magnitude of the trade which, in the course of the next ten years, will have grown up between these two populations on the one side, and the European and American cities on the other. To predict that in the course of time it will *equal in magnitude and value the present entire trade between the nations of the Christian world,* would hardly be extravagant.... It is natural to suppose that immense marts of commerce will soon grow up on our Pacific coast. The shortest route by many hundred miles from the ports of China and Japan to London, and the shortest by more than a thousand miles from these ports to New-York, lies across the Pacific to California, and thence by the routes over Central America. The most direct routes, still shorter, lie directly across our Continent from our Pacific ports. These circumstances cannot fail to attract an immense population to our Pacific States; and, acting in conjunction with the influence of the gold and silver deposits which lie along that whole coast, and the natural tendency of our agricultural population to emigrate and colonize in that direction, an accumulation of population on those coasts more rapid than has ever before been known in the history of human migration cannot fail to result....

But, after all, there can be no doubt that the cheapest lines of communication with our Pacific settlements and the chief tides of travel, will pass over the lower latitudes of the continent. In the course of years this movement will exert an immense influence upon the affairs of Mexico; a region of country which will sooner or later loom up into immense importance under the influence of the trade of China and Japan, and the rapid growth of population upon the Pacific slope. The pestilential vapors of the narrow portions of the continent will always impose more or less disadvantage upon the transits through Panama and Nicaragua, and Mexico will constitute the bridge over which the chief intercourse between the Atlantic and Pacific ports and populations must have their passage. *It is probable that Mexico may lie for several years longer the prey of contending factions, the victim of anarchy and lawlessness;* but sooner or later the necessities of the greatest commerce which the world has yet seen, and the convenience of a mightier migration to and fro than has ever yet been known in international or intercontinental intercourse, will reduce it to the dominion of civilization, government, and law, and convert it, with the aid of its native resources of climate, soil, and mineral wealth, into one of the most flourishing and important regions of the habitable earth.

Japan: Its Resources, Trade, and Currency

The arrival of the Japanese ambassadors in this country with the [Harris] treaty for ratification marks a new era in the commerce of the world, and one which may be productive of great advantages in the future. In the rapid progress of modern industry it has been the case that most of the nations of Eastern Europe and of North America have come to rival each other in almost all the products of manufacturing skill, and while communication and information are prompt and free, a degree of perfect liberality in respect of new inventions and processes has taken the place of that extreme jealousy which formerly guarded every petty trade secret from prying eyes, and which caused the arts to languish for so many ages. Each nation is able, or nearly so, to supply itself with all the comforts luxury required in the way of manufactures. The common want of all has come to be raw materials and raw produce, which the prolific soil of tropical climates gives in the greatest abundance. Hence, intercourse with those nations has become of more general importance. Chinese exclusiveness has been partially broken down, and events have now brought the hitherto little-known empire of Japan within the range of commercial intercourse, and European nations flock round the astonished tycoon in increasing numbers. . . .

The mineral wealth of the empire is represented as very great: Gold, silver, copper, lead, quicksilver, coal, sulphur, salt, and iron to some extent. Marco Polo, in 1298, says the Japanese have gold in the greatest abundance, its sources being inexhaustible; but its export is prohibited.

These metals are the material of many manufactures, but the relative scarcity of iron makes its value nearly as great as copper. Many of the manufactures of the country are carried to great perfection. The lacquering of wood has long been famous, as excelling all other nations; cotton and silk goods are well made, and glass in all its branches of manufacture is carried to a great perfection, but singularly has never been applied to mirrors, which are of polished steel. Their swords are of the same material, and unequaled in quality. Paper of the mulberry tree is used for all purposes—writing and printing, and also for wrappers, and as handkerchiefs. In die sinking and carving, they are very proficient. There exist also tobacco factories, distilleries, and breweries on a large scale. Miako [Kyōto] is the chief seat of manufactures for damasks, satins, taffetas, and other textile fabrics. At Ōsaka cotton goods and iron ware are mostly made. The power of adaptation is great, and every species of European product is speedily reproduced. A native factory produces Colt's revolvers and Sharp's rifles, and one large concern has already built a screw steamer, which plies between Jeddo [Edo] and Nagasaki without European assistance. The internal trade of the country is very active. Many of the merchants are possessed of immense capital, and carry on the most extensive trade. . . .

Thus commerce has fastened its civilizing hand upon that coy empire, and she is fairly introduced into the great family of nations. What she has to contribute to the common weal is yet undecided. She may rival China to some extent in supplying tea and silk, and may be a customer for iron in return. In the process her scale of the metals must undergo a great change. It is quite probable, however, that the expectations of the great nations now flocking thither, to share the fancied advantages, may to some extent be disappointed.

26

From *The Journal of Francis Hall*
(An American Merchant in Yokohama)
1863

Francis Hall (1822–1902), a young New Englander, was one of the first foreigners to arrive in the newly opened port of Yokohama. After running a bookstore in upper New York State, he decided in 1859 to travel the newly opened Japan as a correspondent for the New York Tribune, *but once in Yokohama he went into business. In 1862 he founded Walsh, Hall & Com-*

Japan through American Eyes: The Journal of Francis Hall, Kanagawa and Yokohama, 1859–1866, ed. F. G. Notehelfer (Princeton, N.J.: Princeton University Press, 1992), 514–15.

pany, one of the leading American trading firms in Japan. Quickly amass-
ing a fortune, Hall returned four years later to New York State, where he
lived a life of leisure until his death. The following is a dispatch that Hall
sent to the New York Tribune *in late 1863.*

Yokohama, which is the local appellation, though the port is known generally as Kanagawa, is growing rapidly. Opened to commerce four years
ago, it has changed from a "side beach," which its name signifies, to an
opulent commercial mart. Mr. [Townsend] Harris, the treaty-king, first
came into this bay in March, 1859, and on the present site of the town
were to be seen only the cultivated fields of rice, wheat, beans, bringalls,
and millet, with a few cottages of the contented peasantry among the elms
and evergreen oaks. He returned to Simoda [Shimoda], came back three
months later, on the 1st of July, when the port was to be opened under
the treaty, and as if some new Aladdin had again rubbed his wonderful
lamp, in place of gardens and fields stood the spacious Japanese custom-
houses, blocks upon blocks of official residences, three long streets built
up with shops and filled with curious wares, and besides these a large
number of houses built for rental to the expected comers, to say nothing of a multitude of native cottages. Our own rapidly growing country
never exhibited a transformation so sudden and complete. And now
today the building and extension is as rapid as ever. congRats gRad!
   The fishermen's huts, the farmers' cottages, the broad acres of grain,
have all given way to structures more or less substantial and elegant of
wood, mud, and stone. Yet all partake of the characteristics of the country, bungalow houses; warehouses, i.e. "go–downs," of mud and stone,
tile roofs, neat floors, unpainted fir ceilings, are grafted with curtains of
damask, carpets of Brussels, furniture of rosewood and mahogany from
beyond the seas. Brown-cheeked boys are servitors in place of handy
Biddy [a maid], who I dare say, is more missed than all other home comforts whatever.
   A township block, which, were it regular and compact, would represent an area three-quarters of a mile square, is crowded with foreign
houses and foreign industry. A hundred lot-owners are now lords of the
soil in place of the old swarthy Niponese farmers deposed. Long warehouses and two-story bungalows usurp the place of the brown chalets of
the former peasantry.

   Thus, this spot in the remotest part of the globe, only so recently terra
terribilis, if not terra incognita, is now a dear foster child of commerce.

And commerce comes here full panoplied, as when, centuries ago, she conquered the Mare Mediterraneum, and so passed by to Britain, who now returns to the East. She comes with her sword and cannon, and her resonant fife and drum fill the quiet air of these isles; for today, as I write, twelve hundred British soldiers and marines are parading our streets, to give the Japanese an impress of their strength. She comes with her virtues and vices, and it will take the Eternal Accountant at last to decide whether, "the opening of Japan" brings civilization to a fearful debit or a glorious credit in the books of the Ages.

If I have been prolix and tedious excuse me, for curious thoughts are sometimes suggested, as I witness this contrast of the civilization of the Nineteenth Century with the semi-barbarism of the Fifteenth. I feel as if I were living somewhere out of my time—as if I had left the railway of your active life and gone back to something more ancient than even the old stagecoach of existence. I should not be surprised any day if some one were to ask me to go and see Cleopatra in her barge, or Titus before Jerusalem. If we are in your world, we are certainly not of it, and I am afraid to go to bed, lest I awake in the morning and find that telegraphs, steamers, and railway cars are only dreams.

27

A Yokohama Print of an American Man and Wife

1863

Although no more than two hundred foreigners lived in Yokohama in the early 1860s, there was a sudden boom of woodblock prints purporting to depict their life in the new treaty port. Altogether more than eight hundred were published in 1861–62, a reflection of strong public curiosity about the foreigners and their ways. Utagawa Yoshikazu (fl. 1850–70) was one of the most prolific designers of "Yokohama prints." Working from foreign magazines and book illustrations, he produced prints that identified the national characteristics of the various foreign residents. The caption for this print was written by Kanagaki Robun (1829–1894), a popular author who later sat-

Ann Yonemura, *Yokohama: Prints from Nineteenth Century Japan* (Washington, D.C.: Smithsonian Institution, 1990), 168–69.

This Yokohama print presents an ideal picture of the American husband and wife.

irized the popular faddish attraction to Western culture. It offers a brief expla-
nation of the United States.

The thirty-one states that are known as the republic of the United States, as the name North America makes clear, generally extends from the extreme north to "Ukadan" [the Yucatán] in the south. Although the United States are one part of America, its land is extensive and its population large. Because of its supreme prosperity and strength, it is now simply called North America. In recent years, the country has grown still more, and it administers nearby countries as territorial allies. The increase in productivity is immeasurable. The people are patriotic and, moreover, quite clever. In the world, they are foremost in science, armaments, and commerce. The women are elegant and beautiful.

28

HASHIMOTO SADAHIDE

From *Yokohama kaikō kenbunshi (A Record of Observations in the Open Port of Yokohama)*

1861

Hashimoto Sadahide (1807–1878/79), a printmaker and book illustrator, became interested in the "red hairs" even before the arrival of the Perry expedition. In the early 1850s he illustrated a work on the Opium War by depicting the brutal power of the English, and he established a reputation as a cartographer by producing several world maps. When Yokohama was opened, Sadahide published several panoramic views of the port. His three-volume guidebook, Yokohama kaikō kenbunshi (A Record of Observations in the Open Port of Yokohama), *based in part on his visits to the port, became a best-seller in 1862. What must have fascinated readers was his*

Julia Meech-Pekarik, *The World of the Meiji Print: Impressions of New Civilization* (Tokyo: Weatherhill, 1986), 50–51.

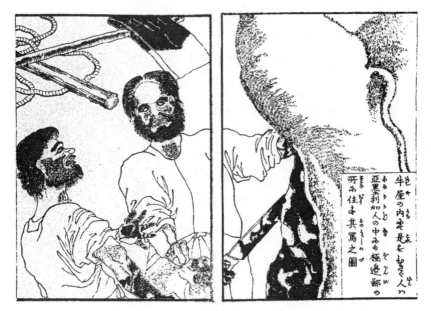

The caption . . . reads: "The people who do the slaughtering in these beef shops, though Americans, live on the extreme edge of town."

depiction of the bizarre customs of the foreigners, such as the eating of beef and pork. Traditionally, the consumption of meat was subject to strong taboos, and the slaughtering of animals was left to outcaste groups. This excerpt from the guidebook, showing a butcher shop where imported cattle brought into Yokohama on the hoof were turned into meat, reflects this strong cultural revulsion.

It appears to be the custom of those countries to hang beef upside down and sell it; whether sheep, pigs, or baby turtles, all are cooked that way and are hung with a rope from the ceiling and cut into pieces. It is fantastic how cleverly they are cut into different parts. Japanese who were watching commented on how gruesome, how unsightly, this was; in the meantime the spectators grew in number and one of them said, "Well, pork stew is popular everywhere nowadays, and when you see pigs raised and slaughtered, it isn't at all like this. The way they kill the squealing, squirming pigs is worse than this, if anything—it's a toss-up if you ask me!" The spectators took this as the pronouncement of a killjoy. Then another opened his mouth: "Who are we to be criticizing this butcher? Japan is our country, all right, but don't we wring oil out of cows? I understand that it is an ingredient in a medicine sold in Edo." Hearing this, others spoke up, saying, "You must be thinking of white butter, but for that you don't slaughter the cow. You feed a white cow white sesame, milk it, and mix the milk with medicine. It is not something available to us lowly creatures and you can't compare it with ordinary bottled milk." All the talk and commotion caused by this troublesome crowd irked the foreigner, who set about ten strange-looking dogs loose on the spectators. There were dogs with long faces and bag-like hanging ears breathing heavily through large open mouths and black dogs that looked like lions. . . . Seeing them coming with their red, open mouths, people started running and the dogs chased after them.

This cleared the entrance to the butcher's shop. Fortunately no one was bitten.

29

YOKOI SHŌNAN

Proposal for Reforming Japan
1862

Yokoi Shōnan (1809–1869), one of the leading advocates of reform in the 1860s, came from a middle-rank samurai family in the domain of Kumamoto. While studying in Edo in the late 1830s, he met Fujita Tōko, an antiforeign scholar from Mito, who stirred in him an awareness that the country had to gird itself to meet the foreign threat. Matsudaira Yoshinaga, the reform-minded daimyo of Echizen, invited Yokoi to teach at his domain academy and serve as an advisor. When Matsudaira assumed a key post in the bakufu in 1862, Yokoi accompanied him, writing memorials that urged the bakufu to form closer ties with the imperial court, reform its financial affairs, and grant the daimyo a larger voice in national affairs. Regarded as too radical, he was put under house arrest on returning to Kumamoto

Dixon Y. Miyauchi ed. and tr., "Kokuzesanron (The Three Major Problems of State Policy)," *Monumenta Nipponica* 23, no. 1–2 (1968): 166–70.

in 1863. This document, based on notes of his lectures, summarizes his reform views. It not only reveals a commitment to opening the country, but also suggests that foreign countries, including the United States, might serve as models for reform.

If the basic principles in governing the nation are to be abandoned and only trade and intercourse are to hold sway, should we consider all Western ways as being desirable and make them the practice of the land?

Because of the fact that in recent years trade has been proposed by foreign countries, the average person believes that this was the start of commercial intercourse, but this is by no means the truth. From the very beginning commerce with foreign countries has been an important part of the trade of a country, and its path has been firmly fixed by principles of heaven and earth. Those who rule others must be nourished by the latter, and those who nourish must be ruled. This is the way of trade, and the same applies to government. Nourishing the people is the main work. . . . The activities of the people are benefited, and their living is made more harmonious. This is the principle of Nature. The rule of the empire of Yao and Shun[1] was none other than this. . . .

In our country from the middle ages wars have followed in succession, the Imperial Court has become weak, and various lords have parcelled out groups of provinces, each defending his own territory while attacking others in turn. The people were looked upon as so much waste, and the severity of forced labor and the arbitrary collection of military rations knew no bounds. Good government was swept away from the land, and it was a period in which one who was skilled in warfare became a great lord and one who was clever in planning became a renowned minister.

Consequently in the Keichō [1596–1615] and Genna [1615–24] periods, . . . all strove to make the foundation of the Tokugawa household supreme and firm, and not once was consideration given to the people of the realm. Although there are said to have been many outstanding rulers and ministers from that time to the present, all have continued the work of administering the private affairs of one household only. The various lords have followed this pattern, and according to the old ways handed down from their ancestors, they have planned with their ministers for the convenience and security of their own provinces with a barrier between neighboring provinces.

[1]The legendary sage kings who allegedly founded the Chinese state.

As a result those who are known as great ministers in the shogunate and in each of the provinces have not all been able to disentangle themselves from the old ways of national seclusion. They have devoted themselves to their lords and their provinces, while their feelings of love and loyalty for the most part ignore the virtues of the good life and on the contrary invite the resentment of the people. All this leads to troubles in ruling the land. Japan has been split up thusly and lacks a unified system. Therefore we must admit that Envoy Perry's observation in his *Expedition to Japan* about the lack of government machinery in Japan when he arrived here in 1855 was truly a discerning one.

Although forbidden, let us discuss the detested things of the present day. From the very beginning the shogunate anticipated moves by the various lords, and the system it used to weaken their military potential was to impose on them the *sankin kōtai* practice, the construction of large and small projects, the fire watches on the two sacred mountain precincts, and guard duty at the highway barrier stations. Moreover, in recent years the guarding of the countryside has been extremely burdensome, yet no consideration has been given to the drain on the provinces and their people. Furthermore, all systems, including currency, are transmitted and executed throughout the land by the power of the supreme government in the interest of the Tokugawa household without in any way benefiting the empire or the people. For Perry to call this 'lack of government' was indeed correct.

Under the system of national seclusion Japan sought safety in isolation. Hence she experienced no wars or defeats. However, the world situation has undergone vast changes. Each country has broadly developed enlightened government.

In America three major policies have been set up from Washington's presidency on: First, to stop wars in accordance with divine intentions, because nothing is worse than violence and killing among nations; second, to broaden enlightened government by learning from all the countries of the world; and third, to work with complete devotion for the peace and welfare of the people by entrusting the power of the president of the whole country to the wisest instead of transmitting it to the son of the president and by abolishing the code in the relationship between ruler and minister. All methods of administrative laws and practices and all men who are known as good and wise throughout the world are put into the country's service and a very beneficial administration—one not completely in the interest of the rulers—is developed. . . .

Thus when the various countries attempt to open Japan's doors according to the way of international cooperation, who would not call Japan a fool for persisting in her old seclusionist views, for ruling for the benefit of private interests, and for not knowing the principles of commercial intercourse? . . .

30

YOKOI SHŌNAN

Evaluation of Foreign Religion
1864

This dialogue between Yokoi Shōnan (see Document 29) and his student, Inoue Kowashi (1844–1895), who later became an important official in the Meiji government, took place in 1864 after Yokoi had returned to his domain of Kumamoto. It shows how culturally conservative even a radical scholar and reformer like Yokoi remained. While there was much Yokoi admired about the West, he still regarded Christianity with deep suspicion. Ironically he was assassinated in 1869 by antiforeign samurai activists who suspected him of hidden sympathy toward Christianity.

Q [INOUE]: . . . Is it true that most of the outside world believes in Christianity?

A [YOKOI]: About 80 percent believe in Christianity.

Q: Do the teachings of Christ stress ethics *(rinri)* and urge people to do good? Or do these teachings take pursuit of profit as their goal?

A: Yes, Christianity does urge people to do good. If one looks into the origins of Christianity, [we learn that] Christ was born to the west of India. Considering that its doctrines were established later than Buddhism, it is certain that [Christianity] is a form of Buddhism and that it gradually spread from [India] to the West. However, its doctrines are much deeper than those of Buddhism. Christianity is divided into eight sects, among which the Purity Sect [i.e., Protestantism] is the newest. It is prevalent in England and America. . . .

Q: Which is worse, Buddhism or Christianity?

Nihon no meicho: Sakuma Shōzan/Yokoi Shōnan, ed. Matsuura Rei (Tokyo: Chūō kōron-sha, 1970), 447–53.

A: Since Buddhism rejects ethics while Christianity upholds them, Buddhism is probably worse. However, I must make something perfectly clear. Confucianism, that is, the teachings of Confucius and Mencius, propagates the Way of the Ancient Kings [Yao, Shun, and Yu], who, being in the position of ruler, actually governed the country. Hence, their governance was an embodiment and a teaching of the Way, and Confucius and Mencius explained to later generations that their governance was an embodiment of the Way. By contrast, since Buddhism and Christianity originally aimed at secretly converting ignorant men and women among the lower orders of society, they conjured up the ideas of Heaven and Hell and contrived to make themselves easy for people to understand.

Q: Well, are the Sages, Buddha, and Christ the same in essence but different only in their country and their position?

A: No, that is not correct, because the Way of the Sages [Confucianism] takes the education of the people as its mission.

Q: I agree that Buddhism is a teaching that undermines ethics more than Christianity does, but even within Buddhism can't one say that the Ikkō Sect, with its Way for Husbands and Wives or Parents and Children, is close to ethics?

A: Christianity resembles the Ikkō Sect, but I think that it is much deeper. ... However, there is one thing that we should be aware of. When Buddhism entered Japan, it penetrated deeply into the people's hearts. No matter whether Buddhism or Christianity is more harmful, Christianity would inevitably provoke a doctrinal war with Japan if it were to enter Japan, and when that escalated into rebellion, the people would suffer the greatest distress. For that reason, I think that we should not permit the entry of Christianity. Since disputes over doctrine frequently give rise to outrageous incidents, they are of the utmost danger. ...

Q: What should we do to protect against Christianity?

A: There is no miraculous medicine. If we maintain the just, rectify our foundations, and make the people's hearts firm, there is no need to worry about Christianity seeping in.

Q: It seems that the more wicked a religion's doctrines are, the more it will lead the ignorant people astray. ... Hence, even if we maintain the just and rectify our foundations, won't Christianity inevitably come into the country if we establish relations with the barbarians?

A: Since the barbarians have recently ... come to understand the frightfulness of doctrinal disputes, they have established strict prohibitions against forcing one's own doctrines on other people. They have done so because great rebellions have occurred in the West as the result of doctrinal disputes. . . . Those who adhere to the Purity Sect [i.e., Protestantism] do not try to destroy the Roman religion [i.e., Catholicism]. This being the case, we can see that they do not insist upon their doctrines against reason.[1] . . .

Q: Are there no aspects of Christianity that are in accord with the Way of the Sages?

A: The Christianity of ancient times, which converted only the ignorant people [gumin], was extremely shallow. However, recently in the West, not only do all the educated classes believe in Christianity, but quite separately they have made discoveries in the study of government, economics, and nature that complement Christianity. To the degree that this study of government, economics, and nature serves greatly to improve the material lot [of the people], one can say that it resembles the Way of the Sages. . . . Standing above the people, the Sages took care of their daily livelihood, . . . encouraged production, made tools and implements, and assured a life of abundance. Indeed, this was the great enterprise that the Sages carried out as the delegates of Heaven. . . .

Today Japan has a population of 35 million, but those "who wear cloth and eat meat," that is, those with a living standard that is above average, number 5 million or 6 million while all the rest are uncertain whether they will have enough to eat. As a result of the closed country mentality, every province and every domain has thought about only its own interests and has failed to manage the distribution [of goods] from the standpoint of the whole country, so goods have not found their way to the marketplace and production is stagnating in every region. Since production has stagnated and manufacturing does not advance, the idle can not find jobs. Spending their days with empty hands and without work, they are pitiful in the extreme. Of every 100 people, about 70 are engaged in farming, but the remaining 30 are unable to do so because they are too old, too young, or too poor. They spend their days with nothing to do. Since 30 percent of the Japanese are without work, it is natural that Japan is a poor country, is it not? The only way to deal [with this problem] is to encourage production in every region. To do that we must increase output and improve the distribution of goods so that stocks of unsold goods do not pile up. To do that well, the best course is to open up trade with the outside world. If we simply open up trade, goods will somehow or other find their way to the market quite well.

[1]In this passage, Yokoi is referring to the spread of religious toleration in post-Reformation Europe.

Today the Westerners are developing techniques to improve their living standard with things like steamships, railroads, telegraphs, and power looms, and they have opened up a new sea route by digging a canal between the Mediterranean Sea and the Red Sea. These are great achievements. Their profits are great, their countries are wealthy and strong [*fūkoku kyōhei*], their living standards are high, and moreover their taxes are low, not only because they possess such technology but because they carry on trade throughout the world. The splendid achievements of their statecraft, I believe, have produced the same results as the Way of the Sages. . . .

Q: You have used the word "statecraft," but that is a word that signifies the "benevolent government" [*jinsei*] of the Sages. Do the Westerners carry on "benevolent government" too?

A: That is correct. There is no doubt that they have achieved the results of "benevolent government." The effect of "benevolence" is to benefit others. . . .

Q: If the Westerners are moved by a benevolent heart and follow the course of benefiting others, Holland should return Jakarta to its native king and England should return India to its former monarchs. But will that really happen?

A: Probably it will not. Since each country in its inmost heart cares most about its own country, and since at bottom none feel sympathy for others, it is not possible for them to pursue the Heavenly Principle *(tenri)* of fairness and selflessness. There is probably nothing to do about that. There is something called "false benevolence." Since the [foreigners'] benevolence is of that sort, it has turned into a means of tyranny. Since India, a land earlier seized by England, possesses fertile land and serves as an important trading center, England will take pains not to release its hold there. Instead, they lower the land taxes and carry on government in a magnanimous fashion, making the people's hearts fond of the English.

Q: So the "statecraft" of the Westerners consists only in the branch, not in the root [i.e., it is statecraft superficially but not essentially].

A: That is correct. Even though their starting point is the calculation of profit, since they are careful to achieve good results they are close to "benevolence" in a superficial way.

Q: When the Westerners say that all countries are one and that all men within the four seas are brothers, does this accord with Heavenly Principles?

A: They are speaking only in general principles. It is inevitable that with respect to [relations between] their country and other countries, or with respect to [relations between] the Westerners themselves and other peoples, they discriminate between the close and the distant. Even the ancient Chinese discriminated between the "civilized" [*ka*] and the "barbarian" [*i*]. However, since all belong to the same human race, and there really are no distinctions between "civilized" and "barbarian" or "East" and "West," I think that carrying on trade fairly and prosperously accords with the principles of nature. . . . In today's world, since the ends of the globe have become closer together as a result of the steamship, and since it is possible to carry on trade freely and without restrictions, in the face of these circumstances it is probably against Heavenly Principles to cling to the outworn notion of keeping the country isolated and closed.

6

The Bakufu Mission of 1860

31

FUKUZAWA YUKICHI

From *The Autobiography of Yukichi Fukuzawa*

1898

Fukuzawa Yukichi (1835–1901), born into a low-ranking samurai family in the domain of Nakatsu, sought to escape from poverty and low status by becoming a Dutch Studies scholar. In 1855, after spending some months in Nagasaki studying Western gunnery, he entered Ogata Kōan's famous academy of Dutch Studies in Ōsaka to take up the study of the Dutch language and basic Western science. When he visited the newly opened port of Yokohama, however, he was disappointed to learn that the foreign inhabitants spoke English, not Dutch, so he immediately turned to the study of English. In 1860 he joined the first diplomatic mission the bakufu sent to the United States. Traveling on the Kanrin-maru, a ship the bakufu had bought from the Dutch, he arrived in San Francisco, where he was finally able to see foreign culture for the first time. These recollections of his experience appeared in his famous and highly readable autobiography, dictated and published in the final years of his life.

The year after I was settled in Yedo [Edo]—the sixth year of Ansei (1859)—the government of the Shōgun made a great decision to send a ship-of-war [the *Kanrin-maru*] to the United States, an enterprise never

---

Fukuzawa Yukichi, *The Autobiography of Yukichi Fukuzawa*, revised translation by Eiichi Kiyooka (New York: Columbia University Press, 1966), 103–06, 110–16.

before attempted since the foundation of the empire. On this ship I was to have the good fortune of visiting America. . . .

This voyage of *Kanrin-maru* was an epoch-making venture for our nation; every member of the crew was determined to take the ship across unassisted by a foreigner. At about that time Captain Brooke, an American officer, had come to Yokohama. He had been engaged in taking soundings in the Pacific Ocean on board a small sailing vessel, the *Fenimore Cooper,* which was wrecked on the southern coast of Japan. The captain and another officer of the ship with a doctor and several sailors, also saved from the wreck, were being kept under the protection of the Japanese government. Now, on learning that a Japanese ship was going to San Francisco, they wished to be carried across.

The government officials agreed to this and were about to grant the permit for the Americans when the staff of the *Kanrin-maru* protested strongly, the reason being that if the American navigators went along, the Japanese staff would feel an implied slur on their own ability to sail. Their opposition grew out of the sense of honor for themselves and for their country, so the Shogunate officials were much concerned for a while. But they finally ordered outright that the ship should take Captain Brooke and his men on board. Probably the elder officials of the government were in reality uncertain of the ability of the Japanese crew and thought Captain Brooke would be of use in case of emergency. . . .

I am willing to admit my pride in this accomplishment for Japan. The facts are these: It was not until the sixth year of Kaei (1853) that a steamship was seen for the first time; it was only in the second year of Ansei (1855) that we began to study navigation from the Dutch in Nagasaki; by 1860, the science was sufficiently understood to enable us to sail a ship across the Pacific. This means that about seven years after the first sight of a steamship, after only about five years of practice, the Japanese people made a trans-Pacific crossing without help from foreign experts. I think we can without undue pride boast before the world of this courage and skill. . . . The Japanese officers were to receive no aid from Captain Brooke throughout the voyage. Even in taking observations, our officers and the Americans made them independently of each other. Sometimes they compared their results, but we were never in the least dependent on the Americans.

As I consider all the other peoples of the Orient as they exist today, I feel convinced that there is no other nation which has the ability or the courage to navigate a steamship across the Pacific after a period of five years of experience in navigation and engineering. Not only in the Orient would this feat stand as an act of unprecedented skill and daring. Even

Peter the Great of Russia, who went to Holland to study navigation, with all his attainments could not have equalled this feat of the Japanese. Without doubt, the famous emperor was a man of genius, but his people did not respond to his leadership in the practice of science as did our Japanese in this great adventure.

Our welcome on shore was certainly worthy of a friendly people. They did everything for us, and they could not have done more. The feeling on their part must have been like that of a teacher receiving his old pupil several years after graduation, for it was their Commodore Perry who had effected the opening of our country seven years before, and now here we were on our first visit to America.

As soon as we came on shore, we found we were to be driven off in carriages to a hotel. While we were resting in the hotel, city officials and various dignitaries came to offer entertainment. We were given quarters in the official residence of the Navy station on Mare Island. Our hosts knew that we Japanese were accustomed to a different diet, so they arranged that our food, instead of being served, should be prepared by our own cook. But the officials being very kind, and desiring to satisfy the Japanese love for seafood, sent fish every day. Also, on learning the Japanese custom of bathing frequently, they had baths prepared daily. Our ship had been damaged by the passing storms, so it was put in dry dock to be repaired—all expressions of American hospitality. This generous treatment in every way brought to mind an old expression of ours—"as if our host had put us on the palm of his hand to see that we lacked nothing."

On our part there were many confusing and embarrassing moments, for we were quite ignorant of the customs of American life. For instance, we were surprised even by the carriages. On seeing a vehicle with horses attached to it, we should easily have guessed what it was. But really we did not identify our mode of conveyance until the door had been opened, we were seated inside, and the horses had started off. Then we realized we were riding in a carriage behind horses. . . .

All of us wore the usual pair of swords at our sides and the hemp sandals. So attired, we were taken to the modern hotel. There we noticed, covering the interior, the valuable carpets which in Japan only the more wealthy could buy from importers' shops at so much a square inch to make purses and tobacco pouches with. Here the carpet was laid over an entire room—something quite astounding—and upon this costly fabric walked our hosts wearing the shoes with which they had come in from the streets! We followed them in our hemp sandals.

Immediately bottles were brought in. Suddenly an explosion—the popping of champagne. When the glasses were passed around, we noticed strange fragments floating in them—hardly did we expect to find *ice* in the warm spring weather. Some of the party swallowed these floating particles; others expelled them suddenly; others bravely chewed them. This was an adventure—finding out that they were ice.

I wanted to have a smoke, but seeing no "tobacco tray" such as in Japan is placed before the smoker to hold the burning charcoal brazier and the bamboo ash-receiver, I took a light from the open fireplace. Perhaps there was an ash-tray and a box of matches on the table, but I did not recognize them as such. I finished my smoke, but finding no ash receiver, I took out some of the tissue paper which we carry in place of handkerchiefs, and wrapping the ashes in it, crushed them very carefully, and placed the ball in my sleeve. After a while I took out the paper to have another smoke; some wisps of smoke were trickling from my sleeve. The light that I thought I had crushed out was quietly setting me afire!

After all these embarrassing incidents, I thought I could well sympathize with the Japanese bride. Her new family welcome her and do everything to make her comfortable. One laughs with her; another engages her in conversation—all happy with the new addition to the family. In the midst of all this the bride has to sit trying to look pleasant, but in her efforts she goes on making mistakes and blushes every time.

Before leaving Japan, I, the independent soul—a care-free student who could look the world in the face—had feared nothing. But on arriving in America, I was turned suddenly into a shy, self-conscious, blushing "bride." The contrast was indeed funny, even to myself.

One evening our host said that some ladies and gentlemen were having a dancing party and that they would be glad to have us attend it. We went. To our dismay we could not make out what they were doing. The ladies and gentlemen seemed to be hopping about the room together. As funny as it was, we knew it would be rude to laugh, and we controlled our expressions with difficulty as the dancing went on. These were but a few of the instances of our bewilderment at the strange customs of American society.

A certain Dutch physician was living then in a place called Vallejo near Mare Island. Since he knew that Holland had maintained the earliest and longest association with Japan, the doctor wished to show some courtesy towards the captain and officers of our ship. The home of the Dutch doctor was a fine dwelling showing his success in that region, but the strange behavior of the household puzzled us. While the mistress of the house stayed constantly in the drawing-room entertaining the guests, the doctor, the supposed master, was moving in and out of the room, directing the servants. This was the reverse of the domestic custom in our country. How strange, we thought. Then, when the dinner was served, came a real shock. On a dish was brought in a whole pig, roasted—head, legs, tail, and all. We at once thought of the fabled land of Adachiga Hara where lived a cruel witch who indulged in gruesome feasts. Still, it tasted very good.

Our hosts in San Francisco were very considerate in showing us examples of modern industry. There was as yet no railway laid to the city, nor was there any electric light in use. But the telegraph system and also Galvani's electroplating were already in use. Then we were taken to a sugar refinery and had the principle of the operation explained to us quite minutely. I am sure that our hosts thought they were showing us something entirely new, naturally looking for our surprise at each new device of modern engineering. But on the contrary, there was really nothing new, at least to me. I knew the principle of the telegraphy even if I had not seen the actual machine before; I knew that sugar was bleached by straining the solution with bone-black, and that in boiling down the solution, the vacuum was used to better effect than heat. I had been studying nothing else but such scientific principles ever since I had entered Ogata's school.

Rather, I was surprised by entirely different things in American life. First of all, there seemed to be an enormous waste of iron everywhere. In garbage piles, on the seashores—everywhere—I found lying old oil tins, empty cans, and broken tools. This was remarkable to us, for in Yedo, after a fire, there would appear a swarm of people looking for nails in the ashes.

Then too, I was surprised at the high cost of daily commodities in California. We had to pay a half-dollar for a bottle of oysters, and there were only twenty or thirty in the bottle at that. In Japan the price of so many would be only a cent or two.

Things social, political, and economic proved most inexplicable. One day, on a sudden thought, I asked a gentleman where the descendants of George Washington might be. He replied, "I think there is a woman who is directly descended from Washington. I don't know where she is now, but I think I have heard she is married." His answer was so very casual that it shocked me.

Of course, I knew that America was a republic with a new president every four years, but I could not help feeling that the family of Washington would be revered above all other families. My reasoning was based on the reverence in Japan for the founders of the great lines of rulers—like that for Ieyasu of the Tokugawa family of Shōguns, really deified in the popular mind. So I remember the astonishment I felt at receiving this indifferent answer about the Washington family. As for scientific inventions and industrial machinery, there was no great novelty in them for me. It was rather in matters of life and social custom and ways of thinking that I found myself at a loss in America.

32

MURAGAKI NORIMASA

From *Kōkai nikki*
(Diary of a Voyage Abroad)
1860

In 1854 Muragaki Norimasa (1813–1880), the son of a high-ranking bakufu retainer, became a financial official with the additional duty of supervising coastal defenses on the northern island of Ezo (now Hokkaidō.) When the Russian admiral Evfimil Vasil'evich Putiatin arrived in Japan in late 1854 to request open trade, Muragaki was sent to Shimoda to assist in negotiating with him. During the late 1850s he served in various posts connected with coastal defense and the development of Ezo, including the office of magistrate of foreign affairs. It was because of this experience that he was appointed vice ambassador on the 1860 mission to the United States. While Muragaki had a reputation as being a lackluster official, his journal observations suggest that he was a man of great curiosity and subtle humor. Until the fall of the bakufu in 1868, he served as an advisor on dealing with the foreigners. In the following excerpt, Muragaki describes his impressions of official Washington, where he was dispatched for ratification of the Harris Treaty, and of New York City.

September 13th.   As I arrived at the [Shogun's] Castle as usual, I was immediately ordered to present myself, dressed in a linen *kamishimo* [a ceremonial kimono], at the Lotus Room. There I was joined by . . . Masaoki . . . Shimmi . . . and Oguri Tadamasa, and, in the presence of [Ii Naosuke] . . . and other high-ranking officials, we were given an order

Kokai nikki: The Diary of the First Japanese Embassy to the United States of America (Tokyo: The Foreign Affairs Association of Japan, 1958), 1–2, 66–68, 70–74, 76–79, 90–91, 96–97, 103–04, 119, 125–26.

by the Shogun's Chamberlain . . . that we should be dispatched to the United States for the ratification of the Treaty. . . .

It was evening when I returned home. It so happened that the night was the second Moon Festival, and to think that I was assigned to the unprecedentedly important duty of going to a distant country as an envoy! Nevertheless, the female members of the household seemed to be much depressed, quite at a loss to understand the importance of the event. In olden days, envoys were dispatched to China, but that is only a neighboring country across a strip of water. The United States of America is more than 10,000 *ri* [leagues] away from Japan, and when it is day in that country, it is night in ours. It should be considered as the greatest honor that a man can ever hope for, to be given such a responsible assignment and to have his name known widely over the five continents. Thus saying, I did my best to comfort my household. However, the more I thought of my responsibility, realizing that failure in accomplishing this unprecedented task of serving as an envoy to the strange land would constitute an irreparable disgrace to our country, the heavier became my heart. However, as the moon began to shine, clear and bright in the sky, we partook of *saké* freely, congratulating ourselves on this memorable event.

> *From now on, the bright Moonlight of our country*
> *Will be admired by the peoples of the strange lands.*

Intercalary[1] March 25th.   Fine weather. At 10 o'clock in the morning, we stopped at a place . . . on the right bank of the River Potomac, on which we were going up westward from the east; and there we purchased some fish, milk and other provisions. The ship left the place immediately, and the same sumptuous meal as yesterday's was served to us.

On either side of the river, we saw no hills, but a drab scenery of flat lands covered with coppices, of which the monotony was occasionally broken by the appearance of shacks. The scenery was very much like what we see along the River Ishikari in the Land of Ezo. The river flowed slowly, and its water was muddy. . . .

Some ten miles from the City of Washington, we saw on the left bank of the river, a large building shaded by trees, which, we were told, was the house where George Washington had lived. Farther up the river, there stood on the right bank, a monument, looking like a fortress. This, we learned, was Washington's tomb. In passing by his tomb, every ship halts awhile, and has its band play music; while all the passengers and

[1]Lunar.

crew take their hats off in homage to the Father of the nation — this custom, well grounded as it is, is worthy of note, as occurring in the nation free of all manner of formality. . . .

At noon, we reached the Navy Yard, located at one end of the city, and built on such a scale as to be worthy of being called the capital's first Navy Yard. The Chief Officer, representing all the officials there, came aboard to bid us welcome. There were crowds of men and women ashore, both in and outside the houses and even on the roofs to see the Embassy from the far country. As we landed, accompanied by Captain Dupont, Commodore Buchanan, who had visited Japan as one of the staff officers of Commodore Perry, came forward, with several other gentlemen, to congratulate us on our safe arrival. The crowd pressing around us on the landing was so immense that hardly any space was left there for us to proceed. Among these spectators, there were seen some "newspapermen," who rushed around, scribbling some notes on paper, which, we were told later, were to be printed and sold on the very same day. We also learned later that the photographic lenses had been set up on the second floor of the building across from the landing place, so as to take the pictures of our arrival. We somehow managed to cross the 180 feet of plank passage laid across the landing to the handsomely decorated carriages-and-four. . . .

Intercalary March 27th.   Fine weather. We had an appointment to call upon General Lewis Cass, the Secretary of State at 12 a.m. Acting upon Captain Dupont's suggestion that we should be accompanied by only a small suite, we wore our travelling costumes, and took but a few servants each. . . .

We were immediately taken upstairs to the anteroom, and after a short while, showed into another spacious room of the size of 20 mats.[2] . . .

We were told that the Secretary of State performed his daily duties in this office. There was his desk strewn with a few books. The interview was quite informal, dispensing with pretentious ceremony. We were then introduced to Mr. Ledyard, General Lewis Cass' son-in-law, and several other high-ranking officials, followed by General Cass' grand-daughter and many other ladies. We were surprised to see ladies present in the government office, but later learned that such was one of the customs in the United States. General Lewis Cass is a tall gentleman of mature age — probably over seventy — with a genial manner, and dignity befitting the

---

[2]Roughly 360 square feet.

high position of Secretary of State. It seemed to be one of those strange customs of a foreign country to receive foreign ambassadors without ceremony or formality, but in a most friendly manner, as if they had been some old acquaintances, without offering a cup of tea even!

When we returned to our hotel, we asked Captain Dupont to give us some idea of the customary etiquette and ceremony which we should observe when being presented to the President tomorrow. He replied that there was no fixed manner of etiquette, but that we might conduct ourselves according to our own etiquette. When we again asked him if we might follow the precedent we set on the occasion of the presentation of Consul General Townsend Harris to the Shogun, he told us that it would be all right for us to do so. We then begged him to arrange for a rehearsal, telling him that it was our custom to rehearse the proceedings previous to any important formal occasion, in the very same place where the ceremony was to be held. To this, he said that there was no such custom in his country, but he would go and ask the President.

Intercalary March 28th.   Cloudy. As the hour for our presentation to the President of the United States was appointed for 12 o'clock, we made all the necessary preparations with the utmost care. Masaoki (wearing a short sword with silk twined scabbard), . . . I (with a short court sword with gold hilt), and Tadamasa (bearing a sword with scabbard twined in front), were dressed alike in [formal court dress] and [formal court hats] with green braided cords, and wore sandals woven of silk threads. . . .

We drove off in open carriages-and-four. . . . Our procession was headed by a score of men in grey uniform (probably city officials), immediately followed by a band of some thirty musicians, and several mounted cavaliers; then came a group of men, bearing upon their shoulders the despatch box with a red leather cover, and accompanied by the officer in charge, a foreman and an interpreter; these were followed by a long line of carriages in good order, on either side of which marched the guards to the accompaniment of music played by the band. The wide main street was literally packed with vehicles, men and women who were eager to get a glimpse of our procession. I could not help smiling, finding myself feeling quite elated at representing Japan in such a grand style in the foreign land; and I looked around almost proudly, even forgetful of my own ignorance, at the wonder registered in the faces of the crowd, as they pressed forward to see our party in strange costumes such as they had never seen nor could have ever imagined.

Through the iron gate of the President's official residence, we continued to drive some 25 yards, accompanied by the cavaliers, soldiers and our servants, up to the main entrance of the building. . . .

. . . As we approached the Audience Room, the doors to its entrance were swung open on both sides. In the center of the room, which measured approximately 6 *ken* by 13,[3] there stood President Buchanan, flanked by high-ranking civil and military officers; at his back were seen many ladies, young and old, all attired in beautiful dresses. Having entered the room and made an obeisance, Masaoki, I and Tadamasa advanced to the center of the room. We made another obeisance and approached where the President stood. Masaoki delivered a short address, conveying to him the Imperial wishes, which was then interpreted by Namura. Having completed his address, Masaoki took the Shogun's letter from the casket, held out by Naruse Masanori, and presented it to the President; the casket was handed over by Naruse to the Secretary of State Cass. We withdrew to the center of the room, whereupon, Morita and the rest of the Embassy were led to the President's seat. We then retired to the anteroom, having expressed our gratification for that occasion.

As we were resting in the anteroom, Captain Dupont came to us, and asked us if the ceremony of presenting the Imperial letter according to our customs was completed. We answered him in the affirmative. Thereupon, he conducted us again to the Audience Room. This time, the President gave his hand to each of us, and delivered a short address, to the effect that the President and the entire American nation rejoiced in establishing amicable relations with Japan for the first time since her declaration of seclusion, and particularly in receiving her first Embassy to the United States, and that they were exceedingly gratified to have received the Shogun's letter of good will.

It was already evening when we returned to our hotel.

We gathered together and talked of our experiences on this memorable day. The President, who, we agreed, was a silver-haired gentleman of over seventy years of age, had a most genial manner, without losing noble dignity. He wore a simple black costume of coat and trousers in the same fashion as any merchant, and had no decoration or sword on him. All the high-ranking civil officials were dressed in the same way as the President, whereas the army and navy officers wore epaulets (the gold tassels attached to the shoulders, of which the length marked the rank,) and gold stripes on the sleeves of their costume (of which the

[3]Roughly 36 feet by 78 feet.

number represented the rank, three stripes signifying the highest;) and they had a sword at their side. It seemed to us a most curious custom to permit the presence of ladies on such a ceremonious occasion as today. . . . In the United States, which is one of the greatest countries of the world, the highest post of the Government is held by the President, who is elected every four years. (It is said that the new President will be elected on October 1st, this year. We heard them suggest a certain gentleman; and upon our inquiry how they could tell before the election, we were told that this gentleman would be the next President, because he was related to the present President. Judging from this, I am doubtful if the constitutional system of this country may last for many more years.) The President is, therefore, different from the King. Nevertheless, as the Imperial letter was addressed to him, we adopted such manners of etiquette as are befitting in the presence of the Monarch, by, for instance, wearing our [ceremonial robes]. We felt slightly put out of countenance, when we discovered that the Americans attached little importance to class distinction, and dispensed with all manners of decorum. We were, however, exceedingly happy and satisfied to have attained the object of our mission abroad, an achievement worthy of any man's ambition, when we learned that the President was highly appreciative of our mission and took pride in showing this occasion to other nations, by permitting various newspapers to carry pictures of our party, dressed in the ceremonial robes.

> *Suffer the folk of a foreign land to look upon*
> *This glory of our Eastern Empire of Japan.*

> *Forgetting their meek ignorance, how proudly today*
> *Shine the countenances of Japan's Embassy.*

Intercalary March 29th.   In the evening, we drove in our carriages, accompanied by Captain Dupont, to the residence of the Secretary of State. . . .

Upon entering Secretary Cass's residence, we found, to our great surprise, that its entrance hall, passages, and rooms were simply packed with several hundreds of ladies and gentlemen. Under chandeliers of many gas lamps, with their brilliant light reflected by innumerable mirrors and glassware, the entire place was illuminated as bright as day, being almost breath-taking. We somehow managed to make our way through the crowd to the room where Secretary of State Cass and his family stood, and were greeted by them in a most cordial manner. Even his grandchildren came to shake hands with us. As we sat on the chairs, every one

in the room came also to take our hands; as their greetings were not interpreted, we did not understand at all what was said, but stood there looking on this scene of confusion smilingly. . . .

. . . After dinner, we were ushered into another large room, the floor
of which was covered with smooth boards. In one corner, music was
played on instruments which looked like violins. Officers in uniform with
epaulets and swords and ladies dressed in *robes décolletées* of light white
material and wide skirts began, couple by couple, moving round the
room, walking on tiptoe to the tune of the music. They went round and
round as nimbly as so many white mice, on their monotonous walk, without making fluttering gestures with their hands even. I was quite amused
to watch the way in which the ladies' voluminous skirts spread to an enormous proportion, as their wearers took quick turns. Upon our inquiring,
we were told that this was what is called a "waltz," and that even officials
of high rank and elderly ladies, as well as young people, were very fond
of this pastime. The dancers went for drinks and light refreshments in
the other room, and came back for another dance. This, we were told,
would continue all night. We stood there gaping at this amazing sight
such as we had never seen or dreamed of. . . . Although taking into consideration, the very fact that this nation attaches no importance to decorum and formalities, it seemed to me a little odd that the Prime Minister
should issue an invitation to the foreign ambassadors. However, there
would be no end to our getting embarrassed, should we allow ourselves
to be disconcerted by minor transgressions on our sense of propriety. I
felt, however, greatly comforted, when I was brought to a full realization
of the fact that with this nation, the basic precept of life was drawn from
neither loyalty nor etiquette, but from the very spirit of friendliness.

So strange is everything, their language, their appearance,
    That I feel as if living in a dream-land. . . .

Ladies of this country are all fair complexioned and beautiful, always
dressed handsomely, wearing gold and silver ornaments. Although we
are getting accustomed to their appearance, we find their reddish hair
uninteresting, as it reminds us of canine eyes. We have come across less
frequently ladies with dark hair and dark eyes. They must have been
descendants of some Oriental races. Naturally, they appeared to me more
beautiful.

Never have I dreamed to find among fair maidens,
    The fairer blooms of different hue and origin.

April 4th.   Fine weather. As it was arranged, we visited Congress this afternoon, accompanied by the same American friends as usual. . . . We were shown to the large hall where affairs of State were being discussed. The hall itself was some twenty *ken* by ten,[4] and had a board flooring and panels all around, with a gallery built above it. Its ceiling was as high as some twenty feet, . . . inlaid with glass sheets of pretty patterns in gold and silver and many other bright colors. On an elevated platform in front, there sat the Vice-President, with two clerks seated on the slightly lower platform in front of him. The members' seats were arranged in semicircle before the platform, where forty or fifty members sat, with files and documents on their tables. One of the members was on his feet, haranguing at the top of his voice, and gesticulating wildly like a madman. When he sat down, his example was followed by another, and yet another. Upon our inquiring what it was all about, we were informed that all the affairs of State were thus publicly discussed by the members, and that the Vice-President made his decision after he heard the opinion of every member. In the gallery, we saw a number of men and women listening eagerly to the debate. We likewise listened but refrained from asking any more questions, although we were courteously invited to do so, because we did not understand a word of the debate, and, moreover, we considered it as rather presumptuous to inquire into the state affairs of another nation.

As we left the hall, we were invited to go up to the gallery. We took our seats there and had a good view of the hall below, where a heated debate was taking place. Even when attending the most important conference on state affairs, they wore their usual narrow sleeved black coat and trousers, and raised their voices in an unmannerly way. Considering all these and that the Vice-President presided over the debate from an elevated platform, the scene, we whispered among ourselves, resembled somewhat that of our fishmarket at Nihonbashi.

April 6th.   Fine and clear. This morning, several hundreds of ladies and gentlemen, introduced as Congress members and their families, came to our hotel to bid us welcome. We received them in the usual manner of hand-shakes before they left. . . .

This was the day that had been appointed previously by letter for President Buchanan's dinner, to which all the members of our Embassy were invited. . . . The President, accompanied by his three nieces and Secre-

---

[4]Roughly 60 feet by 120 feet.

tary of State Lewis Cass and other high-ranking officials with their wives, came to greet us. Our good Captain Dupont explained to us that it was their custom to have the presence of ladies at ceremonial functions, such as the state banquet given this evening. He said that he was giving us this information, lest we should start wondering at this peculiar habit, unknown to us in our country; we thanked him for his consideration. . . . Considering the President's presence, we all ate and drank somewhat in a reserved manner; it was rather amusing to learn and imitate the manner of eating from the lady sitting next. Helen, the President's niece, played the rôle of "hostess" at the table, supervising everything during the dinner, and acting as mistress of the ceremonies. So impressive was her grace and dignity, that she might have been taken for the Queen, and her uncle, the President, for her Prime Minister. This lady graciously invited us to partake of wine, asking numerous questions concerning our country. Most of her questions were very difficult for me to answer, as they were posed entirely from an American view-point. They were: what was the number of our Court ladies; what were their customs and manners like; and so forth. I tried to give noncommital answers as best I could. One question she asked me was: which did we consider to be superior, the American ladies or the Japanese—a question, interesting in that it showed the familiar vein of feminine curiosity. When I replied that the American ladies were the more beautiful of the two with their fair complexion, she and her companions looked well pleased. They must be of a very believing nature. After some 15 different dishes were served one after another, and toasts were drunk to our health and to the host's, a glass bowl filled with water and a small towel was placed before each guest. Wondering what they were for, I looked around, and saw Helen, washing her fingers in the bowl, and then cleansing her lips with the water. I did the same, following her example. We could hardly refrain from laughing to see the look of embarrassment on Morita's face, when, after boldly drinking from the bowl, he was made to realize what it was for by Tadamasa, who, sitting next to him, gave a quick warning by pulling at his sleeve.

April 14th.   Clear. Captain Porter took us at 2 p.m. to a museum called the Smithsonian Institute, where countless rare objects were exhibited, and every possible sort of subject could be studied. Like the other museum we had visited, it was a tall stone building. The Director met us at the entrance, and took us to a large room, where various electrical machines were on display. He ordered all the windows of the room to be closed, and there, in the darkened room, he demonstrated amazing experiments, such as creating lightning before our very eyes. We next entered another large room, containing rows of chairs, which we took for a lecture hall. Another room was a picture gallery, on the walls of which were hung innumerable pictures, depicting American customs and habits in chronological order, and many portraits of the world's most famous personages. On one of the pillars, we saw specimens of human hair displayed in a frame; these, we were informed, were the hair of the successive Presidents. What lack of courtesy! This instance alone speaks for itself.

We saw in glass cases built along the walls of a large hall several thousands of rare objects, viz. stuffed animals and birds, specimens of fish, reptiles and insects. The birds, of which some were as large as swans, looked as if they were alive. Some monkeys bore a striking resemblance to human beings in their physical build; several scores of them had very long limbs. Reptiles and frogs were kept in jars filled with alcohol. As there were more than ten thousands of them, the sight was enough to make us feel uncomfortable. . . . There were stuffed seals, similar to those I had seen in the land of Ezo. We also saw three petrified human bodies or mummies, kept in glass cases in one corner of the hall. They were more than a thousand years old, we were told, but they were not at all like skeletons. Though completely shrivelled and dry, their bodies were perfect, with flesh and skin still retained on them. It was, however, difficult to tell their sex. It is true that these mummies are exhibited for the advancement of study of all the living creatures under heaven. And yet, we did not know what to say on seeing them thus displayed side by side with animals, birds, fish and insects! Literally speaking, I felt "sweat coming out all over my face." In good sooth, I said to myself, these foreigners did not earn their nickname of "barbarians" for nothing!

May 2nd.   Clear; a thunder-storm at noon. The Metropolitan Hotel, which is our temporary home in New York, is much larger than the hotel where we stayed in Washington. On the ground floor there is a large theater, which is crowded with a large number of spectators every evening. A guard stands night and day at the passage leading to our suites on the fifth floor. From the roof of this hotel, we can obtain a good view of the entire city, which, though densely populated and busy-looking, is estimated to be in area not larger than one-third of our capital city of Yedo. The traffic in the streets is great, with pedestrians and carriages of all sorts passing from one direction to another. At night, all the shops and main streets are brilliantly illuminated with innumerable gas lamps, so that it is as light as in the day time. Actually, there are only two of these busy and prosperous streets; the others are much quieter, dotted with open spaces and vacant lots.

Washington is the capital of the United States, but compared with other cities, it has a smaller population and remains quieter; for the majority of the government officials, headed by the President, hail from other towns and villages 400 or 500 miles away, and reside only temporarily in Washington during the tenure of their public service. The subordinate officials often stay in hotels. The shops there serve the residents only with the supplies of daily necessities; commodities other than daily requirements are purchased mostly from New York. (The capital city of a nation should be quiet, like Washington; a simple thrifty way of living will then be encouraged among its citizens.) In Philadelphia, where many wealthy merchants reside, and all kinds of machinery are manufactured, the citizens show their common traits of generosity and modesty, and their merchandises are all of superior quality. As for New York, the best and largest trade port in America, its harbor is crowded with foreign vessels all the year round, and its city, over-run by migrants from other States. As a result, its citizens are invariably callous, while the commodities on sale here are of doubtful quality, despite the fact that their price is surprisingly high. Captain Dupont even warned us to take special caution, when we went out, telling us that the city was full of foreigners and the general spirit of the city itself was none too friendly. The same unfortunate tendency, I fear, exists in all large seaports all over the world.

May 9th. . . . We were advised to pay our respects at the same time to the widow of the late Commodore Perry. . . . Mrs. Perry was an elderly lady of admirable dignity and gentleness. She cordially received us and introduced to us her daughters and grandchildren. In her room were displayed many articles from Japan, some being presents from our Shogun, and others purchased by Commodore Perry during his visits to Japan. Mrs. Perry told us that her husband died only three years ago, after being awarded the highest appreciation of the entire America for his meritorious achievement in opening the door of Japan, which had remained closed to the rest of the world under her seclusion policy. . . . We told her how we wished that the Commodore had been alive to greet us at his home, since we happened to be visiting his country. Upon hearing this, Mrs. Perry was so moved that she could not speak for a while. After having exchanged hearty farewells, we left. . . .

When we returned to our hotel, I sat in my room, musing on the swift changes that had taken place in the affairs of the world during the last few years. The Japanese knew that America was a large continent extending from the North to the South Pole, but were ignorant of the existence of the United States of America; only six years ago when Commodore

Perry came to Japan as the first American envoy, there were some Japanese who argued the necessity of repelling the American fleet by dint of arms; finally Japan and America became treaty nations, after the conclusion of the treaty of amity, which was achieved only through the benevolent spirit of our gracious Ruler. To think that we are here in the United States today as the first Japanese Ambassadors, and welcome guests in the house of the same Commodore Perry! Marvelling at the series of strange events, brought about by the swiftly changing world situation and the unpredictable developments in our own national polity, I at last went to bed, taking with me all the wonders of the past few years.

33

Two American Reports on the 1860 Mission
1860

The first Japanese officials to set foot on American soil created a sensation wherever they went. In Washington, where the mission members met with President James Buchanan, they were feted at balls and receptions (see Document 32), and in New York they paraded down Broadway. Dressed in silk kimonos, with tall black caps perched on their topknotted heads, they charmed and amused American onlookers. As these two newspaper articles show, the American press greeted the Japanese with a mixture of admiration, anxiety, suspicion, and condescension. On the one hand, newspapers portrayed them as representatives of a society that was more orderly and prosperous than the other "slumbering" peoples of Asia; on the other hand, while press reports emphasized their eagerness to learn from the Americans, they also pointed out the potential dangers of "uplifting" the Japanese, particularly by supplying them with military technology.

Our Parting Guests

Our Japanese visitors take their departure for home to-day. It may seem discourteous, but we cannot help saying we are glad they have gone. Their visit has not been without a certain interest to us, but we have had enough of it. They may be, and doubtless are, very respectable persons at home,—but their social intercourse with us has not been especially

"Our Parting Guests," *New York Times,* June 30, 1860. "Our Japanese Visitors," *Harpers Weekly,* May 26, 1860.

fascinating. When persons can neither speak nor understand a syllable of each other's language, and are compelled to converse through the medium of a double interpretation, their intercourse must lack something of the ease and grace essential to cordial and protracted delight in each other's society. The pantomime of the Japanese is expressive enough, but pantomime at the best is a very unsatisfactory style of conversation. One tires of it after a while, even on the stage. In the affairs of daily life, a very little of it will suffice for a long time.

The Japanese, moreover, have very little of that personal beauty, — that majesty of demeanor, graceful dignity of manners or even elegance of outward appearance, which sometimes answer in place of social qualities, and render their possessors favorites in the best social circles. They are small of stature, tawney in complexion, sleepy and feeble in their physical appearance and habits, and with only those characteristics calculated to excite a momentary curiosity. They may be very wise at home, but they have been quite as prudent here in their displays of wisdom as in their expenditures of money. We doubt whether any of our citizens, or any of the corporations which have paid them visits more or less formal, have learned from them anything whatever concerning their country, its government, its people, their habits, commerce, and future policy towards other nations, than they knew before. . . .

The truth is, the Japanese came to acquire knowledge, — not to impart it. An enlightened curiosity, — a desire to explore the secret of the strength and power of that formidable civilization of the West, which has so startled the apathy of the slumbering East by its cannon and its conquests, had quite as much to do with their visit as any liberal wish to cultivate closer relations with other Powers and throw open the gates of Niphon [Nippon] to the commerce of the world. We have done our utmost to gratify and instruct them. We have shown them the wonders of our mechanics, the power of our machinery, and have taught them how to make and use it for themselves. We have given them models of our inventions, have instructed them in the processes of all the useful arts, and have even put into their hands the most formidable engines known to modern warfare. It will not be our fault if, with their quick ingenuity, they do not very speedily become able to fabricate for themselves all the great staples with which we have been hoping to supply them. The blame will not rest upon our shoulders, if they are not able to build and arm their forts with weapons of war as deadly as any known to us, and to resist successfully every attempt of American or English ships to force an entrance into their harbors. It is only a few years ago that the Japanese authorities applied to our Government, through Mr. Townsend Harris, for models of some of our cannon, and instruction as to their use. Our Government declined, from prudential motives, to accede to their request. But we have since grown more liberal, if they have not; and the [Japanese] Embassy takes back complete models of our best howitzers and Dahlgren guns, with full instruction as to the manufacture and use of everything required, both in offensive and defensive warfare. That they will profit by this excessive liberality on our part, we may rest assured. We can only hope that we may not find ourselves among the earliest victims of our over-zealous and mistaken benevolence.

What may be the ultimate results of this extraordinary Embassy, it is, of course, impossible to predict. Thus far the most remarkable fact about it is, that it should ever have been sent. We have received its members with marked and munificent hospitality. Our general Government has incurred an expense of some hundreds of thousands of dollars for its transport and maintenance. Our City has spent at least $100,000 in pro-fessed attempts at its entertainment. We have done everything in our power to make their visit agreeable and profitable to them. What we are to receive in return for all this we shall know in due time. At the latest advices the house of our Minister in Japan was guarded by troops to pro-tect him from assassination. Whether our late visitors will be inclined or able to deal with us in a different spirit, after their return, remains to be seen. Our expectations, we confess, are not particularly sanguine.

Our Japanese Visitors

We devote several of our illustrated pages to the Japanese, who — at the time we write — are in Washington, enjoying the hospitalities of that thriving little town. A large sum of money was voted by Congress to defray the expenses of their reception. . . .

One or two members of Congress have alluded to this "fuss" as a "piece of nonsense." They are the lineal descendants of the people who said that the "fuss" in Boston, eighty odd years ago, about the Tea-duty was "all nonsense," and of the people who shouted aloud that the resis-tance to the Stamp-act, which ushered in the Revolution, was mere gam-mon. The fact is, that this Japanese embassy is a matter of the highest national and commercial importance.

The Japanese are the British of Asia. Like our ancestors of the British Isles, they are of insular origin, and full of insular virtues and insular prej-udices. They despise foreigners; but they know how to take care of them-selves. Many of their customs seem absurd to us; but they are honest in their adoption, and thorough in their observance. Their country pro-duces a number of commodities which would find a sale here, and they consume many articles which we produce. Satisfy them that commercial intercourse with us would be beneficial to them, and a valuable trade will be created. Thus far, their only commercial correspondents have been the Dutch, who have driven hard bargains with them, and impressed them unfavorably with regard to Christian nations. We can undo the mischief that has been done if we produce a favorable impression on our visitors, and commence a trade under proper auspices.

Independently, however, of immediate commercial benefits, the establishment of friendly relations with the Japanese can not fail to be of marked advantage to our Pacific States. The State of Oregon and the future State of Washington will necessarily become intimately connected with their nearest neighbors over the water. Of those neighbors Japan is the one best worth cultivating. The Russians of Northern Asia are hardly more than semi-barbarous, and the Chinese are such a peculiar race, and so entirely foreign to us in every sense of the word, that neither can compare, in respect of neighborly value, to the Japanese. By-and-by there will necessarily grow up an interchange not only of commodities but of men between our Pacific States and the empire of Japan. Our people will go to Japan . . . [and] will endeavor to show the Japanese the best side of the American character. On the other hand, the Japanese — if good relations be established between the two countries — will send out some of their people to plant Japanese colonies in our territory. On this interchange the benefit will be obvious and mutual. Civilized as we boast of being, we can learn much of the Japanese — if nothing more, we can learn the duty of obeying the laws.

34

WALT WHITMAN

A Broadway Pageant (Poem)
1860

Walt Whitman (1819–1892), whose Leaves of Grass *had appeared just a few years earlier, celebrated the arrival of the Japanese mission in this exuberant poem. It overflows with Whitman's confident conviction that the liberating spirit of American democracy represented the future of mankind. Just as the Americans had peopled the New World with "a noble race," Whitman thought they*

Walt Whitman's Drum Taps (New York, 1865), 61–65.

would free Asia from the dead hand of the past. While the poem represents
ancient Asia (including the Assyrians and the Indians as well as the Japan-
ese) as the "mother" of human civilization, it portrays contemporary Asia as
a moribund world awaiting rejuvenation by the westward march of liberty.

(Reception Japanese Embassy, June 16, 1860)

OVER sea, hither from Niphon [Nippon],
Courteous, the Princes of Asia, swart-cheek'd princes,
First-comers, guests, two-sworded princes,
Lesson-giving princes, leaning back in their open barouches, bare-
     headed, impassive,
This day they ride through Manhattan.

     Libertad!
I do not know whether others behold what I behold,
In the procession, along with the Princes of Asia, the errand-bearers,
Bringing up the rear, hovering above, around, or in the ranks marching;
But I will sing you a song of what I behold, Libertad.

     Superb-faced Manhattan!
Comrade Americanos!—to us, then, at last, the Orient comes.

     To us, my city,
Where our tall-topt marble and iron beauties range on opposite sides—
     to walk in the space between,
To-day our Antipodes comes.

     The Originatress comes,
The land of Paradise—land of the Caucasus—the nest of birth,
The nest of languages, the bequeather of poems, the race of eld,
Florid with blood, pensive, rapt with musings, hot with passion,
Sultry with perfume, with ample and flowing garments,
With sunburnt visage, with intense soul and glittering eyes.
The race of Brahma[1] comes!

See, my cantabile! these, and more, are flashing to us from the pro-
     cession;
As it moves, changing, a kaleidoscope divine it moves, changing,
     before us.

[1] Eternal origin of being.

Not the errand-bearing princes, nor the tann'd Japanee only:
Lithe and silent, the Hindoo appears—the whole Asiatic continent
    itself appears—the Past, the dead,
The murky night-morning of wonder and fable, inscrutable,
The envelop'd mysteries, the old and unknown hive-bees,
The North—the sweltering South—Assyria—the Hebrews—the
    Ancient of ancients,
Vast desolated cities—the gliding Present—all of these, and more,
    are in the pageant-procession.

For I too, raising my voice, join the ranks of this pageant;
I am the chanter—I chant aloud over the pageant;
I chant the world on my Western Sea;
I chant, copious, the islands beyond, thick as stars in the sky;
I chant the new empire, grander than any before—As in a vision it
    comes to me;
I chant America, the Mistress—I chant a greater supremacy;
I chant, projected, a thousand blooming cities yet, in time, on those
    groups of sea-islands;
I chant my sail-ships and steam-ships threading the archipelagoes;
I chant my stars and stripes fluttering in the wind;
I chant commerce opening, the sleep of ages having done its work—
    races, reborn, refresh'd;
Lives, works, resumed—The object I know not—but the old, the
    Asiatic, resumed, as it must be
Commencing from this day, surrounded by the world.

And you, Libertad of the world!
You shall sit in the middle, well-pois'd, thousands of years;
As to-day, from one side, the Princes of Asia come to you;
As to-morrow, from the other side, the Queen of England sends her
    eldest son to you.

The sign is reversing, the orb is enclosed,
The ring is circled, the journey is done;
The box-lid is but perceptibly open'd—nevertheless the perfume
    pours copiously out of the whole box.

Young Libertad!
With the venerable Asia, the all-mother,
Be considerate with her, now and ever, hot Libertad—for you
    are all;

Bend your proud neck to the long-off mother, now sending messages
  over the archipelagoes to you;
Bend your proud neck low for once, young Libertad.

Were the children straying westward so long? so wide the tramping?
Were the precedent dim ages debouching westward from Paradise so
  long?
Were the centuries steadily footing it that way, all the while unknown,
  for you, for reasons?
They are justified—they are accomplish'd—they shall now be turn'd
  the other way also, to travel toward you thence;
They shall now also march obediently eastward, for your sake,
  Libertad.

7

The Iwakura Mission of 1871

35

KUME KUNITAKE

Report of the Iwakura Mission

1878

*The five-volume report of the Iwakura mission was compiled by Kume
Kunitake (1839–1931), a former samurai from the domain of Saga
recruited as a secretary to accompany this mission. Kume, who had become
a close advisor to the daimyo of Saga after studying at the bakufu academy
in Edo, was trained in Confucian studies. The report, based on Kume's
observations as well as on journals kept by other members of the mission,
was intended to enlarge public knowledge about the West and to promote
the spread of "civilization." While much of the report simply provides a
straightforward narrative about places the mission visited and the people
it met, interspersed were interpretive passages set off from the rest of the text
that attempted to explain Western customs, institutions, and culture. In that
sense, it was less a diplomatic report than an ethnographic one. For a more
personal account of the mission from Kume's perspective, see Document 36.*

At the time this country became independent . . . its population numbered
a mere 5 million. In the space of one hundred years it has increased sev-
enfold. During the fifty-one years between 1820 and 1871, 7.5 million foreigners immigrated to live here. Among them, those from England are

Kume Kunitake, *Tokumei zenken taishi Bei-Ō kairan jikki* (Tokyo: Hakubunsha, 1877),
33–34, 49–52, 202–05, 250–51, 359–65. ·

the most numerous, followed by the Germans. Since "slaves"[1] were imported from Africa and employed as laborers from the time of the country's foundation, there are many black people. They make up one-seventh of the population. In the central part of the country, there are "Indians," and in the western part they use Chinese as workers. The races are extremely complicated, but every one of them, it can be said, is represented [in America].

However, it was great merchants, powerful aristocrats, and religious believers from Europe who brought land under cultivation using an enormous amount of capital and employing lower classes who flowed in from all directions, so it was people of the white race who became the [country's] leaders. Among them the English are most numerous. Since the country was established under their guidance, English is generally used as the national language, and institutions are for the most part English institutions. Hence, [the Americans] call England their "mother country." In some states German is spoken; in the southern part of the country, French is used widely in the state of Louisiana; and in the southwestern states of New Mexico and Arizona, Spanish is spoken. There are also not a few towns and villages where several languages are spoken. . . .

In the newest states land is abundant but people are scarce; the focus of their statecraft is colonization. So desperate are they to increase the population that they turn to every possible means at hand, even raising bastards and children without parents, and they pay scant attention to the quality of their seed. Immigrants generally come from the ignorant and lazy masses of various countries. Since they come from poor stock, breeding indiscriminately, they are of poor character. Murders or robberies take place everywhere. The hovels of the humble classes are extremely filthy, and much effort is required to educate and protect them.

Penal restrictions on smoking and drinking alcohol are common in Western countries; they take the most extreme form in this country. Taxes [on alcohol] are heavy, so people drink tea instead. That is why tea is so popular in America. Even so, most people will not abandon their taste [for tobacco and alcohol]. This year the value of tobacco consumed domestically was $135.2 million (the value of grain consumed was $200 million, a difference of only $65 million), and the value of alcoholic beverages [consumed] reached $616.8 million. Still, the fact that there are few drunks in the streets is cause for praise. This proves that people all

---

[1]The ideograph used in the text is "black slave." The author inserted an orthographic marker to indicate the English pronunciation of the Japanese word.

know that it is shameful to violate these regulations. Among the Western countries, however, the character of the people is the worst in America to the east and in Russia to the west. . . .

Protestantism is the national religion, but there are also many Roman Catholics, Greek Catholics, Jews, and in California even Buddhist temples. In recent years, granting religious liberty has been the common policy of all the Western countries, but even so Buddhist temples are found only in this country.

In general, the spirit of religion is extremely fervent. In Europe religious fervor is highest in England, but if you travel there from here, one does not think England is so fervent at all. Those who travel from England to America say that English religion is much more subdued. On the sabbath day [in America], most shops are closed in every city, and no trade goes on after Saturday afternoon. Can this be what sustains public morals in this country? . . .

On the way back to our hotel we stopped at Woodward Park[2] in the southern part of the city. For 25 cents anyone can enter. In this park one finds a zoological garden, a botanical garden, a museum, and an art gallery side by side. In its center is a stone fountain and . . . a large stage to hold dances or to put on shows. It is very lively, especially on Sundays.

Inside the gate they have built a display pavilion where animals are housed. [Here one finds] animals, insects, butterflies, cocoons, and so forth, preserved by the drying-out method, divided into categories, and displayed on shelves. In the drying-out method [taxidermy], the outer skin of the animal or fish is flayed, then fashioned into something that looks like its true form when alive. Insects are immersed in alcohol and stored in bottles. . . .

The customs and temperaments of the Orient and the Occident differ from one another, as though they are the opposite of one another. The Westerners enjoy diplomacy, but the Orientals are diffident about it. This is not a relic left over from the closed country period; it is because [the Orientals] do not care much about wealth and do not regard foreign trade as important. The Westerners enjoy getting out into the world and traveling about. Even in a small town like this they build a public garden. The Orientals [on the other hand] enjoy sitting inside, and hence there is a garden in every house, a custom that has its origins in the infertility of the soil. Westerners study the science [*rigaku*] of material things while Orientals pursue the science of the immaterial.

I believe that the differences between the wealth and poverty of the Occident and the Orient arise from these customs. If parks and zoologi-

[2]Woodward's Garden in San Francisco.

cal gardens are to be found in every city in the West, we have our pleasure gardens and animal shows, which even though different [from Western parks and museums] in scale resemble them in a superficial way. However, [Western and Japanese gardens and displays] are entirely different in basic character and origin. Those in the Occident are established to attract attention and to display information, thereby encouraging production and propagating knowledge and learning. Even though they cost an enormous amount, [no one] begrudges the money since the profit [to society] is great. In public parks like Woodward Park, one finds botanical gardens, zoological gardens, museums, and libraries all together, and the varieties of animals and birds . . . are arranged by type. These are different from our own exhibitions, which are put on to astound and astonish people by displaying strange animals and peculiar plants. If one wants to make a picture [of a plant or an animal], the [facilities in America] conveniently allow one to observe the animals and plants directly and to draw their actual form using the real things as models.

In the well-known large cities on the Atlantic coast, and in the European countries, one finds such specialized parks, all fully equipped, of course. The people of these cities pay for their costs. Their profit lies in the fact that they advance the science of the material world, leading to the discovery of practical advances in agriculture, manufacturing, and commerce, and paving the way to wealth and prosperity. One ought not to confuse [Western science] with the Oriental science of the immaterial where people laugh at studying a single plant or a single tree or passively observe the unusual, hoping to take profit from what is immediately under their noses.

Even though public customs in the Orient and the West outwardly resemble one another in certain ways, their focus is usually quite different. This is something that those who wish to understand such things should be aware of. . . .

In America "Congress" is the highest seat of government; the President exercises administrative authority, and the vice president is the head of the legislature; the chief justice holds judicial authority. Such is the general outline of the federal government in the United States, which differs fundamentally in appearance from that of monarchical countries. (In a monarchical country, the monarch exercises both judicial and administrative authority with the assistance of cabinet officers, and the parliament has only the right to legislate.)

When the thirteen colonies broke free from England, at first they established a confederation with representatives from each state discussing public affairs. When the [colonies] won the war [with England] and made a public declaration of their independence to the world, under the leadership of men of learning like Jefferson, Hamilton, Franklin, and other famous men of politics, [the Americans] drafted a constitution for a federal republic. Under this constitution a national assembly was established, the president was to be publicly elected, two members were to be publicly elected from each state to serve in the upper chamber [the Senate] and act as elders of state [*genrō*], and representatives were to be publicly elected by the people of each state to serve in the lower chamber [the House of Representatives]. This proposal for the organization of the central government was sent to the states for discussion [but] with great clamor the gentlemen in every state refused to consent to it. Opposition gushed forth: "The president is nothing but a king by another name"; "The raising of taxes and the levying of military forces ought to be left to the states"; "The confederation government is fine just as it is." For more than a year, this [debate] went on, until Washington brought about an agreement by dint of his moral influence.

Washington later remarked: "At the time the constitution was being discussed, the debate within the country was many times more intense than the eight years of hard struggle against the English, and our patience was almost exhausted." It is well known that truly nothing is more difficult than restoring peace after waging a struggle for survival. Since the constitution was settled upon after many days and months of exhaustive argument, it is thorough in its excellence, and it has made its way into the people's hearts. Indeed, it is treated as though it were an instruction from Heaven. Today, ninety-six years later, even though the states now number thirty-seven, no one has dared to violate it.

However, over the years assertions of independence, attempts to check the authority of the president, and partisan debates among the people have arisen in every state. People in the European monarchies, counting themselves fortunate that they were not a republican people, watched with amusement as the American people fought each other in the midst of peace. Naturally no man-made law is perfect. If the people are given much freedom, then government will be reined in; and the more important freedom becomes, then the more lax the law codes will become. It is in the nature of things that for every plus there is a minus. But the American people have been nurtured by their government, and now that a century has passed by, even small children [in America] regard serving a monarch as a shameful thing. Accustomed [to their system of government], they not only fail to recognize its defect but they so love its beauty that they attempt to turn the whole world into students of their national policy. That is the impression they give even in casual conversations. Their convictions are ultimately unshakeable. This is the soul of a republican people.

In the American federal government, seven secretaries serve under the president, one each in charge of domestic affairs, finances, the army, the navy, commerce, the postal service, and the government's attorneys. However, there is no prime minister. The responsibility of assisting the president lies with the elder statesmen in the upper chamber, whose head is the vice president. All the members are divided into separate sections,[3] and these draft proposals for legislation. In the case of important secret matters, they go into a secret office and discuss them behind closed doors. Once its members are all in agreement, all legislative proposals drafted by the upper chamber are sent to the lower chamber; when the lower chamber agrees to them they are sent to the president. If he disagrees, the proposal is sent back to the national assembly for reconsideration within ten days. If more than ten days elapse, the proposal becomes a national law as decided upon by the national assembly. If two-thirds [of the national assembly] agree upon a proposal sent back for reconsideration, even if the president does not agree with them, it becomes a national law as determined by the national assembly. A law came up for reconsideration only once while Washington was in office, but twelve or thirteen years ago, when Mr. Johnson, the vice president, took office after the death of Mr. Lincoln, he often rejected proposals from the national assembly, which then became national laws [approved] only by the national assembly.

The restraints on the executive branch are many. The upper house even has the authority to impeach administrative officials for unlawful behavior. It can even impeach the unlawful behavior of the president. This constitutional provision was applied to Mr. Johnson, but in the end he was not forced out of office. From this one can imagine just how powerful the national assembly is. Hence, in America it is a very great honor to become an elder statesman and enter the upper house.

Officials are elected by public election, and laws are decided upon by public agreement, so this system appears to be extremely fair. However, in the final analysis, not all the gentlemen elected to the upper and lower houses are endowed with the highest intelligence and talent. Farsighted views do not always reach the eyes and ears of the ordinary person. For that reason, when differences of opinion arise, since matters are decided by majority agreement, it is common that the better policy is rejected and the worse policy adopted. Once specially appointed members draft a proposal, eight or nine times out of ten, they will agree upon the original proposal even if there is some difference of opinion. Hence it is difficult to

---

[3]This passage probably refers to the congressional committee system.

guard against bribery behind the scenes. It is difficult to deny that the private views of administrative officials sway discussions of legislative matters from behind the scenes. These are all regrettable aspects of republican government. . . .

In America women are not prohibited from entering official buildings. Women even gather to watch military drills at the army and naval academies, and when the drill is over, men and women mingle together on the dance platform and give themselves to merrymaking. Such is public custom in a republic.

When we recall that the Orient and the West have been places far apart with no traffic between them since their beginnings, it is not at all strange that their customs and character should be different in every respect and quite the opposite of one another in every detail. From the time our group boarded ship at Yokohama, [we found ourselves] in a realm of completely alien customs. What is appropriate deportment for us seems to attract their curiosity, and what is proper behavior for them is strange to us. But no matter how hard we tried [to understand], what we found most strange in their behavior was the relations between men and women.

With respect to relations between husbands and wives, it is the practice in Japan that the wife serves her husband's parents and that children serve their parents, but in America the husband follows the "Way of Serving His Wife." The [American husband] lights the lamps, prepares food at the table,[4] presents shoes to his wife, brushes the dust off [her] clothes, helps her up and down the stairs, offers her his chair, and carries her things when she goes out. If the wife becomes a little angry, the husband is quick to offer affection and show respect, bowing and scraping to beg her forgiveness. But if she does not accept his apologies, he may find himself turned out of the house and denied meals.

When riding in the same ship or carriage, men stand up and offer their seats to the women, who accept with no hesitation at all. When women take their places sitting down, the men all crowd around them to show their respect. Men are restrained in their behavior when together [with women] at the same gathering, keeping their voices well modulated and always letting women go first in everything. The women do not demur at all. It is only when the women retire that the men begin to become lax in their behavior. If we were to transfer these rules to Japan and apply them to our principles of filiality [i.e., if Japanese children treated their parents as American husbands treated their wives], there would be extraordinary advances in the Way of Filial Piety.

[4]This probably refers to carving roasts and similar traditional husbandly duties.

Even though these customs are generally followed in the West, they are most pronounced in the United States and England. Since England is a country ruled by a queen, this fashion has made gains, and since the United States is a republic, the theory of equal rights for men and women grows stronger.... Recently the idea of giving women political rights has been discussed in the United States, and it is said to have received official approval in certain states. In Washington, D.C., there is a woman who strolls about wearing men's clothes,[5] with a top hat and culottes, but self-respecting women have nothing to do with her.

In sum, the duties of men and women are quite different from one another, and it is obvious that [women] can bear no responsibility for the defense and protection of a country. In the teachings of the Orient, the woman rules within [the home] but she has no role outside it. The distinction between men and women is deep.

... We went to the "Bible" Society. ("Bible" is the term for the Old and New Testaments.) This society was established to gather money contributions from believers in order to send sacred texts throughout the world. We were told that the Bible has been translated into thirty languages and that it is sold in every country. They gave all of us a Chinese translation [of the Bible]. Not only does every household and every person in West own all the sacred texts, but they always have a Bible at hand even when they go on a short trip. Some [Bibles published by the Society], ... made as beautiful and attractive as possible, with extremely magnificent binding, gold rubbings and inlaid jewels, are prized and sought after by women. There are also simple volumes that poor people can own, and also those with raised print for blind people to read. A copy of the sacred texts is always to be found in the reception room of every shop and in the bedrooms of every hotel. In prisons, and in hospitals too, everyone gets a copy of the Bible to read thoroughly. [These Bibles] are sold cheaply, at a price that does not even cover the cost of the paper. They are manufactured with funds collected by the churches, and their purpose is to spread religion, not to make a profit. ...

The Bible is a *sutra* [the Buddhist term for a sacred text] that provides a foundation for popular morals. To make a comparison with the Orient, the Bible is like the [Confucian] Four Books in the sense that it penetrates the hearts of the people, and it is like the Buddhist scriptures in the sense that it is important to both men and women alike. But if we look at

---

[5]This probably refers to Dr. Mary Walker, an early feminist who served as battlefield doctor in the Civil War. In 1865 she was awarded a Medal of Honor, revoked by Congress in 1917, then restored by the Army in 1977.

the degree with which [the Bible] is respected by the peoples of Europe and America, nothing in the Orient can compare with its success and ubiquity. The people's respect for God is the basic source of their diligence, and the excellence of their moral character is the source of their domestic peace. [Their religion] is also what gives rise to their wealth and power. We can liken it to oxygen. . . . Not for one moment can people live without oxygen.

To explain the conditions of the people in the countries of the West, one must by all means understand their religion. When foreigners come to [Japan], they always ask, "What teaching do you revere? What gods do you worship?" If someone responds that he has no religion, [the astounded foreigner] will treat him like a wild man and cut off all contact with him.

If people are without the principles of the Way, they will not respect the laws. They will deceive Heaven, defame their fellow men, and give in to their desires. Truly, this is extremely abhorrent for [it means that they are like] wild beasts. Countless religions are practiced in the world, and their variety is great, but in essence all of them stand in awe of divine protection or counsel the control of sexual desires. Rather than dazzle people with the subtleties of discourse, however, they honor the sincerity [of believers].

People in the West vie with one another in the pursuit of civilization, but we find only absurd tales if we peruse the Old and New Testaments they respect so much. It would not be wrong to regard [tales about] voices from Heaven and criminals raised from the dead as similar to the delirious ravings of madness. . . . They hold that someone crucified was the son of the Heavenly Lord and they kneel, reverently wailing in lamentation. Where do these tears come from? we wonder to ourselves. In all European and American cities, pictures of crucified criminals,[6] profuse with ruby-red blood, are hung everywhere on building walls and rooms, making one feel as though one is living in a cemetery or staying in an execution ground. If this is not bizarre, then what is? The people in the West, however, think it bizarre that no such things exist in the Orient. Even men of great worldliness and insight continually urged that we display them. What could they have in mind?

[The Westerners] accomplish their moral cultivation through the sincerity of their respect for God. This provides the foundation that spurs their striving spirit of study and their mutual harmony. For this reason it

---

[6]After the arrival of the Portuguese and the Spanish, the Japanese adopted crucifixion as a form of public punishment.

is difficult to judge the merits of religion solely on the basis of its forms and doctrines. We must look at a [religion's] actual practices as well. In the Orient, Confucianism is a school of moral cultivation, and Buddhism is a religion. Together they constitute the basic elements of national peace and order, and they have long entered into the hearts of the people. In terms of actual beliefs and actual practices, which has greater depth: Confucianism and Buddhism? or Christianity? The Four Books and the Six Sutras have been known in our country for two thousand years, but only a very few people know how to read them. The rest merely study them without understanding, or with the backing of secular authority, they spread [their teachings] among the ordinary people and propagate the virtues of loyalty, filial piety, benevolence, and righteousness in the countryside.

If Confucian scholars are asked about the particulars of moral cultivation, nearly all of them find it difficult to grasp its essence. And if one looks at the reality of their conduct, one can say with certainty that from ancient times until the present not a single one [has practiced moral cultivation]. Because they are moved by political interest and personal livelihood, they abandon their fidelity, alter their preachings, and follow the fortunes of those in power at the moment.

Buddhist priests are different from Confucian scholars in that they generally follow the rules and submit to the regulations in the Buddhist canon, but only two or three out of a hundred understand what is said in even a few sutras. Nor is what they preach to the people adequate. The faithful may chant the *nenbutsu*[7] and other incantations, but they continue to be driven by their sexual desires. If we weigh the extent to which the caliber of a religion is manifested in the moral conduct of the people, then we should not regret to say that in the whole world [Buddhism] ranks at the bottom.

In the teachings of Christ, there is much that is bizarre. . . . However, when it comes to earnestness of practice, we must blush with shame. Everyone from kings and princes to servants and small children understand what is said in this one book, the Bible. High and low alike carry it to the temple on the weekly day, returning home after hearing sermons and carrying out their worship. Parents teach their children to worship at the temple and study the scriptures, masters preach the same to their servants, and innkeepers urge it on travelers as well. From the moment they leave the womb as infants, they absorb [Christianity] into their blood

---

[7]An invocation of the name of the Amida Buddha so that one can enter the Western Paradise after death.

along with their mother's milk, and they are enveloped in its teachings until they depart from this world. They contribute money for the translation of the scriptures so that it will be easy to read. . . . There are children's churches, and even innocent babes obey the rules [of Christianity]. Wherever there is a village, there is a temple, and wherever people gather, there is a congregation. Even though the level of discourse is not elevated, they are fervent in the pursuit [of their religion], and even if its teachings are bizarre, they are earnest in their beliefs. They cling to their faith, never losing it even if they must brave flood and fire, walk upon unsheathed swords, and endure distress and sorrow. Even what must yield in discussion will not wrest their spirit. In other words, for all that one may mock them, . . . [the religion] has entered their bones from childhood. . . . What we should respect in a religion is not its argument but its practice. . . .

If we ask what lies at the core of the "moral philosophy" recently advocated by scholars in Europe, it is nothing more or less than a borrowing from Christianity. [Christianity] enhances the moral conduct of the Western people, and it smooths their public manners. If [the West] were to abandon this religion without replacing it, it would be the same as if we in the Orient were to cast aside the Way and our governing laws without replacing them.

In recent years the Westerners have translated Confucian texts and studied them exhaustively, and they have found Confucius to be a person of great sincerity and good deeds. By clarifying the good, Confucianism has much in common with Christianity that other religions cannot match. Perhaps one can say that [Confucianism] is "moral philosophy." Although it differs in its thrust from religion, it is of great advantage to the propagation of morals in a country. In the Orient, however, people have abandoned what Confucianism teaches, and they look enviously at teachings that produce good deeds in other countries. . . . In their minds, examining religious teachings is like buying goods in a store; they ask what the advantage is.

With great zeal, the Westerners send us their religious teachings. The most successful has been Greek Catholicism, which is observed in the barbarous lands of Russia, Turkey, and Greece but ignored by civilized countries; then comes Roman Catholicism, especially the Jesuit sect, which Bismarck recently expelled from Germany.[8] However, Protestantism, which is regarded as the true religion in the civilized countries,

---

[8]During the 1870s the chancellor of the German Empire, Otto von Bismarck, waged a "culture war" (Kulturkampf) against the Roman Catholic Church.

is practiced the least in Japan. Ah! What we throw away, [the Western-ers] pick up and polish, while we pounce on what they cast aside! Decades from now, the essence of the Orient will have fled to the West while all the muck from the West will pile up in the Orient. Are not learned men already concerned about this?

36

KUME KUNITAKE

From *Kume hakase kyūjūnen kaikoroku* (*The Memoirs of Professor Kume Kunitake*)
1934

In 1888 Kume Kunitake (see Document 35) became a professor of ancient Japanese history at Imperial University, from which he was forced to resign after writing an article that attacked Shintō, the indigenous religion, as "out-moded." Toward the end of his life, he wrote this memoir of his experiences during the Iwakura mission. In contrast to the impersonality of the official report, his reminiscences give a more intimate sense of the mission's encounter with American society. In many sections, Kume also points out the difficul-ties that the mission members had in coping with Western habits and cloth-ing, such as buttoning and unbuttoning their trousers. He also reveals the dis-comfort they experienced in their encounter with American customs.

During the era of national isolation . . . in popular lore it was thought that the "red hairs" could not bend their legs. On the basis of that fanciful view, the author of *Kaikoku heidan*[1] proposed a peculiar strategy in the event of war with the "red hairs": spreading rounded bamboo poles on the ground where the foreigners landed, then cutting them to pieces with Japanese swords after they slipped and fell and could not get up again.

Once every five years the Dutch *kapitan* stationed at Nagasaki was required to make a formal visit to the capital at Edo, passing through Saga

---

[1]A military treatise written by the Dutch Studies scholar Hayashi Shihei in 1791.

Kume Kunitake, *Kume hakase kyūjūnen kaikoroku* (Tokyo: Waseda daigaku shuppanbu, 1934) 251–55, 263–64.

[Kume's home domain] on his way there. Twice during the [1840s and 1850s], when I was a child, I watched the *kapitan* pass through. With my own eyes I saw his leather shoes sticking out of his palanquin as he stretched his legs. It was from such direct observation that came the notion that the "red hairs" could not bend their legs.

I later went to Nagasaki, where I became acquainted with the customs of the "red hairs." Although a country's customs are for the most part reflected in the way men and women deal with one another, since the only Dutch [in Nagasaki] were men, I was not able to meet any Western women. However, the wife and children of the American minister [Charles E.] Delong accompanied us on our voyage to the United States, so I was able to learn about the relations between men and women in the West and to see at close view the everyday customs within the family. I was extremely surprised at Mr. Delong's behavior. Even though he was not an excessively polite man, after seeing everything he did for his wife, we [Japanese] came to the conclusion that by nature he was infatuated with her. Someone who was knowledgeable about the West said that this was good manners for civilized gentlemen, but we all scoffed, wondering if that were really so.

The separation made between husband and wife in the Orient is a bit difficult to understand, but [in the past it was customary] among the upper classes to have separate women's chambers within the residence. While the husband dealt with affairs outside the house, the woman dealt with affairs inside. It was established form for the husband to engage in his work outside the house during the day but to return at night to the woman's chambers for quiet conjugality. This is what is meant when we refer to the separation between husband and wife. Among those of lower status for whom it was not possible to arrange separate women's chambers, it was proper etiquette among the samurai for the husband and wife to divide the living space and avoid intimacy with one another as much as possible during the day. This was also separation between men and women.

The [American] travelers who crossed the Pacific and stayed in San Francisco with us were all splendid "gentlemen," but as they walked along hotel corridors and elsewhere husbands and wives always went arm in arm, never separated from one another. At the time it was the fashion among women to wear long skirts and a device made of light iron slats, called a "corset," that puffed the woman out below the waist. When the wife walked up and down the stairs, the husband held up the hem of her skirt so that she would not trip on it; when the wife climbed into a horse carriage, the husband lifted her up by the waist, and once she was aboard, he would drape a comforter on her lap; when the wife put on her gloves, the husband would help her fingers into them; and when she wanted to sit, he would push a chair forward and seat her upon it.

When we were invited later on to banquets at the estates of wealthy persons, it was the etiquette for the lady of the house to sit at the main place, welcoming the guests as they arrived at the dinner table, while the master of the house sat at the end of the table, playing the role of chief servant. It was a world of henpecked husbands where everything was topsy-turvy. At government buildings and at military barracks, men and women walked about arm in arm, and the young ladies who accompanied us on a boat trip through San Francisco harbor acted as though they were training themselves in the etiquette of this world of henpecked husbands. It spoiled our pleasure to see them walking about prattling relentlessly and inconsiderately, calling out to the men in shameless flirtation, their faces proud with delight at the beauty of their voices and charming accents, and pronouncing their likes and dislikes or finding fault in the smallest matters.

We thought to ourselves that these women acted in this vulgar way because San Francisco was a gathering place of outlaws or renegades who had come in pursuit of gold and silver and copper, and that such things would not happen in the civilized region on the East Coast. So we restrained ourselves in making judgments about the actual state of customs and morals in the West. Then we arrived in Washington. This was not a city of commerce but a place where officials, military men, and great merchants gathered, so we expected to see the customs and manners of a genteel civilization. But at a great reception to which we invited more than a thousand high officials and men of wealth on February 6 [1872], as the members of the mission stood in the receiving line, the guests arrived proudly in a fashion not at all different from what we had seen in San Francisco, with husbands as usual hand-in-hand with their wives or arm-in-arm with their daughters. When the buffet began, the men shoved through the crowd taking plates of food and glasses of wine for their wives and daughters while the women remained firmly in their chairs, giving orders and having the men bring what they liked. To our eyes the sight of the young men dancing in the embrace of women after the music began was extremely indecent, but we recognized that it was their uxorious custom.

Those very familiar with the West tried to justify [this behavior] by saying that under the barbarian customs of ancient times, men used their physical strength to abuse women cruelly but that Christianity brought a change of heart and established this beautiful new custom. But that is quite doubtful. It is recorded in ancient Chinese works written before the birth of Christ that men of the red-haired, blue-eyed white race worshiped women and followed their words blindly. They were of a character weak in self-control, and it was their unseemly custom to give full expression to their lust and emotion. When we departed for Europe from the docks at Boston, the spectacle of three married couples embracing was the most extreme shamelessness that we had encountered so far. We had felt respect for New England as the cradle of American culture and learning, but we sailed away from the continent into the Atlantic feeling distaste for its unseemly and disgraceful customs.

When he saw that Americans were kind toward their wives but cold toward their parents, Kido [Takayoshi], who was a paragon of filial piety, complained about them at the dinner table, fulminating that "civilization"[2] would bring about the destruction of the great Way.

"Since America is a republic it is inevitable that they do not understand the Way of Loyalty," he said, "but it is terrible that they treat their parents so badly."

"But the Americans are just as affectionate toward their parents as we are," said another person at the table. "There is a fine story of a child's noble deed in yesterday's newspaper. A father who had succumbed to drink went bankrupt and sent all his children to work as servants. One of them, who was perseverant and managed to save some money, prospered greatly running a hotel, and when his down-on-his-heels father appeared at the hotel the son greeted him warmly, put him in a first-class room on the second floor, and provided him with the best in everything else too. For three days he treated the father with great kindness, letting him stay without charge and giving him a small allowance when he left. The newspaper applauded and praised the son's behavior. Judging from that it seems that the Americans practice filial piety too."

"It won't do to equate free food and drink with filial piety," Kido replied with a frown.

"But considered from the legalistic viewpoint of a person who has fallen into the life of a petty man who works with his hands," I said, turning to Kido, "isn't it a principle of filial piety to provide free food and drink?"

Sometime later, on the way back from a visit with an elderly American gentleman of great erudition, Kido said to me, "At the start the elderly scholar I visited today proposed 'The person you love most of all in your family is your wife, is it not?' But I replied 'No, it is my parents rather than my wife.' Then he suggested, 'Of course, parents and children are doubtless close to one another, but that cannot compare with the love between husband and wife. But to make a long story short, when you eventually

[2]For example, the exposure of Japan to Western customs.

return to your country after visiting Europe, won't it be your wife that you first tell of your safe arrival?' Once again I said, 'No. In Japan no matter how fond we are of our wives, etiquette requires that first we inquire about the health of our parents and pay our respects to them, and only after that do we talk to our wives.' There was a strange expression on the scholar's face, as if he were greatly surprised, but after thinking a bit more he muttered, 'In a country with teachings like that people are probably lazy and don't work.' He seemed to be worried that parents might fall into the bad habit of depending on their children and not working for a living."

"To judge from my conversation with this venerable scholar today," said Kido with a sigh, "the Way of Loyalty and Filial Piety will be in peril as civilization advances."

37

An American Report on the Iwakura Mission
1872

While the Iwakura mission attracted less public attention than the first bakufu mission more than a decade earlier, the American public continued to be curious about the visitors from Japan. While press reports often commented on the incongruity of their dress or speech, they also made positive comments on their courteous behavior, their persistent curiosity, and their eagerness to learn.

The Japanese Embassy

GOSSIP ABOUT THE YOUNG LADIES
ACCOMPANYING THEM — IMPRESSIONS
MADE BY THE MEN. FROM THE SAN FRANCISCO
BULLETIN, JAN. 22.

THE MEMBERS OF THE EMBASSY

The Japanese have worn well. Those of our citizens who have unwittingly confounded them with the Chinese have not only been corrected and thoroughly enlightened on the subject, but they have received impressions which will be lasting and probably beneficial to all parties con-

New York Times, February 20, 1872.

cerned. When the steamer *America* arrived here, and the writer scrutinized the visitors, while admiring their manly, independent bearing, he shared in the amusement caused by the peculiar style of clothing worn by some members of the Embassy. The Japanese, apparently unsuspicious of the mirth they created, promenaded around with supreme indifference, yet they quickly noted the unfashionable cut of their garb, and made alterations and amendments without any suggestions. No one had to prompt them on this score. When the Japanese occupied quarters in the hotels, they set about learning the minutiæ of these caravansaries, questioning everybody with whom they came in contact as to rules, regulations and general details. Those who were unfamiliar with the English language managed to make their object known by the cosmopolitan sign language of expression and gesticulation which often answers as well as words. Self-reliance seemed to be a feature of their character, a self-reliance which never rejected advice nor countenanced discourtesy. Without being imprudent or obtrusive, they were cool and self-possessed and accepted statements *cum grano salis.*[1] The majority of the Embassy having theoretical knowledge of the English language, comprehended what was said to them, although often unable to return an answer. At first, the report was circulated that only two members of the Embassy could speak or understand English, and the report was believed. Now it appears that seven of the gentlemen speak English, write English and comprehend English, and before the Embassy leaves the city the number may be increased to ten or twelve. The Japanese can instruct the Americans in etiquette. They bow gracefully, courteously, and, without any apparent effort, treat all men with the respect due from one gentleman to another. Their behavior in private parlors, at public receptions, and upon the streets, has been commendatory to an eminent degree; and when the time for our visitors to depart is reached, there cannot fail to be a general feeling of regret among the citizens.

[1]"with a grain of salt" (Latin).

8
America as "Civilization"

38

FUKUZAWA YUKICHI

From *Seiyō jijō (Conditions in the West)*
1867

During his travels to the United States and Europe in the 1860s, Fukuzawa Yukichi (see Document 31) collected a large library of books on all aspects of Western culture and society, which he used in the writing of Seiyō jijō *(Conditions in the West), a readable three-volume introduction to Western customs, history, geography, and institutions that became an immediate best-seller. The first volume sold more than 150,000 copies. Even officials in the new imperial government used it as a basic handbook about the West. The frontispiece of this volume introduces the reader to the "five races of the world." "George Washington, already a well-known figure in Japan, represents the white race, and the other four figures, dressed in 'native' costume, represent the red, yellow, brown, and black races. The caption, however, reads: 'Within the four seas, the five races are brothers.' " (For more details on Fukuzawa's views of civilization, see Document 39.)*

Fukuzawa Yukichi zenshū, Vol. 1 (Tokyo: Iwanami shoten, 1958), 278.

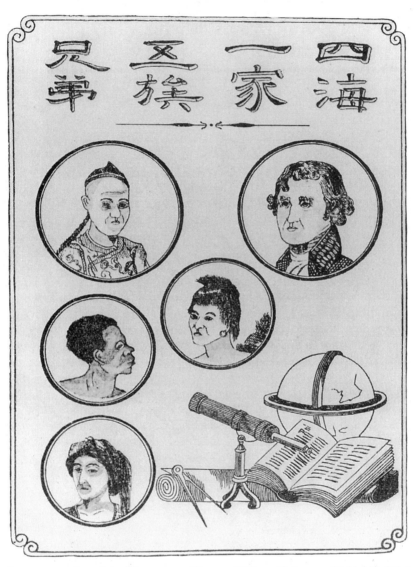

A representation of the "five races of the world" from Fukuzawa Yukichi's *Seiyō jijō (Conditions in the West)*.

39

FUKUZAWA YUKICHI

From *Bunmei no gairyaku*
(An Outline of a Theory of Civilization)
1875

Established as the country's leading authority on the West, Fukuzawa Yukichi (see Documents 31 and 38) founded Keiō Academy (later Keiō University) to train young men in the "new knowledge" of the West. He also published numerous works, including Bunmei no gairyaku (An Outline of a Theory of Civilization), *aimed at deepening public understanding of what "civilization" meant. As this excerpt makes clear, Fukuzawa believed that Japan could acquire national wealth and strength only if it understood and assimilated the basic principles of "civilization," but he was by no means an uncritical observer of Western culture.*

. . . I argued that such designations as light and heavy and good and bad are relative. Now, the concept 'civilization and enlightenment' *(bummei kaika)* is also a relative one. When we are talking about civilization in the world today, the nations of Europe and the United States of America are the most highly civilized, while the Asian countries, such as Turkey, China, and Japan, may be called semi-developed countries, and Africa and Australia are to be counted as still primitive lands. These designations are common currency all over the world. While the citizens of the nations of the West are the only ones to boast of civilization, the citizens of the semi-developed and primitive lands submit to being designated as such. They rest content with being branded semi-developed or primitive, and there is not one who would take pride in his own country or consider it on a par with nations of the West. This attitude is bad enough. What is worse, though, those with some intelligence start to realize, the more they find out what is happening, the true condition of their native lands; the more they come to realize this, the more they awaken to the distance separating them from the nations of the West. They groan, they grieve; some

Fukuzawa Yukichi's "An Outline of a Theory of Civilization," tr. David A. Dilworth and G. Cameron Hurst (Tokyo: Sophia University Press, 1973), 13–15.

are for learning from the West and imitating it, others are for going it alone and opposing the West. The overriding anxiety of Asian intellectuals today is this one problem to the exclusion of all others.[1] At any rate, the designations 'civilized', 'semi-developed', and 'primitive' have been universally accepted by people all over the globe. Why does everybody accept them? Clearly, because the facts are demonstrable and irrefutable. I shall explain this point further below. For there are stages through which mankind must pass. These may be termed the ages of civilization.

First, there is the stage in which neither dwellings nor supplies of food are stable. Men form communal groups as temporary convenience demands; when that convenience ceases, they pull up stakes and scatter to the four winds. Or even if they settle in a certain region and engage in farming and fishing, they may have enough food and clothing, but they do not yet know how to make tools. And though they are not without writing, they produce no literature. At this stage man is still unable to be master of his own situation; he cowers before the forces of nature and is dependent upon arbitrary human favor or accidental blessings. This is called the stage of primitive man. It is still far from civilization.

Secondly, there is the stage of civilization wherein daily necessities are not lacking, since agriculture has been started on a large scale. Men build houses, form communities, and create the outward semblance of a state. But within this facade there remain very many defects. Though literature flourishes, there are few who devote themselves to practical studies. Though in human relations sentiments of suspicion and jealousy run deep, when it comes to discussing the nature of things men lack the courage to raise doubts and ask questions. Men are adept at imitative craftsmanship, but there is a dearth of original production. They know how to cultivate the old, but not how to improve it. There are accepted rules governing human intercourse, and, slaves of custom that they are, they never alter those rules. This is called the semi-developed stage. It is not yet civilization in the full sense.

Thirdly, there is the stage in which men subsume the things of the universe within a general structure, but the structure does not bind them. Their spirits enjoy free play and do not adhere to old customs blindly. They act autonomously and do not have to depend upon the arbitrary favors of others. They cultivate their own virtue and refine their own knowledge. They neither yearn for the old nor become com-

---

[1] Even the obstinate Chinese have been sending students to the West in recent years. You can see how concerned they are about their country. [Fukuzawa's note]

placent about the new. Not resting with small gains, they plan great accomplishments for the future and commit themselves wholeheartedly to their realization. Their path of learning is not vacuous; it has, indeed, invented the principle of invention itself. Their business ventures prosper day by day to increase the sources of human welfare. Today's wisdom overflows to create the plans of tomorrow. This is what is meant by modern civilization. It has been a leap far beyond the primitive or semi-developed stages.

Now, if we make the above threefold distinction, the differences between civilization, semi-development, and the primitive stage should be clear. However, since these designations are essentially relative, there is nothing to prevent someone who has not seen civilization from thinking that semi-development is the summit of man's development. And, while civilization is civilization relative to the semi-developed stage, the latter, in its turn, can be called civilization relative to the primitive stage. Thus, for example, present-day China has to be called semi-developed in comparison with Western countries. But if we compare China with countries of South Africa, or, to take an example more at hand, if we compare the Japanese people with the Ezo, then both China and Japan can be called civilized. Moreover, although we call the nations of the West civilized, they can correctly be honored with this designation only in modern history. And many of them, if we were to be more precise, would fall well short of this designation.

For example, there is no greater calamity in the world than war, and yet the nations of the West are always at war. Robbery and murder are the worst of human crimes; but in the West there are robbers and murderers. There are those who form cliques to vie for the reins of power and who, when deprived of that power, decry the injustice of it all. Even worse, international diplomacy is really based on the art of deception. Surveying the situation as a whole, all we can say is that there is a general prevalence of good over bad, but we can hardly call the situation perfect. When, several thousand years hence, the levels of knowledge and virtue of the peoples of the world will have made great progress (to the point of becoming utopian), the present condition of the nations of the West will surely seem a pitifully primitive stage. Seen in this light, civilization is an open-ended process. We cannot be satisfied with the present level of attainment of the West.

Yes, we cannot be satisfied with the level of civilization attained by the West. But shall we therefore conclude that Japan should reject it? If we did, what other criterion would we have? We cannot rest content with the stage of semi-development; even less can the primitive stage suffice. Since these latter alternatives are to be rejected, we must look elsewhere. But to look to some far-off utopian world thousands of years hence is mere daydreaming. Besides, civilization is not a dead thing; it is something vital and moving. As such, it must pass through sequences and stages; primitive people advance to semi-developed forms, the semi-developed advance to civilization, and civilization itself is even now in the process of advancing forward. Europe also had to pass through these phases in its evolution to its present level. Hence present-day Europe can only be called the highest level that human intelligence has been able to attain at this juncture in history. Since this is true, in all countries of the world, be they primitive or semi-developed, those who are to give thought to their country's progress in civilization must necessarily take European civilization as the basis of discussion, and must weigh the pros and cons of the problem in the light of it. My own criterion throughout this book will be that of Western civilization, and it will be in terms of it that I describe something as good or bad, in terms of it that I find things beneficial or harmful. Therefore let scholars make no mistake about my orientation.

40

NISHIMURA SHIGEKI

"An Explanation of Twelve Western Words (Part I)"

1875

This article appeared in the Meiroku zasshi, *a journal published by a group of early Meiji intellectuals who wished to spread ideas from the West and encourage debate over important public issues. Nishimura Shigeki (1828–1902), the author of the article, was son of a bakufu retainer who had studied with Sakuma Shōzan in the early 1850s and then served as an advisor to the family of Hotta Masayoshi. After the Meiji Restoration*

Meiroku zasshi: Journal of Japanese Enlightenment, translated with an introduction by William Braisted assisted by Adachi Yasushi and Kikuchi Yūji (Tokyo: University of Tokyo Press, 1976), 446–49.

Nishimura continued to serve as chief administrator of his domain, but he also published many translations and introductory works on Western history, world geography, education, economics, and moral philosophy. In 1873 he was appointed to a post in the education ministry of the imperial government and eventually he became a tutor to the young Meiji emperor.

Bummei kaika is the translation of the English word "civilization." The Chinese have translated "civilization" in the sense of advancing toward propriety. Should we translate the word into our vulgar tongue, we would speak of the improvement of human character. It is said that "civilization" was originally derived from the Latin word *civis*. *Civis* conveys the sense of people living in cities. Should you inquire why a word meaning city dwellers changed to refer to the improvement of human character, it apparently was because, as compared with those in the country, city dwellers generally were more learned, more advanced in manner, and more refined in conduct.

Now to take up and analyze the word "civilization," what comes to mind is only the character of the people and mankind's social intercourse, never the wealth, ability, and power of the people. . . .

. . . In the words of the renowned English scholar [John Stuart] Mill, "civilization" is the opposite of "savagery" when one speaks from the point of view of man's conduct as an individual or from the point of view of group relations. According to the French scholar [François] Guizot, civilization in its original meaning had the sense of progress and development, and we should, therefore, speak of civilization by referring to the advance of group relations and individual human conduct together until they reach the level of perfection. When it refers to the conduct of man as an individual, civilization includes the idea of progress and development of knowledge, behavior, benevolence, brotherly love, ability, and taste. In the view of these two scholars, civilization's form appears on two paths: one is through the course of group relations, and the other through the conduct of man as an individual. To further clarify its meaning, civilization refers to the peace and happiness gained by both man as an individual and society as a whole as they gradually advanced in dignity. . . .

The concept of what is called the advanced level of human social intercourse or the elevated character of the individual must vary according to country. People in European countries assume that the conditions of social intercourse in their countries are the most civilized, and they regard as barbarians or half-civilized the peoples of other lands the roots of whose social intercourse are not the same as the European. After all, what will be the result if we look at the matter objectively? If we want to judge fairly, it is necessary to know the true meaning of the word "civilization." It may be that, in the long run, the above explanations of civilization [by Mill and Guizot] will not prove erroneous. If we assume that they, after all, convey the true meaning of civilization, then there is no doubt that the most civilized people in the world are the Europeans or those who migrated from Europe.

If you inquire into the fundamental roots of the Europeans and those who have migrated from Europe, their civilization ultimately arose from two elements. The first was the doctrine of Christianity; the second, the conditions of social intercourse in Rome at its zenith. Thereafter, with the introduction of legal systems of land registry in various countries, conditions of social intercourse advanced still another step ahead with really noteworthy results. Since the roots of social intercourse in India, China, and Arabia are entirely different from those of Europe, it is quite reasonable for the shape of their civilizations to be very different from that of the Europeans.

When one reads the history of man from furthest antiquity to the present, it seems clear that civilization has advanced step by step. Its progress, however, has not always been at the same rate. Having stopped at a given point, it may remain quite stationary or thereafter retreat. Or it may rest for a moment in order later to progress greatly. Looking at ancient history, there was invariably a conspicuous state in any given period, such as Rome, Greece, or the Frankish Empire. The level of civilization in these countries was closely related to the progress of civilization in the world. Rising one after another in this fashion, these great states during their flourishing periods always generated progress by steering the course of civilization in advance of the world. But when their time was up, their power greatly declined, and their progress gradually came to an end. If one country stopped progressing, however, another arose to become the leader of nations and to advance the course of civilization. This periodic rise and fall of states was sometimes a regional, sometimes a continental, and sometimes a world-wide phenomenon. I shall refrain here from reviewing the complex course of the rise and fall of states within each region and continent. If you review the path of rise and decline throughout the world, the areas that have advanced civilization after achieving prosperity at a particular time were Africa in ancient times, then Asia, and now, similarly, Europe. (I shall omit Japan, leaving the affairs of our country for a separate discussion.) In the future, America may come next and thereafter Australia. This is not my conjecture. I am only elaborating views drawn from the words of Western intellectuals.

41

SUGI KŌJI

The Federated States
of North and South America

1874

This essay by Sugi Kōji (1828–1917), a former bakufu retainer and government official who became member of the Meiroku zasshi *group, comments on the differences between the "civilizations" of North and South America. It echoes a view prevalent in the United States at the time—that the "Anglo-Saxon" peoples, who were more advanced in the pursuit of liberty and free institutions, had reached a higher plane of moral and political progress than their neighbors to the south. It was just such views that were deployed to justify the American annexation of Texas and other territories from Mexico in the 1840s. It is ironic that Japanese intellectuals uncritically accepted the same attitudes that had justified American intrusions on their own sovereignty.*

Although the rise and fall of nations seems to be determined by fate, their course generally depends on whether those guiding the people adopt appropriate methods. In the past, the colonies of North America revolted against England, and those of South America arose against Spain to establish their independence. Since the founding of these nations, the federated states of North America [the United States] have progressed day by day, but those of South America have successively fallen into disorder. When one asks the reason for this, it lies simply in whether governments respect the rights and liberties of the people.

As England from the outset honored the wishes of her colonists, accorded them religious freedom, and allowed them political liberty, the people already understand the principles of self-government. The colonists established their independence once the English king and his ministers resorted to oppression and lost popular support, and the subsequent stability of their country may be attributed to the fact that the people already individually understood their rights.

Meiroku zasshi: Journal of Japanese Enlightenment, translated with an introduction by William Braisted assisted by Adachi Yasushi and Kikuchi Yūji (Tokyo: University of Tokyo Press, 1976), 93–94.

Such was not the case with Spain, which denied her colonists self-government. In addition to fettering his people's minds by driving them into the Roman Church that he honored, the Spanish monarch long drew his subjects' blood with his violent tyranny. Unable to bear this oppressive rule, the people established their independence. Internal griefs again arose, however, despite the departure of external troubles. The consequent disturbances in these countries may be ascribed to the fact that they were established without a common and single purpose since the poison of oppression had penetrated their bodies deeply, their rights had suffered, and men's minds were upset. Even such wise and noble men as Bolivar and San Martín[1] were ultimately unable to unite their countries. In Mexico, for example, the form of government has been changed more than nine times, and there have been more than three hundred instances in which a party has been formed or destroyed.

After all, England was the one that encouraged luxuriant stems and branches by cultivating the roots. In the case of Spain, however, the stems and branches were weakened by failure to nourish the roots. How correct it is to state that England sowed good seeds in North America and that Spain planted bad seeds in South America!

[1]Simón Bolivar (1783–1830) and José de San Martín (1778–1850), heroes in the South American struggle for independence.

42

INOUE RYŌKICHI [?]

A Japanese Student's Views of the United States

1872

These two essays were probably written by Inoue Ryōkichi (also known as Inoue Rokusaburō) (1852–1879), a native of Fukuoka, who arrived in Boston in 1867 at the age of sixteen. After entering Worcester Military Academy with a scholarship from the new Meiji government, he decided to

The Japanese in America, ed. Charles Lanman (New York: University Publishing Company, 1872), 66–72, 82–85, 94–100.

study law under Oliver Wendell Holmes and became the first Asian to receive a degree from the Harvard Law School. Although he had nearly completely forgotten his native language when he returned to Japan in 1875, he was appointed a professor of law at the newly established national university in Tokyo. Brilliant but plagued by poor health, Inoue committed suicide at the age of twenty-six by jumping into a well. His essays reflect the ambivalence that many returned Japanese students felt about the United States.

The Practical Americans

Is it a disgrace to the Americans that they are a practical people?

Before entering into the discussion which the theme demands, let me define the position from which I am obliged to look at this delicate question. Japan, before the late revolution, was undoubtedly the most aristocratic nation in the world. As is usually the case under such circumstances, the downtrodden mass of the people strikingly manifest that characteristic which is the subject of my present essay—namely, an acquaintance only with those ways of life which relate to the supply of the actual wants and necessities of mankind. This is because, the greater portion of the nation's wealth being in the hands of the ruling class, the lower classes have to make the most of everything within their reach. I, like any other thoughtless born-aristocrat, despised this tendency of the commons. I acknowledge now that this was very unjust, but still something of this spirit will no doubt influence me in the decision of the great question now before us, and I request my kind readers constantly to bear in mind this circumstance.

The Americans, who unmistakably inherited the virtues as well as the vices of their ancestors, are a nervously energetic, enterprising people. When they threw off the British yoke, what remained was to develop the hidden resources of the country; and how well they have performed this the present prosperity of the country sufficiently attests. In the course of this stupendous undertaking they were being continually brought into contact with new difficulties, and they have always proved themselves equal to any emergency.

The world is indebted to the Americans for the steamboat, telegraph, and many other very useful inventions. It may be broadly asserted that whatever had a practical application was studied and improved by them. A glance at its educational system enables one to form some idea of the people. The cities have their business colleges, while agricultural colleges dot the face of the country. Then there are schools of engineering, architecture, medicine, and other departments of the useful arts, and these are faithfully attended to, while the general education of the youths is designed to make practical men. The fine arts, which refine, ennoble, and delight mankind, are sadly neglected. The fact is, an American does not want to be a painter, sculptor, poet, or rhetorician, but a rich man. Wealth is the sole object of ambition of the people at large. I must say now that I am entering on very serious grounds. I am not so presumptuous as to attempt to trespass on theology, but I must confess I shall go very near the frontiers of it. The Americans who point the fingers of scorn against the rest of Christendom as lukewarm in the cause of religion, and freely condemn without fair trial the rest of mankind as ignorant of the duties of man, seem to think that money-making is the most important business of life; and, taking this as a standard, I shall finish the rest of my essay accordingly. It is not possible that the Americans should be such enthusiastic champions of Christianity, and yet reject its teachings in their ordinary life.

But Christianity teaches them that their souls live after their bodies, and therefore they must better the condition of their minds by the cultivation of virtues in this world. The money-loving Americans are doing just the opposite of this. So-called business men, who constitute a large portion of "the life and the blood" of American society, seemingly have no souls, for they are exposed for sale, if not already exchanged, for hard cash. When their souls are disposed of they receive the millions of money they desire; but what is to be done with it? . . .

If money-making is the source of enjoyment to them, as drunkenness and gluttony are to some men, I have only to say that their taste is a corrupted one. It is but just to say that the riches of these men are gained by hard, patient labor; hence they are more to be pitied than condemned, for the question again returns, "What is to be done with these riches, and what have they made themselves by the operation?"

Another set of men, thinking this a rather unprofitable way of making money, adopt a system which combines both theft and perjury, and insures to those men a life of misery, which they richly deserve. I refer to those who seek fortune by a lucky marriage—an excellent mode of self-selling! A man who is so degraded as to go through a formal loving of an innocent, confiding woman for the sake of her money, shows a disposition which, if an opportunity presented, would sell country, religion, anything and everything which mankind so sacredly prizes. All these things arise from that intense love of money which is so deeply ingrafted in the hearts of the Americans. If they should pay more attention to philosophy and the fine arts, they would be far more intellectual as a people; but as long as they are admirers of wealth, no matter how gained, they are merely practical and inconsistent people. Inconsistent, because priding themselves on their republican simplicity, they are the most willing slaves of fashion; or pretending to be true republicans, they are never so happy as when they have an opportunity of paying respect to a prince or a duke. Where is the trouble? The answer is plain. They are too practical.

When Franklin, than whom there cannot be a more practical American, with all the simplicity of Cincinnatus[1] presented himself before the court of Versailles, even the ultra-royalists could not withhold the veneration due the man for true dignity, and he commanded the respect of even the bitterest enemies. Compared with this glorious spectacle, the idea of the Americans of the present day, with much money, trying to imitate the manners of other countries whose teachers they might well become, and making bad blunders, is really disgraceful. In their eagerness to educate all the young persons to be practical, they almost neglect their moral training. Man is both an intellectual and moral being. He must be so educated as to develop both these capacities. If his intellect is trained more than his moral nature, he will be a dangerous man, for his power for evil is increased beyond measure.

In this connection I may again observe a strange inconsistency of the Americans. Though they thus neglect their moral training at home, they send missionaries to teach the wretched heathen to be good, and at the same time send a company of practical men who show their practicability by extracting the riches in every way, and when they could, by cheating those men whom their fellow-countrymen undertake to teach — to be what?—to be good!

So I might go on, but I think I have said enough to make you acknowledge, at least to yourself, that it is a disgrace to the Americans that they are a practical people.

The Strength and the Weakness of Republics

The republican form of government is now generally conceded to be "theoretically the best," but its claim to be also the strongest is still disputed, or at least not yet firmly established. The Declaration of Independence by the American Colonies, the French Revolution, and vari-

---

[1]Lucius Quinctius Cincinnatus (b. 519 B.C.), a general who, according to legend, led Romans to victory over the Aequi in a single day, then returned to his work as a farmer.

ous important subsequent events, until the present time, all unite in proclaiming to the nations of the world the right of a people to govern itself, and by so doing demonstrated clearly the absurdity of the divine rights of the kings to rule.

The whole political heaven is, as it were, being charged with republican electricity. The explosion will come sooner or later. Meanwhile, the diffusion of intelligence among the people makes them more enlightened and more jealous of their rights than ever before; despots tremble on their thrones, and as they make concessions most reluctantly, most readily do the people call for more. Judging from such circumstances, it would appear that all the nations of the world, as if by common consent, are converging rapidly toward that point where Republicanism reigns supreme.

It is then a matter of the utmost importance to us to endeavor to discover in what lie the strength and the weakness of republics.

In a republic, every citizen is interested in any measure before the government, and it would be safe to set this down as one of the great elements of strength.

The government is influenced, to a great extent, not by the opinions of a king, or, what is worse, those of a few ambitious politicians, but by the mighty voice of an almost infallible people. It is evident that the government thus situated will be more faithful in the execution of its duties than in monarchical countries, where the character of the government depends a good deal on the disposition of the sovereign. Another strong point in a republic, is the bicameral feature of its government. One body acts as a check on another, and, if their characters are different, for instance, the first radical, and the second conservative, the course of legislation will be neither too progressive, with which the people cannot keep pace, nor so conservative as to interfere with the enterprises of the country. The right to struggle for fame, for learning, and wealth, is the grandest heritage of humanity, and this right is most scrupulously respected in almost all the republican countries of the present day; hence, the poorest and humblest can have fair play to become superior in position to any other.

This state of things keeps the people ever in activity.

. . . If we go back a few years in the history of the world, we shall find the true strength of republicanism displayed in the American [Revolutionary] war. We do not purpose to look at that memorable contest in all its bearings, but will content ourselves with an observation illustrating one of the secrets of the success of the Americans. Every historian has dwelt with enthusiasm on the retreat of Washington through New Jersey with a few thousand of the barefooted and famishing soldiers. Was it the devotion to their illustrious commander which enabled those brave men to encounter so cheerfully the manifold dangers of that disastrous campaign?

No, noble Washington did much, but the real strength of the army lay in the fact that every soldier was also a citizen, imbued with a hatred of the tyrant, and conscious of fighting in the cause of freedom and humanity.

When we see so much dignity in common soldiers, we shall not be dazzled by the sublime spectacle of the Revolutionary Congress defying the power of the strongest nation in the world, often fleeing before the victorious foe, yet firm and unyielding, and, at last, after a long struggle, giving the country a glorious peace, and placing her by the side of the proudest nations of the world!

Thus far, we have looked at the strong sides of the republic. Now we shall investigate some of the causes of its weakness. "When you assemble a number of men to have the advantage of their joint wisdom, you inevitably assemble with those men all their prejudices, their passions, their errors of opinion, their local interests and selfish views." The history of every republic too clearly illustrates the above remarks of Franklin. Grant that all the legislators chosen are conscientious men; they determine to be true to their sacred trust. But alas! they do not, nay, cannot, agree as to the best method of promoting the interests of their constituents, for nothing is dearer to a man than his theory; and especially is this true of such upright men as we suppose them to be. And then, a particular member, in pleading the cause of his constituents, may badly interfere with carrying out of a measure which will be beneficial to the whole people as a nation. It may be contended that the majority will rule; but, if our supposed member happen to be also an influential man, he may so exert his powers as to cause the very majority to enter into his views.

. . . It will be admitted that the officers of a republic are not always the best and ablest men of the land, but that they sometimes are the most cunning, perhaps the most unprincipled.

By the most unprincipled, we refer to that class of politicians called demagogues. These persons rarely succeed in securing the confidence of the respectable portion of the people, and when they do so, they cannot retain it long.

To the mere outsiders, they would seem to be wholly incapable of doing any serious injury to the state. But when we study the effect of their proceedings, we shall be very likely to change our opinion. Too often have the glories of the state been tarnished by the disgraceful conduct of these men, too often their impudence, vulgarity, and reck-lessness have so prevented an enlightened statesman from carrying out his plans, that they deserve to be set down as at once worse than traitors. . . .

. . . In a republic, a constant change of officers exerts a very baneful influence, and is the cause of bitter political and party strife. Thus there can be no stability in the government. And the stability, it must be remembered, is an important element of the strength.

Beholding a republic with her weakness and strength before us, and a monarchy with hers in the same position, we shall fear the latter as our enemy, for she is strong, but the former we shall love as we love the truth; we shall encourage as we would an inexperienced youth, for her strength is not yet as fully developed as that of her elder sister, monarchy!

43

WILLIAM ELLIOT GRIFFIS

From *The Mikado's Empire*

1876

William Elliot Griffis (1843–1928), who tutored several Japanese students (including two nephews of Yokoi Shōnan) while attending Rutgers University, wrote voluminously on Japan. In 1870 he was invited to teach science and mathematics in Fukui domain, once led by the reformist daimyo Mat-sudaira Yoshinaga. When the domains were abolished in 1871, Griffis departed for Tokyo, where he became a teacher at a new government school. After returning to the United States in 1874, he wrote The Mikado's Empire *(1876), a general history of Japan, which ended with his personal experi-ences and observations of the country in the early 1870s. Published in a dozen editions, the book was perhaps the most influential single work on Japan in the last quarter of the nineteenth century. The following excerpts reflect Griffis's firm assurance that Japan would soon take its place among the "civ-ilized" nations of the world.*

William Elliot Griffis, *The Mikado's Empire,* 2 vols., 12th ed. (New York: Harper and Broth-ers, 1912), 322–24, 572–74, 576–78.

In its prime object the [Iwakura] embassy was a magnificent failure. Beyond amusement, curiosity, thirst for knowledge, its purpose was constant, single, supreme. It was to ask that in the revision of the treaties the extra-territoriality clause[1] be stricken out, that foreigners be made subject to the laws of Japan. The failure of the mission was predicted by all who knew the facts. From Washington to St. Petersburg, point-blank refusal was made. No Christian governments would for a moment trust their people to pagan edicts and prisons. While Japan slandered Christianity by proclamations, imprisoned men for their belief, knew nothing of trial by jury, of the habeas-corpus writ, or of modern jurisprudence; in short, while Japan maintained the institutions of barbarism, they refused to recognize her as peer in the comity of nations.

Meanwhile, at home the watch-word was progress. The sale of orphan female children to brothel-keepers, the traffic in native or European obscene pictures, the lascivious dances, even to nudity, of the singing-girls, the custom of promiscuous bathing in the public baths, and of the country coolies going naked or nearly without clothing, were abolished. Public decency was improved, and the standards of Christendom attempted. The law entered that the offense might abound. Many things absolutely innocent became at once relatively sinful. It was an earnest effort to elevate the social condition. With a basis of education and moral training in the minds of the people to underlie the Government edicts, complete success may be hoped for; but even in the mikado's empire the moral character of a people is not made or unmade by fiat. Marvelous progress has, however, been made. The slanderous anti-Christian [notice boards] were also taken down, and the last relic of public persecution for conscience' sake removed. . . . In this year (1872) I made a tour of one month, over nine hundred miles, to Shidzŭöka, Kiōto, Fukui [Shizuoka, Kyōto, Fukui] and along the Sea of Japan, to near Niigata, thence through Shinano and Kodzuké [Kozuke]. I went to spy out the land and see how deeply civilization had penetrated. A week's journey was also made through Kadzusa [Kazusa] and Awa, another in Shimōsa and Hitachi, and three separate trips for purposes of research in Sagami, Idzu [Izu], and Suruga. My intense enjoyment of the classic ground was shadowed by the vivid realization of the poverty of the country, the low estate of the peasantry, the need of something better than paganism, and the vastness of the task of regenerating an agricultural nation. The task, though great, is not hopeless. I was pleased to find education thoroughly extended, schools

[1]A clause exempting foreigners from Japanese law.

everywhere, and boys and girls alike studying with the help of such new improvements as slate and pencil, blackboard and chalk, charts and text-books on geography, history, reading, etc., translated from standard American school-books.

The objects of the revolution of 1868 have been accomplished. The shōgunate and the feudal system are forever no more. The mikado is now the restored and beloved emperor. The present personage, a young man of twenty-four years of age, has already shown great independence and firmness of character, and may in future become as much the real ruler of his people as the Czar is of his. The enterprise of establishing Shintō as the national faith has failed vastly and ignominiously, though the old Shintō temples have been purged and many new ones erected, while official patronage and influence give the ancient cult a fair outward show. Buddhism is still the religion of the Japanese people, though doubtless on the wane.

A mighty task awaited the new Government after the revolution of 1868. It was to heal the disease of ages; to uproot feudalism and sectionalism, with all their abuses; to give Japan a new nationality; to change her social system; to infuse new blood into her veins; to make a hermit nation, half blinded by a sudden influx of light, competitor with the wealthy, powerful, and aggressive nations of Christendom. It was a problem of national regeneration or ruin. It seemed like entering into history a second time, to be born again.

What transcendent abilities needed for such a task! What national union, harmony in council, unselfish patriotism required! . . . At home were the stolidly conservative peasantry, backed by ignorance, superstition, priestcraft, and political hostility. On their own soil they were fronted by aggressive foreigners, who studied all Japanese questions through the spectacles of dollars and cents and trade, and whose diplomatists too often made the principles of Shylock[2] their system. Outside, the Asiatic nations beheld with contempt, jealousy, and alarm the departure of one of their number from Turanian ideas, principles, and civilization. China, with ill-concealed anger, [K]orea with open defiance, taunted Japan with servile submission to the "foreign devils."

For the first time, the nation was represented to the world by an embassy at once august and plenipotentiary. It was not a squad of petty officials or local nobles going forth to kiss a toe, to play the part of

---

[2]Unprincipled moneylender from Shakespeare's *The Merchant of Venice.*

figure-heads or stool-pigeons, to beg the aliens to get out of Japan, to keep the scales on foreign eyes, to buy gun-boats, or to hire employés. A noble of highest rank and blood of immemorial antiquity, vicar of majesty and national government, with four cabinet ministers, set out to visit the courts of the fifteen nations having treaties with Dai Nippon [Japan]. . . . They arrived in Washington, February 29th, 1872, and, for the first time in history, a letter signed by the mikado was seen outside of Asia. It was presented by the ambassadors, robed in their ancient Yamato costume, to the President of the United States. . . . The one hundred and twenty-third sovereign of an empire in its twenty-sixth centennial saluted the citizen-ruler of a nation whose century had not yet bloomed. On the 6th of March they were welcomed on the floor of Congress. This day marked the formal entrance of Japan upon the theatre of universal history.

Let us now award to every nation due honor. The Portuguese discovered Japan, and gave her slave-traders and the Jesuits; the Spaniards sent friars, slavers, and conspirators; the Dutch ignobly kept alive our knowledge of Japan during her hermit life; the Russians, after noble and base failures to open the country, harried her shores. Then came Perry, the moral grandeur of whose peaceful triumph has never been challenged or compromised. The United States introduced Japan to the world, though her opening could not have been long delayed. The American, Townsend Harris, peer and successor to Perry, by his dauntless courage, patience, courtesy, gentleness, firmness, and incorruptible honesty, won for all nations treaties, trade, residence, and commerce. . . . It is but fair to note that Americans have, in certain emergencies, derived no small advantage from the expensive show of English and French force in the seas of China and Japan, and from the literary fruits of the unrivaled British Civil Service.

Let us note what Americans have done. Our missionaries, a noble body of cultured gentlemen and ladies, with but few exceptions, have translated large portions of the Bible in a scholarly and simple version, and thus given to Japan the sum of religious knowledge and the mightiest moral force and motor of civilization. . . . The first grammar of the Japanese language printed in English, the beginnings of a Christian popular literature and hymnology, the organization of Christian churches, the introduction of theological seminaries, and of girls' schools, are the work of American ladies and gentlemen. The first regular teachers in their schools, and probably half their staff in their colleges, are Americans. In the grand work of agricultural and mineral development, in the healing art, and in jurisprudence, education, and financiering, Americans have done valuable service.

Can an Asiatic despotism, based on paganism, and propped on a fiction, regenerate itself? Can Japan go on in the race she has begun? Will the mighty reforms now attempted be completed and made permanent? Can a nation appropriate the fruits of Christian civilization without its root? I believe not. I cannot but think that unless the modern enlightened ideas of government, law, society, and the rights of the individual be adopted to a far greater extent than they have been, the people be thoroughly educated, and a mightier spiritual force replace Shintō and Buddhism, little will be gained but a glittering veneer of material civilization and the corroding foreign vices, under which, in the presence of the superior aggressive nations of the West, Dai Nippon must fall like the doomed races of America.

A new sun is rising on Japan. In 1870 there were not ten Protestant Christians in the empire. There are now (May, 1876) ten churches, with a membership of eight hundred souls. Gently, but resistlessly, Christianity is leavening the nation. . . . With those forces that centre in pure Christianity, and under that Almighty Providence who raises up one nation and casts down another, I cherish the firm hope that Japan will in time take and hold her equal place among the foremost nations of the world, and that, in the onward march of civilization which follows the sun, the Sun-land may lead the nations of Asia that are now appearing in the theatre of universal history.

Glossary

Here are definitions of some key terms that you will encounter in the introduction and documents.

bakufu   Government of the shogun; shogunate

bateren   Catholic priests

Buddhism   Major organized religion in Tokugawa Japan; originated in India

Confucianism   Dominant system of social, political, and ethical thought in Tokugawa Japan; originated in China

daimyo   Local or regional territorial lord(s); governed majority of population

Edo   Shogun's capital in eastern Japan; the site of the bakufu; now called Tokyo

emperor   Semidivine monarch living in Kyōto; exercised no real power before 1868 but appointed shogun

Ezo   Northernmost island; now called Hokkaidō

Kyōto   Emperor's capital in central Honshū

Meiji Restoration   Revolution that overthrew the Tokugawa dynasty in 1868 and established a new imperial government

mikado   Emperor

Nagasaki   Main port for foreign trade under the Tokugawa; located in western Kyūshū

Ōsaka   Major commercial city in central Honshū

samurai   Warrior class; dominant political and social elite in Tokugawa Japan

shogun   De facto ruler or monarch; appointed by emperor; suzerain for the daimyo

Tokugawa   Dynasty of shoguns, 1600–1868

tycoon   Shogun

Way A teaching or doctrine, such as the "Way of the Sages" (i.e., Confucianism)

Yokohama Treaty port south of Edo

A note on name order: In Japan, surnames come first, personal names second. In this book Japanese people are usually referred to by surname. Occasionally, however, famous persons are referred to by their personal names (e.g., Manjirō for Nakahama Manjirō) as Western artists like Michaelangelo are.

Chronology of Japan's Relations with the West

THE DEVELOPMENT OF NATIONAL ISOLATION

1542 The Portuguese arrive in Japan.

1549–51 St. Francis Xavier establishes the Jesuit mission in Japan.

1571 Nagasaki becomes the main port for trade with the Portuguese.

1592 Spanish Franciscan missionaries arrive in Japan.

1597 European missionaries and Japanese converts are first persecuted.

1602 Spanish trading vessels arrive in Japan.

1603 Emperor appoints Tokugawa Ieyasu as shogun.

1609 The Dutch establish a trading post at Hirado.

1614 The bakufu persecution of Christians begins.

1624 Spanish vessels are denied entry into Japan.

1633–39 The bakufu issues decrees banning travel or residence abroad, prohibiting construction of oceangoing vessels, and restricting foreign trade to Nagasaki.

1637–38 The Shimabara rebellion occurs in Kyūshū.

1639 The Portuguese are denied entry into Japan.

1641 The Dutch are restricted to Deshima trading post at Nagasaki.

1720 The bakufu relaxes ban on the importation of Western books.

NEW WESTERN INTRUSIONS

1792 Adam Erikovich Laxman, a Russian envoy, visits Ezo with a request to open trade.
The bakufu orders the strengthening of coastal defenses.

1797 First American trading ship arrives in Japan.

1803 An American ship arrives in Nagasaki demanding trade.

1804 Nikolai Rezanov, a Russian envoy, arrives in Nagasaki with a proposal to open trade.

1806   The bakufu orders that foreign ships in distress be given provisions, then sent on their way.

1808   An English frigate, the *Phaeton,* enters Nagasaki demanding provisions.

1811   Vasilii Golovnin, a Russian explorer, is captured while while exploring the Kurile Islands.
The bakufu establishes an office to translate Western scientific books, encyclopedias, and other works.

1825   The bakufu issues a "no second thoughts" edict requiring the forcible expulsion of foreign ships.

1829   Tokugawa Nariaki begins a reform program in his domain of Mito.

1833–37   Bad harvests lead to widespread famine and peasant uprisings.

1837   The *Morrison* enters Edo Bay in an attempt to repatriate Japanese castaways.

1839   Opium War breaks out.

1842   Ch'ing government is defeated by the British; signing of the Treaty of Nanking opens new ports in China; the bakufu rescinds "no second thoughts" edict.

1844   The Treaty of Wanghsia gives the United States rights to trade in the new ports in China.

THE AMERICANS AND THE "OPENING" OF JAPAN

1844   The Dutch king urges the shogun to open Japan.

1846   Commodore James Biddle attempts to open treaty negotiations at Uraga.

1846–48   War fought between Mexico and the United States.

1848   Gold is discovered in California (January).
Mexico cedes California to the United States (February).

1849   Commander James Glynn attempts to open treaty negotiations at Nagasaki.

1853   Perry Expedition makes first visit to Japan (July).
The bakufu solicits the opinions of daimyo on the American request for a treaty (August).
A Russian expedition under Admiral Putiatin arrives in Nagasaki demanding treaty negotiations (December).

1854   Perry Expedition makes second visit (February–March).
The bakufu and the United States sign a Treaty of Peace and Amity (March).

1855   The Russians obtain a treaty with the bakufu.

1856   Townsend Harris, the first American consul, arrives in the port of Shimoda.

1857   The bakufu signs new treaties with the Dutch and the the Russians.

1858   Townsend Harris successfully negotiates a draft trade treaty with the bakufu (February).
The imperial court resists the ratification of the Harris treaty (February–April).
The bakufu ratifies the Harris treaty (July).
The Dutch, Russians, and British obtain a treaty similar to the Harris treaty (July); so does France (September).

THE END OF NATIONAL ISOLATION

1859   Ports are opened to foreign trade and foreign residence at Yokohama, Nagasaki, and Hakodate (June); foreign diplomats take up residence in Edo.

1860   The bakufu sends its first diplomatic mission to the United States.

1860–64   An antiforeign movement gains strength among the samurai class; its adherents attack foreigners in the treaty ports; the British legation in Edo is attacked and Western ships are bombarded by the domain of Chōshū.

1867   The last Tokugawa shogun resigns from office.

1868   A new imperial government under the Meiji emperor is established (January).
Imperial government military forces crush resistance.

1871   The old system of feudal domains is abolished.

1871–73   The Iwakura mission travels in the United States and Europe (November 1871–September 1873).

1873   Bans on Christianity are loosened in Japan.

1874   Publication of *Meiroku zasshi* begins.

1876   The Japanese participate in the Centennial Exposition at Philadelphia.

1879   Former President Ulysses S. Grant visits Japan and meets the Meiji emperor.

Selected Bibliography

The reference work with the best coverage of nineteenth-century Japanese history is Marius B. Jansen (ed.), *The Cambridge History of Japan, Vol. 5, The Nineteenth Century* (Cambridge: Cambridge University Press, 1989). More detailed treatment of particular historical actors, terms, or incidents can be found in the *Kodansha Encyclopedia of Japan,* 9 vols. (Tokyo: Kodansha International, 1983).

Sir George B. Sansom, *The Western World and Japan* (Alfred A. Knopf, 1950) provides a good general background on Japan's relations with the outside world from the earliest contacts through the nineteenth century. For more recent interpretations, particularly of Japan's relations with its Asian neighbors, see Ronald P. Toby, *State and Diplomacy in Early Modern Japan: Asia in the Development of the Tokugawa Bakufu* (Princeton, N.J.: Princeton University Press, 1984) and Kazui Tashiro, "Foreign Relations during the Edo Period: *Sakoku* Re-examined," *Journal of Japanese Studies* 8 (Summer 1982). The standard account of the Dutch experience in Nagasaki is C. R. Boxer, *Jan Compagnie in Japan, 1600–1850* (The Hague: Martinus Nijhoff, 1950.)

The two countries most interested in "opening" Japan in the early nineteenth century were England and Russia. For a survey of British relations with Japan during this period, see William G. Beasley, *Great Britain and the Opening of Japan, 1834–1858* (London: Luzac, 1951) and Grace Fox, *Britain and Japan 1858–1883* (Oxford: Clarendon Press, 1969). The most comprehensive treatment of the Russian probes into Japan is George Alexander Lensen, *The Russian Push toward Japan: Russo-Japanese Relations, 1697–1875* (Princeton, N.J.: Princeton University Press, 1959).

The following books offer general surveys of relations between Japan and the United States during the nineteenth century: Payson J. Treat, *The Early Diplomatic Relations between the United States and Japan, 1853–1868* (Baltimore: Johns Hopkins University Press, 1917); Tyler Dennett, *Americans in East Asia* (New York: Macmillan Company, 1922); T. Wada, *American Foreign Policy toward Japan during the Nineteenth Century* (Tokyo: Tōyō bunko, 1928); William L. Neumann, *America Encounters Japan: From Perry to MacArthur* (Baltimore: Johns Hopkins University Press, 1963); Foster Rhea Dulles, *Yankees and Samurai* (New York: Harper and Row, 1965); and

210

Charles E. Neu, *The Troubled Encounter: The United States and Japan* (New York: John Wiley and Sons, 1975). On cultural relations, Robert Schwantes has written a useful survey: *Japanese and Americans: A Century of Cultural Relations* (New York: Institute of Pacific Relations, 1955).

A general account of the Japanese castaways is to be found in Katherine Plummer, *The Shogun's Reluctant Ambassadors* (Tokyo: Lotus Press, 1967). The most interesting personal account is Hamada Hikozō's autobiography: Joseph Heco, *The Narrative of a Japanese* (Yokohama: Yokohama Printing and Publishing, 1895). There are several biographies of Nakahama Manjirō, including Hisakazu Kaneko, *Manjirō: The Man Who Discovered America* (New York: Houghton Mifflin, 1956). On the American side, an interesting tale of an American adventurer, the son of a Hudson's Bay Company official and a Native American mother, who deliberately went to Japan as a castaway in 1848, can be found in William S. Lewis and Naojiro Murakami, *Ranald Mac-Donald* (Spokane: Eastern Washington Historical Society, 1923).

The emergence of Dutch Studies in the eighteenth century is covered in Grant Goodman, *The Dutch Impact on Japan* (Leiden: E. J. Brill, 1967) and Donald Keene, *The Japanese Discovery of Europe, 1720–1820* (Stanford, Calif.: Stanford University Press, 1969). Early nineteenth-century debates over how to deal with new Western intrusions are covered in Richard T. Chang, *From Prejudice to Tolerance: A Study of the Japanese Image of the West* (Tokyo: Sophia University Press, 1970), Harry D. Harootunian, *Toward Restoration* (Berkeley: University of California Press, 1970), and Bob Tadashi Wakabayashi, *Anti-Foreign Thought and Western Learning in Early Modern Japan* (Cambridge, Mass.: Harvard University Press, 1985).

The political situation in Japan on the eve of the Perry mission is discussed succinctly by Conrad Totman, "Political Reconciliation in the Tokugawa Bakufu: Abe Masahiro and Tokugawa Nariaki, 1844–1852" in Albert Craig and Donald Shively (eds.), *Personality in Japanese History* (Berkeley: University of California Press, 1970). Totman's magisterial work *The Collapse of the Tokugawa Bakufu, 1862–1868* (Honolulu: University of Hawaii Press, 1980) traces the slow deterioration of the Tokugawa regime after the opening of the ports.

The official report of the Perry Expedition, *Narrative of the Expedition of an American Squadron to the China Seas and Japan, Performed in the Years 1852, 1853, and 1854* (Washington, D.C.: Beverly Tucker, Senate Printer, 1865), offers the most detailed description of the mission. (A one-volume commercial edition was published by D. Appleton Company the same year.) Incidents not recorded in the official narrative may be found in J. W. Spalding, *The Japan Expedition: Japan and around the World* (New York: Redfield, 1855) and Bayard Taylor, *A Visit to India, China, and Japan* (New York: G. P. Putnam and Co., 1855). Many secondary works have been written about the expedition; the most recent is Peter Booth Wiley, *Yankees in the Land of the Gods* (New York: Viking, 1990). Samuel Eliot Morison's highly readable *"Old Bruin": Commodore Matthew Calbraith*

Perry, 1794–1858 (Boston: Little, Brown, 1967) is the standard biographical work on Commodore Perry.

The private diaries and journals of many participants in the Perry expedition have been published. Commodore Perry's own journal provides his vivid personal perspective: Roger Pineau (ed.), *The Japan Expedition, 1852–1854: The Personal Journal of Commodore Matthew C. Perry* (Washington, D.C.: Smithsonian Institution, 1968). Other published journals include: S. Wells Williams, "Journal of the Perry Expedition to Japan," *Transactions of the Asiatic Society of Japan* 37 (1910); Boleslaw Szczesniak (ed.), *The Opening of Japan: A Diary of the Discovery of the Far East* (Norman: University of Oklahoma Press, 1962); Sakanishi Shio (ed.), *A Private Journal of John Glendy Proston* (Tokyo: Sophia University Press, 1940); Henry F. Graff (ed.), *Bluejackets with Perry in Japan* (New York: New York Public Library, 1952); Allen B. Cole (ed.), *With Perry in Japan: The Diary of Edward Yorke McCauley* (Princeton, N.J.: Princeton University Press, 1942); and Allen B. Cole (ed.), *A Scientist with Perry in Japan: The Journal of Dr. James Morrow* (Chapel Hill: University of North Carolina Press, 1947). A Japanese account of the negotiations with Perry is "Diary of an Official of the Bakufu," *Transactions of the Asiatic Society of Japan,* ser. II, vol. 7 (December 1930).

The negotiation of the commercial treaty between Japan and the United States is chronicled in M. E. Costenza (ed.), *The Complete Journal of Townsend Harris* (New York: Doubleday, 1930). The are two biographies of Harris: William E. Griffis, *Townsend Harris: First American Envoy to Japan* (Boston: Houghton Mifflin, 1885); and Carl Crow, *He Opened the Door of Japan* (New York: Harper and Row, 1939). A readable popular account of Harris's experience in Japan is provided by Oliver Statler, *The Shimoda Story* (New York: Random House, 1969). The journal of Harris's Dutch secretary and interpreter can be found in Henry Heusken, *Japan Journal, 1855–1861* (New Brunswick, N.J.: Rutgers University Press, 1964).

An extensive literature examines life in the early treaty ports. The most interesting contemporary account is probably the journal of Francis Hall, a young American businessman who spent 1859–66 in the new port of Yokohama: Fred G. Notehelfer, *Japan through American Eyes* (Princeton, N.J.: Princeton University Press, 1992). Another interesting contemporary account by an English journalist is J. R. Black, *Young Japan: Yokohama and Edo* (London: Trubner, reprint edition, 2 vols., 1968). A readable account of the early interaction between Japanese and treaty port foreigners can be found in Pat Barr, *The Coming of the Barbarians* (New York: Dutton, 1967). Harold S. Williams wrote several popular works on treaty port life: *Tale of the Foreign Settlements* (Tokyo and Rutland, Vt.: Charles E. Tuttle, 1955); *Shades of the Past, or Indiscreet Tales of Japan* (Tokyo and Rutland, Vt.: Charles E. Tuttle, 1959); and *Foreigners in Mikadoland* (Tokyo and Rutland, Vt.: Charles E. Tuttle, 1963).

The best introduction to bakufu diplomacy during the 1850s and 1860s is William G. Beasley (ed.), *Select Documents on Japanese Foreign Policy,*

1853–1868 (London: Oxford University Press, 1955); the editor's introductory essay is followed by a collection of translated Japanese documents. Students will find it profitable to consult several other of Professor Beasley's works, including *The Meiji Restoration* (Stanford, Calif.: Stanford University Press, 1972) and "The Foreign Threat," *The Cambridge History of Japan, Vol. 5, The Nineteenth Century,* ed. Marius B. Jansen (Cambridge: Cambridge University Press, 1989). Another useful essay on the subject is Conrad Totman, "From *Sakoku* to *Kaikoku:* The Transformation of Japanese Foreign Policy," *Monumenta Nipponica* 35 (Spring 1980).

Masao Miyoshi has written an informative and readable study of the 1860 bakufu mission to the United States: *As We Saw Them: The First Japanese Embassy to the United States* (Berkeley: University of California Press, 1979). A briefer treatment can be found in William G. Beasley, *Japan Encounters the Barbarian: Japanese Travellers in America and Europe* (New Haven, Conn.: Yale University Press, 1995). The diaries of two members of the mission, Muragaki Norimasa and Yanagawa Masakiyo, have been translated into English: *Kōkai Nikki: The Diary of the First Japanese Embassy to the United States of America* (Tokyo: The Foreign Affairs Association of Japan, 1958) and *The First Japanese Mission to America, 1860,* ed. Junichi Fukuyama and Roderick H. Jackson (Kōbe: J. L. Thompson and Co., 1937). *The Autobiography of Yukichi Fukuzawa* (New York: Columbia University Press, 1966) covers Fukuzawa's reminiscences about the mission's visit to the West Coast of the United States.

William G. Beasley covers the Iwakura mission in another chapter of *Japan Encounters the Barbarian: Japanese Travellers in America and Europe.* The only firsthand account of the Iwakura mission translated into English is Sidney D. Brown and Akira Hirota (trans.), *The Diary of Kido Takayoshi,* Vol. 2 (Tokyo: Tokyo University Press, 1985). Marlene Mayo has written several articles on the mission, including "Rationality in the Meiji Restoration: The Iwakura Embassy," in B. S. Silberman and H. D. Harootunian (eds.), *Modern Japanese Leadership* (Tucson: University of Arizona Press, 1966) and "The Western Education of Kume Kunitake, 1871–1876," *Monumenta Nipponica* 28 (1973). Charles Lanman, a Washington newspaperman who worked for Mori Arinori, the Japanese minister to the United States, provides a contemporary introduction to the visit of the Iwakura mission to the United States, including essays by Japanese students, in *The Japanese in America* (New York: University Publishing Co., 1872). A new edition issued in 1931 under the title *Leaders of the Meiji Restoration in America* (Tokyo, 1931) includes biographical notes on the Japanese introduced in the book. Mori Arinori also prepared a briefing book for the mission members titled *Life and Resources in America* (Washington, D.C., 1871).

The cultural and intellectual impact of the opening of Japan, especially the influx of Western liberal thought, has been dealt with by a number of authors. Sir George Sansom's *The Western World and Japan* provides a readable survey, but the best scholarly introduction is Carmen Blacker, *The Japanese*

Enlightenment: A Study of the Writings of Fukuzawa Yukichi (Cambridge: Cambridge University Press, 1964). A more recent essay is Hirakawa Sukehiro, "Japan's Turn to the West," in Volume 5 of *The Cambridge History of Japan.* The *Meiroku zasshi,* a journal published by a group of westernized ex-samurai intellectuals in the early Meiji period, has been translated in its entirety as *Meiroku zasshi (Journal of Japanese Enlightenment),* tr. William R. Braisted (Tokyo: Tokyo University Press, 1976). Shunsuke Kamei has written an interesting essay describing America's appeal as a liberal polity: "The Sacred Land of Liberty: Images of America in Nineteenth Century Japan" in Akira Iriye (ed.), *Mutual Images: Essays in American-Japanese Relations* (Cambridge, Mass.: Harvard University Press, 1975).

Several studies have been written on American and other foreign advisors to the new imperial government: William E. Griffis, *The Mikado's Empire* (New York: Harper Bros., 1876); William E. Griffis, *Verbeck of Japan: A Citizen of No Country* (New York: Notable American Author Series, 1900); Edward Beauchamp, *An American Educator in Early Meiji Japan* (Honolulu: University of Hawaii Press, 1976); Hazel H. Jones, *Live Machines: Hired Foreigners and Meiji Japan* (Vancouver: University of British Columbia Press, 1980); and Ardath W. Burks (ed.), *The Modernizers: Overseas Students, Foreign Employees, and Meiji Japan* (Boulder, Colo.: Westview Press, 1985).

(Acks. cont'd from p. iv)

Fukuzawa Yukichi, excerpt from *The Autobiography of Yukichi Fukuzawa* by Fukuzawa Yukichi. Copyright ©1966 by Columbia University Press. Reprinted with permission of the publisher. Excerpt from *Bunmei no gairyaku (An Outline of a Theory of Civilization)*, 1875. Translated by David A. Dilworth and G. Cameron Hurst. Tokyo: Monumenta Nipponica, Monograph 51 (1973).

William Elliot Griffis, excerpt from *The Mikado's Empire.* 2 vols. Twelfth Edition. New York: Harper and Brothers, 1912, pp. 322–24, 572–74, 576–78.

Francis Hall, excerpt from *Japan through American Eyes: The Journal of Francis Hall, Kanagawa and Yokohama, 1859–1866,* edited by F. G. Notehelfer. Princeton: Princeton University Press, 1992, pp. 514–15.

Hamada Hikozō, from *Hyōryūki (The Record of a Castaway).* From Arakawa Hidetoshi, *Ikoku hyōryūkishū.* Tokyo: Yoshikawa kobunkan, 1962.

Francis L. Hawks, Official Report of the Perry Expedition, 1856. From *Narrative of the Expedition of an American Squadron to the China Seas and Japan, Performed in the Years 1852, 1853, and 1854, Under the Command of Commodore M. C. Perry, etc.* New York: D. Appleton and Company, 1856, pp. 445–46, 447, 452–53.

Honda Toshiaki, from *Keisei hisaku (A Secret Strategy for Ruling the Country).* Reprinted from *The Japanese Discovery of Europe, 1720–1830* by Donald Keene with the permission of the publishers, Stanford University Press. Copyright ©1952 and 1969 by Donald Keene.

Hotta Masayoshi, "Memorial on the Harris Proposal." From *Select Documents on Japanese Foreign Policy, 1853–1868,* translated and edited by W. G. Beasley. Oxford: Oxford University Press for the School of Oriental and African Studies, 1955, by permission of Oxford University Press.

Ii Naosuke, Memorial on the American Demand for a Treaty, 1853. From *Select Documents on Japanese Foreign Policy, 1853–1868,* translated and edited by W. G. Beasley. Oxford: Oxford University Press for the School of Oriental and African Studies, 1955, by permission of Oxford University Press.

Inoue Ryōkichi, "A Japanese Student's Views of the United States" from *The Japanese in America,* edited by Charles Lanman. New York: University Publishing Company, 1872, pp. 66–72, 82–85, 94–100.

"The Japanese Embassy. Gossip About the Young Ladies Accompanying Them — Impressions Made by the Men." *New York Times,* February 20, 1872.

Kirishitan Monogatari (Tales of the Christians). Excerpt from *Deus Destroyed: The Image of Christianity in Early Modern Japan* by George Elison. Copyright ©1973 Harvard University Press.

Excerpt from *Kōkai nikki: The Diary of the First Japanese Embassy to United States of America.* Tokyo: The Foreign Affairs Association of Japan, 1958.

Kume Kunitake, "Report of the Iwakura Mission" from *Tokumei zenken taishi Bei-Ō kairan jikki.* Tokyo: Hakubunsha, 1877, pp. 33–34, 49–52, 202–05, 250–51, 359–65. Kume Kunitake, *Kume hakase kyūjūnen kaikoroku (The Memoirs of Professor Kume Kunitake).* Tokyo: Waseda daigaku shuppanbu, 1934, pp. 251–55, 263–64.

Mitsukuri Shōgo, excerpt from *Konyo zushiki (A World Atlas),* 1845–1846. Reprinted from Series 2, Vol. 18 of *Transactions of the Asiatic Society of Japan,* Tokyo, 1940 by permission of the Asiatic Society of Japan.

Nakahama Manjirō, excerpt from *Ikoku hyōryū kikenshū,* edited by Ishii Keno. Tokyo: Shinjimbutsu ōraisha, 1971, pp. 256–58, 260–68.

"The Newly Opened Trade with the East—Its Results upon our Pacific States and upon Mexico." *New York Times,* December 3, 1858.

Nishimura Shigeki, excerpt from *Meiroku zasshi: Journal of Japanese Enlightenment,* translated and with an introduction by William Reynolds Braisted assisted by Adachi Yasushi and Kikuchi Yūji. Tokyo: University of Tokyo Press, 1976, pp. 446–49.

"On the Opening of the Treaty Ports (1860)" from *Hunt's Merchants' Magazine* 43, no. 1 (July 1860), pp. 60, 62, 67.

"Our Japanese Visitors," *Harper's Weekly,* May 26, 1860.

"Our Parting Guests," *New York Times,* June 30, 1860.

Aaron Haight Palmer, "Letter to the Honorable John Clayton, Secretary of State, Enclosing a Paper, Geographical, Political, and Commercial on the Independent Oriental Nations; and Submitting a Plan for Opening, Extending, and Protecting American Commerce in the East &c." Washington, D.C.: Gideon and Co., Printers, 1849, pp. 5, 12, 14–16, 17–20.

Matthew C. Perry, from *The Personal Journal of Commodore Matthew C. Perry,* 1853–1854. Reprinted from pp. 159, 164, 168–69, 176–77, 182–83. Washington, D.C.: Smithsonian Institution Press. Reprinted by permission of the publisher. Copyright ©1980.

Rai San'yō, "Dutch Ship" from *Japanese Literature in Chinese* by Burton Watson, vol. 2. Copyright ©1976 by Columbia University Press. Reprinted with permission of the publisher.

"Report of a Rape" from *Correspondence Relative to the Naval Expedition to Japan.* 33 Cong. 2 Sess. Exec. Doc. 34, pp. 172–73.

Sakuma Shōzan, *Kaibōsaku (A Plan for Coastal Defense)* from *Nihon no meicho: Sakuma Shōzan/Yokoi Shōnan* (Chūō koronsha,, 1970).

Sugi Kōji, "The Federated States of North and South America" from *Meiroku zasshi: Journal of Japanese Enlightenment,* translated and with an introduction by William Reynolds Braisted assisted by Adachi Yasushi and Kikuchi Yūji. Tokyo: University of Tokyo Press, 1976, pp. 93–94.

Tokugawa Nariaki, Memorial on the American Demand for a Treaty, 1853. From *Select Documents on Japanese Foreign Policy, 1853–1868,* translated and edited by W. G. Beasley. Oxford: Oxford University Press for the School of Oriental and African Studies, 1955, by permission of Oxford University Press.

Walt Whitman, "A Broadway Pageant" from *Walt Whitman's Drum Taps.* New York, 1865, pp. 61–65.

Samuel Wells Williams, from "Narrative of a Voyage of the Ship *Morrison,*" 1837 from *The Chinese Repository,* Vol. VI, No. 8 (December 1837), pp. 356–57, 361–63, 376–78.

Yokoi Shōnan, "The Numayama Dialogue" from *Nihon no meicho: Sakuma Shōzan/Yokoi Shōnan* (Chūō koronsha, 1970), and "Proposal for Reforming Japan, 1862" from "Kokuzesanron (The Three Major Problems of State Policy)," by Dixon Y. Miyauchi, editor and translator. Tokyo: *Monumenta Nipponica* 23, no. 1–2 (1968), pp. 166–70.

Yoshida Shōin, from *Kyōfu no gen (Testimony of a Madman)* from *Nihon no meicho: Yoshida Shōin* (Chūō koronsha, 1973).

ILLUSTRATIONS

Page 106: Broadsheet of Sumo Wrestlers Delivering Rice, 1854. Reprinted with permission of the Tsuboushi Memorial Theatre Museum, Waseda University (Material No. 111-136-S22-1123).

Page 108: Broadsheet on the "Capture" of the Americans, 1854. Reprinted with the permission of the Tsubouchi Memorial Theatre Museum, Waseda University (Material No. 111–1364).

Page 110: Kawaraban shinbun: Edo/Meiji sanbyaku jiken ("A Comic Dialogue Between American and Catfish"). Reprinted with permission from the Kurofunekan Museum, Niigata Prefecture, Japan.

Page 112: "A Black Ship Scroll with Dialogue" from *The Black Ship Scroll* by Oliver Statler. Published in Japan by John Weatherhill, Inc., Tokyo, and in the rest of the world by Charles E. Tuttle Co., Inc., Rutland, Vermont. Copyright in Japan, 1963 by the Japan Society of San Francisco (Japan Society of Northern California). All rights reserved.

Page 134: "A Yokohama Print of An American Man and Wife (1863)" from *Yokohama: Prints from Nineteenth Century Japan* by Ann Yonemura. Washington, D.C.: Smithsonian Institution, 1990, pp. 168–69. Reprinted with permission from the Daval Foundation—Collection of Ambassador and Mrs. William Leonhart, Washington, D.C.

Page 135: Hashimoto Sadahide, excerpt from *Guidebook to Yokohama,* from Julia Meetch-Pekarik, *The World of the Meiji Print.* New York: Weatherhill, 1986, pp. 50–51.

Page 186: "The Five Races of the World" from *Seiyō jijō (Conditions in the West)* by Fukuzawa Yukichi. Reproduced by permission of Iwanami Shoten, Publishers, Tokyo.

Index

Abe Masahiro, 122
Aizawa Seishisai, 16, 17, 28, 52, 102
  excerpt from *Shinron* of, 52–56
Amaterasu, 15, 52
American Businessman's View of Japan, An
    (Palmer)
  background to, 68
  excerpt from, 68–70
American culture
  advantages to the Japanese of adopting
    laws, customs, and institutions of, 3
  American ethnocentrism concerning, 9
  bakufu diplomatic mission of 1860 and
    descriptions of, 24–25, 150–61
  centrality of religion in, 31
  as cultural model for Japan, 3, 9–10, 30,
    33–37
  goal of Perry's expedition for export-
    ing, 2
  identification as the "Occident" or
    "West," 29
  Iwakura mission of 1871 and descrip-
    tions of, 168–83
  Japanese doubts about aspects of,
    35–36
  Japanese identification with, by the
    mid-1870s, 27
  Japanese interpretation of, 28–29
  reports of Japanese visitors on, 79–81,
    196–97
  social importance of education in,
    31–33, 195–96
American politics and government
  bakufu diplomatic mission of 1860 and
    descriptions of, 24, 150–61
  influence on Japanese government
    of, 3
  Iwakura mission of 1871 and descrip-
    tions of, 172–74
  Japanese interpretations of, 27–29,
    74–75, 137–40, 143–44

manifest destiny doctrine and, 11
  as political model for Japanese reform-
    ers, 36–37
  protection of American sailors and, 11,
    12, 71, 72
  reports of Japanese visitors on, 85–86,
    197–200
  vision of future power in the Pacific
    and, 10–11
American Revolution, 8, 36
  Japanese on, 75–76, 84–85, 171–72,
    198–99
Americans
  bakufu diplomatic mission of 1860 and
    knowledge of, 22–25, 26, 79, 150–61
  Hamada's report on, 23, 83–89
  isolation policy and ignorance of, 18–19
  Iwakura mission and knowledge of,
    25–26, 30–31, 32–33, 168–83
  Japanese curiosity about, 19, 20, 95,
    162
  Japanese interpretation of, 27–33
  Japanese knowledge of, in the 1840s, 8
  Japanese reports about, 73–89
  Japanese students and knowledge of,
    26–27
  knowledge of Japanese among, 37–40
  Perry's expedition and familiarity with,
    19–20
  popularity of broadsides and prints
    describing, 20–22, 27, 106–15
  trade and firsthand observation of, 21,
    135–37
  Yokohama print depicting, 133–35
  See also Westerners
American sailors, 146
  arrest and confinement of, 69–70
  New York Times report of Japanese cru-
    elty to, 71–72
  protection of, 11, 12, 71, 72
  report of a rape by, 115–16

218

"Explanation of Twelve Western Words
(Part I), An" (Nishimura)
background to, 190–91
text of, 191–92
Ezawa Tarōzaemon, 58
Ezo, 7, 12, 15, 150, 189
Honda's proposal for colonizing, 48,
49–50
Russian trade with, 54–55

*Federated States of North and South Amer-
ica, The* (Sugi)
background to, 193
text of, 193–94
Feminism in Japan, and American
women, 37
Fillmore, Millard, 8, 13
France, 13
Frank Leslie's Illustrated Newspaper,
21–22
Franklin, Benjamin, 75, 172, 197, 199
Fujita Tōko, 102, 137
Fukushima Yoshikoto, 24, 25
Fukuzawa Yukichi, 23, 29–30, 31, 34, 35,
145, 185, 187
excerpt from the autobiography of,
145–50
excerpt from *Bunmei no gairyaku* of,
187–90
frontispiece of *Seiyō jijō* of, 186

Germany, 33, 34, 36
Glynn, James, 12
Golovnin, Vasilii, 7
Gotō Islands, 108
Government. *See* American politics and
government; Japanese politics and
government
Grant, Ulysses S., 34
Great Britain. *See* England
Griffis, William Elliot, 39, 200
excerpt from *The Mikado's Empire* of,
200–04
Guizot, François, 30, 192
Gun making, 2, 4

Hall, Francis, 131–32
excerpt from the journal of, 132–33
Hamada Hikozō (Joseph Heco), 23, 30, 83
excerpt from *Hyōryūki*, 83–89
Hamilton, Alexander, 77, 172
Harris, Townsend, 83, 117,122, 125, 126,
132, 162, 203
excerpt from the journal of, 117–22

Harris Treaty, 150
Hotta on support for, 13, 122–25
negotiation of, 13–14, 120–22
Perry and, 13
protests against, 14, 125–28
Hashimoto Sadahide, 22, 135–36
excerpt from *Yokohama kaikō kenbunshi* of, 136–37, 136 (illus.)
Hawks, Francis L., 97
text of *Official Report of the Perry Expedition* by, 97–99
Hawthorne, Nathaniel, 97
Heco, Joseph. *See* Hamada Hikozō
(Joseph Heco)
Hokkaidō, 7, 36, 39
Holland, 59–60
bakufu order to expel foreign ships
from, 57–58
cultural contacts between Japan
and, 6
early trade between Japan and, 68, 69,
101
restrictions on trade with, 5–6, 91,
98
sailors from seen as barbarians, 15
Holmes, Oliver Wendell, 195
Honda Toshiaki, 48
excerpt from *Keisei hisaku*, 48–50
Honshū, 7
Hōreki period, 75
Hotta Masayoshi, 13, 18, 100, 122, 190
text of *Memorial on the Harris Proposal*
of, 123–25
Hyōgo, 14
Hyōryūki
background to, 83
excerpt from, 83–89

Ii Naosuke, 17–18, 99–100
text of *Memorial on the American
Demand for a Treaty* of, 100–02
Imperialism of free trade, 2
Inō Tadataka, 7
Inoue Kowashi, 140
Inoue Ryōkichi (Inoue Rokusaburō),
194–95
text of *A Japanese Student's Views of the
United States* of, 195–200
International relations
Dutch Studies scholars and knowledge
of, 16–17
technological revolution and trade and,
1–2
Ishuyo, Simeon Dorofeivitch, 49